THE SUNRISE
of the SOUL

Meditations on Prayerful Stillness, Silence,
Solitude, and Service in the
Spirit of St. Francis of Assisi

Gerard Thomas Straub, OFS

Foreword by Jonathan Montaldo

San Damiano Books

PARACLETE PRESS
BREWSTER, MASSACHUSETTS

PAX ET BONUM COMMUNICATIONS, INC.
FORT PIERCE, FLORIDA

2020 First Printing

The Sunrise of the Soul: Meditations on Prayerful Stillness, Silence, Solitude, and Service in the Spirit of St. Francis of Assisi

Copyright © 2020 by Pax et Bonum Communications, Inc.,
Post Office Box 970, Ft. Pierce, FL 34954

ISBN 978-1-64060-468-1

Library of Congress Cataloging-in-Publication Data

Names: Straub, Gerard Thomas, 1947- author.
Title: The sunrise of the soul : meditations on prayerful stillness,
   silence, solitude, and service in the spirit of St. Francis of Assisi /
   Gerard Thomas Straub, OFS ; foreword by Jonathan Montaldo.
Description: Brewster, Massachusetts : San Damiano Books, Paraclete Press,
   2020. | Summary: "The fruit of the last 24 years of Straub's new life,
   away from the glamour of Hollywood and into a crowded slum in Haiti
   where he operates a home of hope and healing for 69 abandoned kids"—
   Provided by publisher.
Identifiers: LCCN 2020001406 (print) | LCCN 2020001407 (ebook) | ISBN
   9781640604681 (trade paperback) | ISBN 9781640604698 (mobi) | ISBN
   9781640604704 (epub) | ISBN 9781640604711 (pdf)
Subjects: LCSH: Meditations. | Contemplation. | Spiritual life—Catholic
   Church. | Church and social problems—Catholic Church—Meditations. |
   Poverty—Religious aspects—Catholic Church—Meditations. | Francis, of
   Assisi, Saint, 1182-1226. | Straub, Gerard Thomas, 1947- | Television
   producers and directors—United States--Biography. | Secular Franciscan
   Order--United States—Biography. | Church work with children—Haiti. |
   Abandoned children--Haiti. | Haiti—Social conditions.
Classification: LCC BV4832.3 .S884 2020 (print) | LCC BV4832.3 (ebook) |
   DDC 242—dc23
LC record available at https://lccn.loc.gov/2020001406
LC ebook record available at https://lccn.loc.gov/2020001407

10 9 8 7 6 5 4 3 2 1

Published by Paraclete Press
Brewster, Massachusetts
www.paracletepress.com

Printed in the United States of America

CONTENTS

Other Books by Gerard Thomas Straub

Salvation for Sale
Dear Kate (a novel)
The Sun & Moon Over Assisi
When Did I See You Hungry? (photo/essay)
Thoughts of a Blind Beggar
Hidden in the Rubble
The Loneliness and Longing of Saint Francis

Films by Gerard Thomas Straub

We Have a Table for Four Ready
Room Enough for Joy
Glidepath to Recovery
When Did I See You Hungry?
Embracing the Leper
Holy Pictures
Rescue Me
Endless Exodus
Poverty and Prayer
The Patience of a Saint
Where Love Is
The Faces of Poverty
Room at the Inn
The Narrow Path
The Fragrant Spirit of Life
Poverty and Prayer II
A Distressing Disguise
Cathedrals of the Poor
Mud Pies & Kites
We Anoint Their Wounds
The Wings of Love
The Smile of a Sick Child
Rooted in Love
Silenzio
The Loneliness and Longing of St. Francis of Assisi
A Place for Kids to Be Kids

"Contemplation cannot construct a new world by itself. Contemplation does not feed the hungry; it does not clothe the naked; it does not teach the ignorant; and it does not return the sinner to peace, truth, and union with God. But without contemplation we cannot see what we do in our apostolate. Without contemplation we cannot understand the significance of the world in which we must act. Without contemplation we remain small, limited, divided, partial; we adhere to the insufficient, permanently united to our narrow group and its interests, losing sight of justice and charity, seized by the passions of the moments, and, finally, we betray Christ. Without contemplation, without the intimate, silent, secret pursuit of truth through love, our action loses itself in the world and becomes dangerous."

—THOMAS MERTON
from the preface to the Argentine edition of his complete works[1]

"Prayer and action can never be seen as contradictory or mutually exclusive. Prayer without action grows into powerless pietism, and action without prayer degenerates into questionable manipulation. If prayer leads us into deeper unity with the compassionate Christ, it will always give rise to concrete acts of service. And if concrete acts of service do indeed lead us to a deeper solidarity with the poor, the hungry, the sick, the dying, and the oppressed, they will always give rise to prayer. In prayer we meet Christ, and in him all human suffering. In service we meet people, and in them the suffering Christ."

—HENRI J. M. NOUWEN
from *Compassion: A Reflection on the Christian Life*[2]

A Journey
Through Faith and Fire

I learned a hard lesson in my years of reading Thomas Merton. I can write and speak beautifully about the spiritual life without living one. I teach but shall not sit for examinations. I ooze sentiment without paying its price. I sip scotch while lost in reverie and Gregorian chant. I forget my backstory as I preach spiritual exercises.

Wanting to be heard and "seem" good but never seen for the catastrophe I am, I have earned my seat in the choir of false teachers. We have never been in short supply. St. Symeon warned his listeners to sniff out charlatans who proclaim paths to holiness without having subdued their own passions. Beware of actors who only play a part. Avoid the purveyors of pulp spirituality. The Zen hermit Ryokan was equally succinct in chasing ideas without acting on them: "Book after book you can read to advance your knowledge, but I urge you to cling to the one word of truth: read your heart as it truly is."

More important for my own salvation than my encounters with Gerard Thomas Straub's prolific books and films that chronicle his testimonies as an eyewitness to the crimes of our neglect of the poor and the earth's expendables has been my reading the "living text" of his behavior. Having abandoned a life of luxury and ease, after realizing his life was as empty as the church he had entered by chance in Rome, through his life he has not ceased to preach to me, as St. Francis of Assisi insisted his followers teach, "without words."

Gerry reads his heart as his heart truly is. He writes excessively but records his spiritual poverty. He renounces the facile role of guilty bystander to wrestle with the dark angels of his own and the world's sins. Gerry is always on his knees, waiting for a mercy he knows he can't manufacture for himself, much less for those whose impoverishment cannot quickly be relieved. He has discovered a mirror for his spiritual dereliction in the thousands of faces his camera has recorded in the world's slums. He has bent down his camera and his pen to serve the poor. His "holy pictures" are not pretty.

Gerry Straub is the "real thing." He does not "seem." Every day he confronts himself. His tears at what he finds in himself and the world that abandons the hungry and naked are not faked. He daily takes to heart the warning that Thomas Merton wrote to his troubled monastic novice Ernesto Cardenal: "We are not entitled to a happiness that the rest of the world cannot share."[3]

Reading Marcus J. Borg's *Reading the Bible Again for the First Time* (2001), I thought of Gerry when I read, "I now see the prophets as more (but not less) than radical cultural critics with a passion for social justice. I now see them as God-intoxicated, as filled with the passion of God. And so I speak of them as God-intoxicated voices of radical social criticism and God-intoxicated advocates of an alternative social vision. Their dream is God's dream."[4]

I only judge myself in Gerry's light to realize that the true contemplatives are not the professional inmates tending monasteries, ashrams, and temples but are the religious reprobates on the front lines who serve without fanfare those who are poor, not just the "spiritually poor," like we rich pretend to be, but the poor who can't easily find a cup of clean water. Even Jesus had attendants and his Mary Magdalene: He too had to learn through hard experience to become poor enough unto death to realize his "true self."

Gerry has painstakingly (the precise word) built a house in Port-au-Prince that now cloisters almost seventy children in the middle of an entire nation "at risk." His photographs and journals of his young kids and his coworkers living at the Santa Chiara Center for Children in Haiti are icons for those all over the world who are famished for love and our concern.

Gerry accomplishes this work of radical hospitality by the grace of benefactors who support him at every turn, those who show up for him just in time when the funds are low. Almost daily the denizens of Santa Chiara Children's Center don't know where the money to purchase food for next week will come from. These benefactors everywhere who are aiding the contemplatives serving on the earth's front lines and field hospitals are novices in waiting for their own solemn professions when they too will go into exile from their lives of luxury to hit the streets of their neighborhoods with their own feet. Those who financially support the true contemplatives in action are in training to answer up when their names are called to live among those whom God loves best. They have all been baptized in the Holy Spirit, but not all have yet received the gift of fire and become flame.

Gerry recounts the story of his continuing conversion in the first part of this book. It is a compelling personal history without the more exciting gory details. His life's story is the sermon he was born to preach. His spiritual reflections that follow as his book's core are well phrased but contain nothing new. He shares a tradition of spiritual narrative that would find a home as paragraphs in one of the most popular of Christian books, *The Imitation of Christ*. I urge you, however, to read these reflections slowly and, following Marcus Borg's advice, "as if for the first time." Consider this book as an occasion of grace that might impel you to do what Gerry does. But, no sugarcoating it, you will suffer if you allow Gerry Straub's life and words to set you on fire.

If while reading his book, it dawns on you that this guy is suffering a dark night of soul, you will have entered the landscapes of his life in Haiti. There's no cheap grace here. Meister Eckhart insinuated that the place to which all chosen by the Spirit must finally arrive is a turf so desolate that even God cannot find a space to settle down in it. True contemplatives, Thomas Merton surmised though personal experience, are unsettled and unsatisfied with human life as it is and with themselves just as they are most of all. The journey of contemplatives in action is an arduous pilgrimage through which they sleep on the ground. Gerry's dark nights in this book are not for show or religious soap opera. Does the phrase "being immolated" mean anything to you? He's not pretending he smells smoke, he's at the stake.

Karl Barth got it just right about a guy like Gerry when he wrote in his *Epistle to the Romans* (1968) that the true value of an apostle like St. Paul is negative rather than positive. Listen up and hard to this: "When pilgrims on the road of God meet one another, they have something to say. A man may be of value to another man, not because he wishes to be important, not because he possesses some inner wealth of soul, not because of something he is, but because of what he is not. His importance may consist in his poverty, in his hopes and fears, in his waiting and hurrying, in the direction of his whole being towards what lies beyond his horizon and beyond his power. The importance of an apostle is negative rather than positive. In him a void becomes visible."[5]

Gerry's flame will naturally burn out. If fate is kind, he will die surrounded by his kids in Haiti. They will put his ashes in the backyard with a rock to mark it, let off a couple of white balloons and sing a hymn, before they celebrate with cake and ice cream to forget what they just did. In time they will ignore the rock. In time the new kids won't know Gerry's name. If his death gets a paragraph in a paper, it won't be in the *New York Times*.

Seek out true teachers while they have the light. Their lives are transparent, hiding in plain sight for us behind their words. Let their testimony burn you whether you are spiritually impoverished in Los Angeles or Manila, in Cape Town or Rome. There are true contemplatives among us in every city and village. Look for them if you are far enough along in the spiritual life that you have bottomed out and need to be saved.

I am as certain that Gerard Thomas Straub and his testimony will be forgotten as I am that all he has done and is doing for the least of those among us is eternal. In the fire of the Holy Spirit in which Gerry and his Haiti burn, may we, who are equally most unworthy, be with them so enkindled.

JONATHAN MONTALDO
New Orleans, Pentecost 2019

(*Note well: Neither the publisher nor Gerry Straub invited me to write this foreword. I was moved to write it by reading his book in manuscript and offered it for publication with the sole proviso that not one word I wrote be changed. I mean what I write here based on my decade of reading Gerry's heart as it truly is. If he sues me in a court of law for hyperbole, dissembling, and aggravated embarrassment, I am certain to be exonerated, so help me God, by a jury of our peers. My words are cheap, but the life they honor is priceless.*)

A Cry to God for an Undivided Heart

O God, how I long for your radiant sweetness and abundant goodness to overflow in my heart. But I stand in the way of such a divine visitation. My unruly behavior withdraws the welcome mat your extravagant grace seeks.

A stone heart is hard to enter.

Having once, ever so fleetingly, felt Grace's loving and merciful embrace, I long to feel it again. Help me, Lord, prepare my heart to receive her once more. I lack the peace and purity that is the welcome mat she seeks.

To be pure of heart
requires an undivided heart,
a heart fixed on you
and you alone.

A pure heart beats with love for the Other and every other. A pure heart is unsullied by pride, envy, or lust. A pure heart only gives and never takes. A pure heart is a humble heart. A pure heart is a peaceful heart, a heart unruffled by the ups and downs of life.

Peace and purity are soulmates living together in the heavenly chamber your never-ending grace creates within us as we surrender more and more of ourselves to your all-embracing love.

O Lord, help me transform
my stone heart
into a
pure heart
that beats for you
and you alone.

My Busy, Noisy Life

I live in a slum in Haiti, where I operate a home for sixty-nine abandoned children ranging in age from eleven months to fourteen years. Twenty-four of my kids are infants and toddlers still in diapers. One infant was only two days old in late January 2018 when his distraught mother left him in a garbage dump. The newborn baby boy was found by a woman who brought him to me. The city government gave me custody of the infant. I named him Peter Francis, and he is still with me, now running all over the place. Stillness and silence are in short supply in a home with so many kids.

Before I opened the Santa Chiara Center for Children in Port-au-Prince in May 2015, I had spent the previous fifteen years making documentary films on global poverty. I've photographed and filmed in the most horrific and deadly slums in India, Kenya, Uganda, El Salvador, Honduras, Mexico, Peru, Brazil, Jamaica, and the Philippines. I've filmed the homeless in Philadelphia, Detroit, San Francisco, and Los Angeles. I've documented the destitute in Toronto, Budapest, and Rome.

After eighteen years of virtual nonstop work (with one nine-month-long sabbatical in 2010 that I was forced to take due to post-traumatic stress disorder and some personal challenges), I needed to recapture my love of stillness and silence that had marked the first five years after my dramatic and unexpected conversion in 1995 in an empty church in Rome, when I abandoned my atheism and returned to the Catholic Church of my youth. So, in May 2018, I spent two weeks in Rome and Assisi. In Rome the Franciscan friars from the Irish Province housed and fed me. In Assisi, a Franciscan friar gifted me with a private apartment in the heart of the city. For two weeks, I essentially sat in stillness and silence. I read a lot, and some of what I wrote ended up in this book. I also walked the streets of Rome and Assisi that I love so much. I returned to Haiti renewed and rejuvenated. My friar friends knew this time apart was essential for my survival in such a harsh and violent part of Haiti where I lived.

My work for the last twenty years, in my books and documentary films on global poverty, as well as in my ministry to abandoned kids in Haiti, has given me the unique opportunity to see the depths and deadly destructive power of chronic, debilitating poverty. Those were hyperactive years of nonstop work on behalf of the poor. On two occasions, the constant action, albeit good and much-needed work, pushed me to the brink of burnout. Moreover, the frenetic activity, including giving over 250 "poverty and prayer" presentations at churches, high schools, and universities across the United States and in Europe, masked my own inner poverty. I spoke a lot about prayer, but rarely prayed. I deluded myself into thinking I was praying with my pen and with my camera. I easily trick myself.

Perhaps I'm being too harsh. In the years following my conversion, I spent considerable time in solitude. I spent four days living with Franciscan friars in a hermitage founded by St. Francis high above Assisi, Italy. I made silent retreats at a Benedictine monastery in New Mexico and in a Cistercian monastery in Kentucky. I was even given permission to spend a week of solitude in Thomas Merton's hermitage at the Abbey of Gethsemani. But once I began making films on global poverty in Africa and South America, the time I spent in stillness and silence became less frequent. That would prove to be a big mistake.

Living in a home with sixty-nine kids in Haiti means stillness and silence are virtually nonexistent. After four years of intense work in Haiti, I've begun to commit myself to the rejuvenating power of authentic solitude in order to turn my attention to my own inner spiritual poverty. In Haiti, I now pass two hours (from four to six in the morning) a day in the predawn darkness alone in the silence of my office. During this time, I also read spiritual literature and write.

A friend is an Orthodox priest and monk. His early monastic life was spent in a Trappist monastery. I asked him if he would pen a "short and concise" explanation of *lectio divina.* He wrote me back: "*Lectio Divina* is a reverential listening to what the heart is saying in response to the text of the Scriptures. *Lectio Divina* is not a theological analysis. It is not a confirmation of the creed to which one adheres. It is a way of discovering what the heart wants, what it thinks, especially those realities ordinarily hidden from one's conscious awareness. *Lectio Divina* is, as St. Benedict states, 'to listen with the ear of the heart.'"

I have used this method when reading the Bible and spiritual books written by contemporary authors I admired. It centers me face-to-face with intuitions and feelings within me that I had no idea were there. For me, spiritual books read in the manner of *lectio divina* become a spiritual retreat, leaving me with new insights for my own pilgrimage. As you read this book, I hope you will listen to what your heart is saying in response to what I wrote. *Cor ad cor loquitur*: let heart speak to heart.

The Sunrise of the Soul has short pieces and aphorisms that give you license to pause often and reflect on what you've read, even (or especially) if you disagree with something I wrote. Some of the book is laid out in "poetic" form because it helps me read each line more slowly and carefully. I hope the poetic format of some of the text makes the book more conducive to cultivating a meditative experience for you. I respectfully suggest you read this book in an unhurried and relaxed manner that is in harmony with *lectio divina*, which gives you permission to close the book if something in my text triggers a thought within you, and then follow that thought until it reaches a conclusion, at which point you may open the book and continue reading. This is a way of reading different from the ordinary search in books for facts and entertainment. It's a way of reading geared toward enabling you to discover your heart's reactions and deeper desires.

I pray these humble words will be useful on your prayerful journey to God.

GERRY STRAUB
Feast of St. Francis of Assisi
Port-au-Prince, Haiti

Chiesa di Sant'Isidoro, Rome

PART ONE

An Empty Church in Rome

Unfinished Symphony

I'm tired of telling my story, the unlikely story of going from the glamour of Hollywood to the horror of the worst slums on earth. I've told it more than 250 times in presentations and retreats I've given during the last nineteen years—most recently on July 15, 2019, during a retreat I gave in Haiti to the superiors of the Missionaries of Charity serving in Haiti, the Dominican Republic, Cuba, Jamaica, Puerto Rico, and Miami. I've told the story in varying degrees of detail in at least three published books, as well as in essays published in three other books. The initial draft of the manuscript I submitted to the publisher of this book had the story tucked away in the epilogue. I had placed it there mostly to preserve it, as my other books containing the story were all out of print. A good friend of my mine suggested that I needed to put the story at the beginning of this book, because it puts into context everything that follows it. If you're familiar with the story, skip to Part Two. However, I've added new material (never before published) about my teenage years to this incarnation of the story.

This book is the fruit of the last twenty-four years of my unexpected life and a journey of transformation that took me from an empty church in Rome to a crowded slum in Haiti. The journey is far from over and will never be finished. As Karl Rahner reminded us, "In the torment of the insufficiency of everything attainable we ultimately learn that here, in this life, all symphonies must remain unfinished."[6]

A Meeting Place of Grace

For years, I produced soap operas on all three major networks, including the wildly popular *General Hospital* on ABC. I was a big success. I had a glamorous job. I made tons of money. But something was missing. I had this emptiness inside of me. I tried to fill it with all kinds of things. But the emptiness would not go away. As I would discover, only God could fill my emptiness. God was who was missing in my life. But because of my power, prestige, and money I felt no need for God. My story is about how a saint from medieval Italy walked into the life of a modern, skeptical American and turned it upside down or, more correctly, turned it right side up.

I grew up in a Norman Rockwell painting. My parents had been married forever, raised four kids, two boys and two girls, in a safe, middle-class neighborhood in the New York City borough of Queens. We may have been the last family on the block to get a color television, but we never were hungry or cold. We had all we needed, including lots of aunts, uncles, and cousins whom we saw on a regular basis. My father was with my mother when she died. Life was peaceful and ordered. We ate our meals together. We prayed together and worshiped together. Ours was a devout Catholic family. My parents loved the Church and fully participated in its sacramental life. Daily Mass and the rosary were part of the fabric of our lives. I attended a Catholic grammar school and was an altar boy. I had an aunt who was a Dominican nun, a cousin who was a sister of St. Joseph, and a cousin who was a Redemptorist missionary priest who spent his life in Mexico. Catholicism was not only in my blood but also an intricate part of the architecture of my mind.

When I was a young boy, a Vincentian missionary priest visited my parish grammar school, St. Benedict Joseph Labré in the Richmond Hill section of Queens, New York, seeking vocations to the priesthood. He captivated my mind with a vision of going to China to save souls. I bought the sales pitch, and after grammar school, I entered a Vincentian minor seminary in Princeton, New Jersey. Back in 1960, Princeton seemed, for a young teenager, as far from Queens as China. My dream of going to China died in the minor seminary, where I only lasted for two semesters. The death of my dream died at the hands of doubt. I began to doubt that God was calling me to China to save souls. Bigotry in my quiet Queens neighborhood opened the doors of doubt. The all-white neighborhood was being "invaded" by blacks. I can still vividly remember hearing someone say, "The niggers have crossed 103rd Avenue." We lived near 97th Avenue, which meant our block would soon have African Americans living on it, which in turn meant property values would decrease. In church I heard about Jesus and love. Outside of church I heard about property values and hate. Love your neighbor unless they are black. Why go to China to save souls, I wondered, when people on my block seem unchanged by the Gospel? That question led to the death of my dream to go to China.

(In my sixty-eighth year, I fulfilled my childhood ambition to be a missionary. Haiti is not China, and I'm not a Vincentian priest, which was the original dream. Nonetheless I'm a missionary. Actually, I don't see myself as a missionary, as I am not trying to convert anyone. I am merely a dad to more than five dozen kids who are in desperate need of love and hope. I realize now that when I was growing up, religion was a duty instead of a relationship. Dutiful religion lacks passion and easily becomes a social ritual. Relational religion is not relegated to a weekly worship but constantly interfaces with all aspects of our life and points us to a deeper understanding of love.)

After graduation (near the bottom of the class) from St. John's Prep in Brooklyn in 1964, I landed a four-week, summer job at CBS in New York. That fall, the Beatles were appearing on *The Ed Sullivan Show*. CBS had received sacks of mail requesting tickets. My job was to answer all that mail. I completed the task in two weeks, and was told I didn't need to come in for the last two weeks but I'd be paid for them anyway. Not come in? CBS was the most exciting place I'd ever been. As long as I had an ID badge good for two more weeks, I showed up every day, walking the corridors, poking my head into the studios, marveling at the cameras, lights, and sets. It was a magical world that captivated my imagination.

One day, a man spotted me wandering the halls and asked, "Hey, kid, are you lost?" I told him I completed my four-week job in half the time and that I was using the balance of the time exploring this exciting place. Two days later, he spotted me again and said, "Hey kid, do you want a real job?"

To my parents' horror, I jumped at the chance of getting a lowly clerical job at a television studio rather than going to college. I'm not saying it was a smart thing to do. It was crazy but fortuitous, as I was later selected for an executive training program. I was given a new job every three months. By the time I was twenty-one, I was an executive at the CBS Television Network in New York. Television would become my life.

By the age of thirty-five, I had produced the most popular soap on the air: *General Hospital*. In subsequent years, I was the supervising producer of a soap taped at CBS Television City in Hollywood and I was the executive producer of an NBC soap opera taped at Rockefeller Center in New York starring a young Alec Baldwin. I was very successful yet unsatisfied. I was surrounded by people with lots of money and lots of unhappiness. Money and power are addictive, and I was ripe to imbibe them.

One day, a vice president of NBC called me into his office and said, "Do you know what your problem is?"

"No," I said, "but I'm sure you're going to tell me."

"Your problem," he said, "is that you think you're an artist. You are. But the thing is we don't want art. We want filler to keep the commercials from bumping into each other."

Of course, I knew television was all about the commercials. The commercials were about creating desires by convincing viewers they needed products to make them happier and sexier. What the vice president meant was that economics was more important than art. My soap opera could be replaced by a game show that could be produced at a fraction of the cost and still garner the same profit. I vividly recall sitting in my office watching an episode of the show and thinking, "Who would watch this garbage?" To be honest, I never could have mustered the courage to walk away from the garbage. Mercifully, the show was cancelled, and replaced with a game show.

Armed only with a desire to write, I set out on a journey to discover whether there was a deeper meaning to life. I wanted to understand how I went from spending part of the first year in high school in a minor seminary, harboring dreams of taking the gospel to China, to becoming a Hollywood television producer cranking our mindless soap operas. I retreated to a small town in upstate New York, not far from the Vermont border. I spent my days reading philosophy and theology books. I wrote two books in support of atheism, one of which was a dark, depressing novel about a man who had become so exhausted from his search for God that he elected to kill himself. The book was an angry scream at the church. Critics called it a philosophical novel, which meant no one bought it. It sold about three hundred copies, fifty of which I purchased. When I ran out of money, I would return to Hollywood for a few months, just long enough to earn enough money to finance another stretch of time away from Hollywood in the natural beauty of Carmel-by-the-Sea. Clint Eastwood was the mayor of Carmel when I lived there.

My next book explored the connection between creativity and spirituality. Titled *The Canvas of the Soul*, the novel's protagonist was an unpublished writer obsessed with the lives of Vincent van Gogh and St. Francis of Assisi. I was more interested in Vincent than Francis, because no artist so thoroughly documented the creative process as did Vincent in a series of letters to his brother Theo. Francis, on the other hand, was just a pious fairy tale from the Middle Ages who had nothing to say to my modern, skeptical, secular life. My protagonist's obsession with Francis would soon foreshadow my own.

After nearly two years of writing, I was hopelessly stuck and reaching the point where I had to abandon my literary dream and return to the Hollywood dream factory and crank out more mindless soap operas that pandered to the most sordid of human desires. Before throwing in the literary towel, I decided to make one more stab at finishing *The Canvas of the Soul*. I thought that visiting Arles in the South of France, where Vincent had his most creative years, and Francis's hometown of Assisi in Italy would inspire me to finish my book.

During my long years away from God and the Catholic Church, I had remained friends with a Franciscan friar who had always accepted my unbelief, and always made time to talk with me. I asked him if he knew where I could stay in Rome and Assisi. He called the guardian of the friary at Collegio Sant' Isidoro, a four-hundred-year-old seminary in Rome operated by Franciscan friars from Ireland, and I was given permission to stay there for a week.

I arrived at the gate of the friary one morning in March of 1995. A woman working in the office escorted me to my tiny, spartan room. She said I could join the friars for dinner, but the day was mine to wander the streets of Rome. So, after unpacking, I headed out, excited to see the ancient city. As I walked past a door open to Sant'Isidoro's church, a beautiful statue caught my eye. I entered the church, but not to pray. I simply wanted to look around. Before hitting the noisy, hot streets, I decided to sit and rest for a while in the quiet, peaceful space.

This empty church and an empty man met in a moment of grace. As I rested in the silence something happened, something highly unexpected: *God broke through the silence.* And everything changed. In the womb of the dark church, I picked up a copy of the Liturgy of the Hours and opened it randomly to Psalm 63. In boldface above the psalm it said, "A soul thirsting for God." As I read the words of the psalm my soul leapt with joy:

God, you are my God, I am seeking you,
my soul is thirsting for you,
my flesh is longing for you,
a land parched, weary and waterless;
I long to gaze on you in the Sanctuary,
and to see your power and glory.

Your love is better than life itself,
my lips will recite your praise;
all my life I will bless you,
in your name lift up my hands;
my soul will feast most richly,
on my lips a song of joy, in my mouth praise.

Without warning, I felt the overwhelming presence of God. I didn't see any images or hear any words. What I felt was beyond images and words. I felt immersed in a sea of love. I knew—not intellectually, but experientially—that God was real, that God loved me, that the hunger and thirst I had felt for so long could only be satisfied by God. In that moment of revelation, I was transformed from an atheist into a pilgrim. I went from denying God to wanting to experience more of God.

I adopted St. Francis as my spiritual guide. Day by day, this medieval saint showed a modern skeptic how to enter the heart of God. Over the years, the hillside town of Assisi would become my spiritual home and would open the mystical windows of my soul.

All the friars at Sant'Isidoro were very welcoming. I tried to enter their daily routine, attending morning and evening prayers and the daily celebration of the Eucharist. But my participation was passive. I didn't receive Communion. I hadn't been part of the Church for at least fifteen years. One evening, the guardian asked me if I wanted to talk. I said yes. We walked to his office and had a three-hour period of prayer and reconciliation. It was both intense and liberating. We ended up by kneeling and praying together in the empty church. The next day I received the Eucharist.

In the span of a few days, in a place far from Hollywood, the direction of my life changed.

One of the friars was studying at the Pontifical Gregorian University. The school was founded by St. Ignatius of Loyola, and its alumni included more than twenty canonized saints. The friar convinced the Jesuit priest who headed the communications department to invite me to visit a class where the students could question a Hollywood producer. That led to my being invited to return to the school in the fall to teach a two-week course on creative writing for film and television.

When I returned in September of 1995, the department head asked to see my syllabus. I gave him a blank stare. He asked again. More silence. I could see it dawning on his face that I had no idea what a syllabus was. Again, he asked, this time more agitated, "Where is your syllabus, you know, your course outline, what you expect to do every hour of the forty-hour course."

I shrugged and said, "I don't have a syllabus."

Consternation crossed his face, and he said, "Well, what are you going to do every day?"

I said, plainly and truthfully, "I'm just going to make it up as I go."

The Jesuit looked at me as if I had two heads and said, "I'm sorry, but that's a little too Franciscan for us." He assigned a young Jesuit seminarian to help me write a syllabus.

I overcame that rather shaky beginning and was invited back four more times, and over the next few years, the course grew from forty hours to eighty hours crammed into four weeks. My syllabus at the Gregorian grew into a small book on creating art.

During that first year teaching at the Greg, I met Fr. John Navone, a Jesuit priest who was a literary figure and a professor of theology at the school. I told him about my novel *The Canvas of the Soul*. He loved the idea and said he would be happy to read it and offer his feedback. In December of 1995, I received a ten-page letter from him, in which he cut my novel to pieces as only a Jesuit could, bluntly telling me how the novel did not work on any level. But, on the bottom of the ninth page he wrote, "However"—I turned to page ten—"the writing on St. Francis is the best I have ever read. Throw this book out and write a book about St. Francis." I followed his advice and tossed out over two years of work and began writing a book about the saint that took over four years to finish.

As I was writing *The Sun and Moon Over Assisi*, the hardest thing for me to understand was the saint's love not only for the poor but for poverty itself. It made no sense to me. I had lived such a pampered life; I didn't even know any poor people. St. Francis may have chased after Lady Poverty, but I had chased after Brother BMW.

For St. Francis, voluntary poverty was a way for him to always be dependent on God for everything. I could perhaps understand that on a theoretical level, but on a practical level, it was very difficult to grasp, especially in our culture that promotes personal strength and independence.

In order to better understand the saint's love for poverty, I lived for a month with Franciscan friars serving at St. Francis Inn in Philadelphia. It was another transformational experience. Every conception I had about the homeless and the addicted turned out to be a misconception. I met real people, people just like me in so many ways. It's easy to label a homeless person as lazy, or an alcoholic or a drug addict as weak. The labels removed my obligation to do anything: it's their fault they are homeless; it's their fault they are addicted. Christ didn't label people or judge them. He reached out to them, he excluded no one.

The people I had blithely dismissed as worthless and those who were dedicating their lives to serving them moved me to want to make a film about the St. Francis Inn. I asked a friend of mine from *Good Morning, America* to help assemble a crew. We made the film in four days. Amazingly, the humble film was broadcast by PBS stations across the country. For many years, the film was shown every Thanksgiving on many PBS stations. In 2006, the Hallmark Channel aired the film, which is called *We Have a Table for Four Ready*.

Over the years, the friars have received over $200,000 in donations from people who saw the film, and they now have a waiting list of people who want to volunteer. With the money, the Franciscans built a larger soup kitchen to better serve their guests; they added a second floor containing a chapel. Every day, about sixty poor people, including many recovering addicts, attend the Eucharist at the St. Francis Inn.

This film revealed a new meaning for my life. I knew what I had to do: *put the power of film at the service of the poor.*

Shortly after *The Sun and Moon Over Assisi* was published, I met the head of the Order of Friars Minor in Rome. He had read the book and liked it very much. He asked me to visit him. I told him that I was still struggling with the subject of poverty and its meaning for my life. I asked his permission to spend time living with the friars as they ministered to the poor, so I could create a photo-essay book on the Christian response to poverty.

The minister general blessed my plan. Within three weeks, I landed in Calcutta, India, and over the course of the next fifteen months I visited thirty-nine cities in eleven nations. All of that travel resulted in a photo-essay book titled *When Did I See You Hungry?* as well as a short film narrated by Martin Sheen. Making the film profoundly changed my life.

I knew early on that my time in the horrific slums in India, Kenya, Jamaica, and the Philippines had forever changed me. A doctor later put a name on what was happening inside me that made everything different: Post-traumatic stress disorder, PTSD, whose symptoms are flashbacks, sleeplessness, dissociative episodes, and sudden, inexplicable surges of emotion. My shorthand term for when the haunting memories would grab hold of me was "panic attack." When one hit, I could not function for hours.

A scene of suffering in a slum would flash across my mind and I would begin to cry. What made it worse was that I had taken thousands of vivid, pain-filled photographs during the eighteen months I was traveling the world trying to understand the global plague of poverty that was killing millions of people, including countless children dying from malnutrition and curable diseases. Filming people living in garbage dumps around the world filled me with an unshakeable and profoundly deep sadness. Lost and forgotten, their desperate lives were not important enough or worthy enough to save; they were disposable people. When I returned home from one of these hellholes of poverty, I spent hours on hours studying the photographs, painstakingly selecting the ones that would be featured in my photo-essay book, *When Did I See You Hungry?* It was a nonstop horror film constantly playing in my mind.

As the years rolled on, I continued making films and taking photographs in Uganda, Kenya, Brazil, Peru, Mexico, Honduras, El Salvador, and Haiti, each place deepening the reality of the unjust, unwarranted, unnecessary suffering caused by our inability to share or care that our brothers and sisters—children of God all—could have something to eat or a cup of water to drink. Not helping those in need became, for me, the biggest sin of a heartless humanity.

In January of 2001, I formed the San Damiano Foundation. San Damiano was the little church outside the walled city of Assisi where St. Francis heard God ask him to rebuild the church. We made films that featured individuals and organizations that are helping the poor. They used the films to raise funds. I showed the films at universities, high schools, and churches in order to raise awareness about the plight of the poor and the need for Christians to do something to relieve the suffering. We sought nothing from those we helped. I begged for the funds needed to make the films. Professionals often donated their services. As I mentioned, Martin Sheen narrated one film. Bono contributed a song to another. In the first four years, the San Damiano Foundation had produced seven films. It was emotionally draining and hard work. I made very little money, but I had never been happier or more fulfilled. Between the San Damiano Foundation and Pax et Bonum Communications, which was formed in 2010, I made twenty-four films. Except for a film on prayer and a film on nonviolence, all were about chronic, debilitating poverty.

Living among the poor in homes that had no electricity or running water wasn't the hardest part of my job. The hardest part was begging for the funds to produce the films. In an odd way, I learned how to finance my films at the St. Francis Inn. There's a friar there named Brother Xavier. He is a simple man, and all the street people love him. One day, he was cooking lunch for five hundred homeless people. A volunteer entered the kitchen and asked, "What are you making, Brother Xavier?" He answered, "Potato soup." The volunteer looked around the small, cramped kitchen and didn't see any potatoes. So he asked, "Where are the potatoes, Brother?" Brother Xavier answered, "We have no potatoes." The volunteer asked, "Then how are you making potato soup?" He said, "The Lord will supply."

You can imagine the volunteer rolling his eyes and thinking, "What a sweet, pious thought," but the people were lining up in the yard and we would need to serve them in an hour. A few minutes later, there was a knock at the side door. It was an off-duty Philly cop. He had been at the farmer's market and spotted fifty-pound bags of potatoes on sale. He knew he would be passing the inn, so he bought two bags and threw them in his trunk.

I made my films the way Brother Xavier makes potato soup. I trusted God would supply what I needed. I used Brother Xavier's "business plan" when I decided to open the Santa Chiara Children's Center in Haiti.

These are the bare essentials of my story. I end here with one suggestion. Do not be afraid of enjoying the full freedom of giving your life away. In *New Seeds of Contemplation*, Thomas Merton reminded us, "We do not detach ourselves from things in order to attach ourselves to God, but rather we become detached from ourselves in order to see and use all things in and for God."[7]

Interior of Thomas Merton's hermitage
Photo taken by Gerry Straub in December 2000

Chiesa di Santo Stefano, Assisi

PART TWO

SOLITUDE
Reflections on Prayer and Service

Holy Pictures

I spend three weeks of every month in Haiti; the other week is spent in Florida handling administrative chores and begging for funds for the Santa Chiara Children's Center. When I'm in Haiti, I attend Mass every morning at six-thirty in the small chapel of the Missionaries of Charity, who operate a hospital for over a hundred malnourished children. I gave a copy of my book *The Loneliness and Longing of St. Francis* to Sr. Immacula, the regional superior, and it had an unintended consequence. In late October 2018, Sr. Immacula invited me to give the Missionaries of Charity serving in Haiti a two-day retreat on prayer, including clips from my global poverty films. The two-day retreat in May 2019 would be divided into four presentations, each running two hours. The prospect at first seem daunting, even frightening.

It seemed a bit crazy for me to talk about poverty and prayer to a group of holy and courageous women who, following in the saintly, heroic footsteps of St. Teresa of Calcutta, have dedicated their lives to caring for the poor and to praying. In preparation for the presentation, I watched a film I made in 2003 that was very different from all my other films, whose sole focus was on poverty in all its ugly manifestations around the world. The film was titled *Holy Pictures*, and it was a visual meditation on stillness and silence. I had not watched the film in more than a dozen years. I was alone in my apartment in Florida when I watched it. During the fifty-eight-minute film, I felt I was being slapped in the face with the reality I was not living the message of the film. As the images and words washed over me, they provided me with the incentive to more seriously enter into periods of stillness and silence. I suddenly saw Sr. Immacula's invitation as an opportunity to renew my withering prayer life. The *Holy Pictures* script slowly morphed into this book. In the first few pages of Part Two, an old filmscript is given new life as I basically present the narration from the film, after which the balance of the book moves beyond the motion picture as it probes more deeply the necessity of contemplation and action, as well as the spirituality of St. Francis of Assisi, which perfectly combined prayer and service.

The Wings of a Hummingbird

The mists of worldly vanities need to be burned off by the light of the Son.

So much of life seems like an illusion—a dream or a nightmare. Spacious, sweeping landscapes, however, are real. They are open-air cathedrals. Open space has a spiritual dimension to it. Vast, unspoiled landscapes are sacred places, spiritual spaces. They are sacramental, healing, unifying—and very real. They echo the landscape within.

> *Christ is radically present*
> *in the entire universe*
> *as its ultimate fulfillment.*

In creation we contemplate a manifestation of God's face, of God's presence—and our souls are set afire with charity for all of creation, leading us to embrace the whole world, a world deformed by sin yet transfigured by grace. Nature has the power to awaken the soul.

> *On the wings of a hummingbird*
> *my spirit flies*
> *to an awareness of the sacred.*

An incredibly beautiful world lies silent all around us all of the time, and it remains unseen, a lost paradise, until some quiet miracle opens our eyes and we see everything afresh. By grace, seeing deeply into a flower or a weather-beaten old barn or even the tormented face of a homeless person, we catch a glimpse of paradise, a vestige of God.

> *Through creation we can pick up*
> *the footprint of God.*

Beauty is a vestige of God. God made the flower, and your response to it calls out God's presence in you both. Listen to the silence of nature and you will hear a symphony singing the praises of God.

We do not need to run
and catch God;
we need to stop running
and be caught by God.

The One who has always been is always only present. We are the ones too busy to be present to God's presence. The frenzied pace of life today easily leaves us feeling disoriented and unbalanced. The crush of time and competition has nearly squeezed contemplation out of existence. Without regular periods of stillness and contemplation, we are doomed.

Simplicity is the key to unraveling
the complexities of modern life.

Where Hope Abounds

Many people are questioning the very meaning of their lives. Many are eagerly seeking God because their lives seem empty even though their homes are filled with every gadget and convenience imaginable. But their search finds little trace of God or peace, because they do not realize that God cannot be found in noise and restlessness. As the saints and mystics of all faiths down through the centuries have learned, God is a friend and lover of silence. For us, silence has become a foreign language. Yet God transcends language and intellect.

In the sea of dysfunction and destruction that engulfs so much of modern life, there is an island where hope abounds, a sacred space that nurtures the soul. That island has a name: prayer. Intimacy with God grows freely on this island.

We must guard against
the onslaught of distractions
our culture hurls at us each day.
We need to incorporate structured time
for spiritual reading and reflection.

So much of life distracts us from Life. We live in a whirlwind of noise. Our homes and cars have become elaborate entertainment centers. Cell phones allow us to talk while driving or walking in the woods. Cable television serves up news, sports, and movies twenty-four hours a day. Computers link us to the internet and chat rooms and websites featuring triple-X porn stars. Crass commercialism is always screaming at us, insisting we need what we don't need.

Finding silence is harder than finding a needle in a haystack. Our culture is so riddled with turmoil and confusion it's easy to seek refuge in the noise of mindless entertainment, channel surfing through endless hours of tedious programs. We need to welcome the chance to be alone with God; but the barren silence scares us, and we quickly miss the security blanket of noise.

We need time alone
in order to be present to God.
We need a desert experience.
In the barrenness of the desert,
whether literal or figurative,
we can experience the fullness of life.
The desert is a place of silence
where we find the quiet to hear.

God Is Near

We need to create time for stillness, carving places in our daily schedules for contemplation, meditation, or prayer. We need to be less concerned with *doing* so many things, and instead develop our innate capacity for simply *being*—being fully present to the integrity and capacity of each moment.

More often than not, I seem to be far from God. But in those moments, frequent as they are, God is near—so near, I do not have to struggle to find God, for God is already seeking me, rushing to embrace me. Only in stillness can I sense God's movement, God's presence. Whether we are aware of it or not, God's love is continually coursing through our very veins.

Prayer cleanses your heart
and separates you
from the transitory allurements of the world.

Hungry for Answers

Perhaps the single biggest need busy people face today is quiet. It is impossible to be touched by God on a deep level if we do not recover the essential gift and grace of quiet and silence that makes us aware of God's holy presence.

Far more than the absence of noise,
silence is an opportunity,
our gateway to God.

Waves of demeaning entertainment wash over us every day. We're surrounded by people with addictive lifestyles. Many of us suffer from a sense of psychological isolation and social alienation. Many people are sinking into a quicksand of poverty that is slowly choking their lives. We thoughtlessly pollute the environment. Acts of violence are commonplace around the world and in our backyards. Morality has become a private affair. Terrorism is rattling everybody's nerves. In the Middle East, war is always on the horizon. We live in a time of grave incivility, divisiveness, and cultural loneliness. Day by day our joy is being stripped from us. We are hungry for God, hungry for answers to our endless stream of problems. But our really big questions about God only have one answer: silence.

The Unity of Life

Our real pilgrimage through the depths of silence leads to our hearing a true, clean word that saves our lives and returns us to living in peace. The quest for God is a journey, a pilgrimage to the depths of the soul. The quest requires a listening heart, an ear quickened to the silent voice of God, and a vigilant spirit actively waiting and watching. To be a pilgrim is to live on life's threshold, walking on the edge of reality, striving for what lies beyond the reality we see with our flawed human eyes.

Jesus often sought
the emptiness of the desert
to experience a fuller union with God.

God never shouts to be heard over our noise. Only silence gives God a chance to speak. To effectively listen to God—or even to another human being—one needs to be silent and attentive. If we are truly listening to God or another, truly paying attention, there will be no hint of self-reflective consciousness—there will only be silent receptivity. To listen is to be silent.

We need to empty our hearts,
to sit in stillness.

Silence allows us to live within, helps us to concentrate on the serious, profound inner mysteries of life. Noise takes us out of ourselves and distracts and scatters our thoughts.

Silence is not simply a wordless state; it is an attentive waiting. Deep, spiritually active silence allows us to hear the unity of life. Silence stills the intellect and opens the portal of the heart. Holy silence takes our humble prayers to new and exalted heights of contemplation.

Be still and hear the voice of God.

It is in stillness that we find our emptiness, the emptiness that can only be filled by welcoming God into our hearts. Seeing my own emptiness and impermanence prompted me to fall to my knees and pray.

Alert Stillness

> *When you lose touch with inner stillness, you lose touch with*
> *yourself. When you lose touch with yourself, you lose touch*
> *with the world.*
> —Eckhart Tolle, *Stillness Speaks* [8]

Prayerful silence is more than a lack of words; it is a state of alert stillness. The point is not to rest, but to concentrate and focus the heart and mind on God. Beneath the appearance of passivity is an active state of attentiveness. Silence is an expression of love and strength.

Within the silence of our hearts
lies a mystery beyond our hearts.

In deep silence, we are fully awake, fully open, and one with God. To enter the silence of meditation is to enter our own poverty as we renounce our concepts and intellect and sit alert, waiting to hear from God . . . even if we must wait a lifetime.

Prayer helps us transcend our preoccupation with the self, and teaches us how to embrace the other. Grace prompts us to pray, and praying opens us up to even more grace.

Our journey to God begins in earnest when we still our senses, desires, and mind. In stillness, real movement begins.

Stillness stills unruly passions.

Contemplation quiets our restless, relentless quest for sensual pleasure. The cornerstone of the spiritual life is shaped by stillness, prayer, love, and self-control.

Concentrated Attention

Spirituality is *not* otherworldly; it is found in our relationships, work, attitudes, illness, and dreams. Simply put, spirituality is rooted in ordinary emotional, physical, and mental life. The difficulty lies in achieving the concentrated attention needed to observe what is going on, moment by moment, in ourselves and around us, to uncover that spiritual dimension.

Spiritual growth hinges
on our ability to see the divine
woven into mundane human reality . . .
a feat that will take a lifetime.

God humbly came to the earth he created.

As the opposite of pride, humility reflects honesty, a holistic sense of reality, and a keen awareness of the awesomeness of the universe and the profound mystery of God. Growth in humility is a sign of maturing holiness.

The best way to approach God is to proceed in humility, simplicity, and poverty, and to enter the silence of God's presence, and then patiently sit in prayer and wait until God elects to speak in a manner we can hear and understand. The primary focus of prayer is to lead the mind to stillness. Prayer helps us become more aware of God's presence. The goal of prayer is communion with God.

Approach God with open hands,
a searching mind, and a loving heart.

Prayer is the breath of life. Prayer acknowledges our dependency on God. Prayer is an act of humility, stemming from a mindfulness of our inadequacy. Prayer and humility go hand in hand: prayer deepens humility and humility deepens prayer.

Prayer creates the unruffled calmness
required to encounter God.

Gentleness is the daughter of prayer.

Prayer helps us flee from the storm of inner thoughts and the noise that engulfs modern life. Prayer should lead us to wholeness and simplicity. Prayer helps you see the extraordinary hidden in the ordinary. Prayer is the only vision correction we need.

Prayer is the sunrise of the soul.

A Simple Heart

Our prayer life needs to move from being mechanical and extrinsic to being mystical and intrinsic. Prayer is the natural expression of the friendship that exists between myself and God, a friendship initiated in love by God. A simple heart is a heart where God is. A simple heart is a pure heart, a heart willing to surrender itself to the will of God.

The only thing standing between
me and God
is me.

To pray is to surrender your own power. When you enter into prayer you must leave your self behind. Contemplation cultivates a spirit of receptivity and a listening heart. To enter fully into silence, we need to drop all preoccupations, being awake only to the presence of the moment.

Without solitude and silence,
I easily lose my self. And God.

Solitude is a presence, not an absence. Solitude allows the soul to look on the pieces and see the unity.

Without silence, we are deaf.

A Garden Enclosed

If we really want to pray we must first learn to listen, for in the silence of the heart God speaks.
—T. S. Eliot

Thomas Merton reminded us that we are not all called to be hermits, but we all "need enough silence and solitude" in our lives to enable the deep inner voice of our own "true self to be heard at least occasionally."

True silence is a garden enclosed,
where alone the soul can meet its God.

Silence is a gift from God, to let us speak more intimately with God. If we are constantly talking, God will be unable to teach us anything. If you don't listen, you will never learn.

Thomas Merton said, "If our life is poured out in useless words, we will never hear anything in the depths of our hearts, where Christ lives and speaks in silence. We will never be anything, and in the end, we shall be found speechless at the moment of the crucial decision: for we shall have said everything and exhausted ourselves in speech before we had anything to say."[9]

Without silence, the inward stillness in which God educates and molds us is impossible.
—Evelyn Underhill[10]

Periods of Solitude

Solitude is not the same as withdrawal, which has negative connotations. Solitude has positive qualities. In solitude, I stopped running from myself and became friends with myself; solitude helped me to enjoy my own company.

Solitude helps free you from the illusions of the false self.

In solitude, I learned that I'm not alone; moreover, it taught me there is no such thing as aloneness. Spiritual growth doesn't come from fleeing the world, but from entering into it fully. For the sake of our spiritual health, we each need periods of solitude. We also need to develop an inner solitude that can be entered no matter where we are.

Entering into solitude with the idea of affirming ourselves, separating oneself from others, even interiorly, in order to be different, or by intensifying our individual self-awareness, is not in harmony with the purity required for spiritual growth.

Solitude gives you the ability to hear an inner voice
longing to tell you the truth about yourself.

For the Christian, pure solitude is a place of self-emptying in order to experience union with Christ; in the interior abyss we become detached from our petty false self and open ourselves up to the vastness of the infinite Presence. Detachment reflects the realization that God alone matters. Detachment teaches us not be seduced by perishable things.

Solitude is the incubator of transformation.

Everyone has the potential to be a mystic—to awaken to the deep mystery within them and beyond them. Mysticism is not relegated to a select few.

My friend Fr. John Dear, a modern-day prophet of nonviolence, said, "Solitude plucks us out of the world's frenzy and centers us in nonviolence. Solitude silences the loud voices within us to allow the still, small voice of God to speak. Solitude gives God the time and space to disarm our inner wars."[11]

Contemplation takes us out of the world
so we may see the world better, more clearly.

The late Trappist monk Fr. Thomas Keating said, "Keeping returning to silence. It's God's first language; everything else is a poor translation. In order to hear that language, we must learn to be still and to rest in God."[12]

Silence gives us space for receptivity; it allows us to hear the speechless language of God and to respond with our hearts. Only an open and serene heart can absorb God's love.

In the state of emptiness,
you are better able to encounter
the fullness of God.

Only in silence can you hear the vast, boundless depths of the Spirit speaking more and more clearly about the unlimited love and mercy of God.

Be still. Be quiet. Be.

The End of Isolation

On the road to God,
words eventually dissolve into silence.

To become more and more silent, to enter deeply into creative silence, takes courage. The wordless is foreign to us. Yet God transcends language and intellect. In silence, we are able to meet our deepest self. When we have found our authentic self, we are free to give ourselves away, to give ourselves back to God.

St. Maximus the Confessor, a great saint of the Eastern church, said, "Love and self-control free the soul from passions; spiritual reading and contemplation deliver the intellect from ignorance; and the state of prayer brings it into the presence of God Himself."

The end of isolation is found in prayer.

Through prayer, we become aware that God is present. Through prayer we become at home with the living presence with whom we can share everything. In the presence of God, we become aware of our complete dependence on the Creator. Prayer fosters within us a spirit of humility and the realization that we cannot truly live without God.

Punctuate your day with thoughts of God, recalling God's unselfish, self-giving love for us. Do not be seduced by perishable things. Detachment reflects the realization that God alone matters.

The world demands more and more from us.
God only asks for empty hands.

At its essence, prayer is not about asking for favors. The primary purpose of prayer is to assist us in continual abandonment to God.

A free moment is a moment free to speak to God.

Prayer is essentially loving God, which is why we need to deepen our prayer life in order to deepen our love.

Quiet your fears; rest in God.

Serve While Seeking

While most of us are busy ourselves striving for power and trying to control events and even people, the Gospel perpetually proclaims a far different approach to life: God has created us to live a life of dependence and receptivity, and our acceptance of that spiritual reality is required for true human growth and fulfillment.

Fifteen centuries ago, in a time of great uncertainty and social change, St. Benedict, the father of Western monasticism, wrote a rule for his monks that stressed the balance between prayer and work. Serve your brother, Benedict advised, while you seek God. Benedict believed a person's most basic inclination and need was to seek God, and so he insisted a monk's day have sufficient time for private meditative reading and prayer.

The more we worship God the more we grow in humility. The more we grow in humility, the more gentle we become. The more gentle we are, the less aggressive we become. Stripped of aggression, the more pure we are. As we grow in purity, the more receptive we are to the gift of God's spirit. The more filled we are with God's spirit the more loving and compassionate we become.

Nothing can separate us
from love
if love
is not what
we have
but what
we are.

Your Neighbor's Yard

The faults of my neighbor must be of no concern to me nor be the subject of my idle chatter, whose only purpose is to spotlight my goodness and flatter my ego.

> *Let words fly from your mouth*
> *on the gentle yet strong*
> *wings of humility.*

Goodness, from a Christian perspective, does not come from morality but from communion with God and neighbor.

> *The path to God*
> *runs through*
> *your neighbor's yard.*

True Freedom

Humanity tends to view greatness in relation to one's ability to dominate. Jesus offers a different perspective. For him, greatness lies in the ability to give oneself away. The wonder of the universe and the totality of our humanity is within ourselves. It is a gift of life that we must give away in order to possess it.

> *To be in communion*
> *with God and each other*
> *we must liberate ourselves*
> *from ourselves,*
> *from our hungry egos,*
> *in order to be free enough*
> *to give ourselves*
> *to the Other*
> *and each other.*

Flip Sides of the Same Coin

Contemplation without action is merely conceptualization. Action without contemplation is merely busyness.

St. Francis of Assisi spent half his converted life in deep contemplation, often in far-off, remote mountaintop hermitages. It was during this time that the Lord spoke to him in the depths of his heart and he came to understand what course of action the Lord was asking him to undertake. The saint's quiet time gave direction to his outward ministry and gave him the strength and courage to complete it.

Christ certainly desires that we spend time in prayer, apart from the roar of the crowd in the silence of our most private space, communicating with the Father. But Christ also requires us to feed the hungry, to shelter the homeless, to visit the sick and imprisoned, to extend a helping hand to the poor, to embrace the leper.

Contemplation and action are
flip sides of the same coin of faith.

Contemplation creates an awareness of God's presence in the here and now, and that awareness elicits a response. In contemplation, we're prompted to reach out in compassion to the suffering and weak, and embrace all of humanity.

Contemplation means to witness and respond.

Contemplation frees us from self-serving and prepares us to lead a life of service to others without unconsciously desiring our own success.

I understand contemplation to be any way that we can unveil the illusions that masquerade as reality and reveal the reality behind the masks.
—Parker J. Palmer[13]

A Broken World

We are slow to compassion because we are quick to exploit others for our own gain. We are slow to compassion because of our own misguided sense of scarcity where nothing is ever enough because we do not trust the abundance of God.

As we grow in compassion, we are able to see more clearly the beauty of all life and we also increase our desire to transform everything ugly into something beautiful.

Action is as important as prayer; each of us must take responsibility for meeting the world's need, for we are the accomplices of evil if we do nothing to prevent it.

Ours is a broken world in turmoil, a world in desperate need of the restoration and wholeness promised by Christ. As disciples of Christ, we need to be doing the redemptive work of Christ.

To be a follower of Christ is to be a friend of the poor and the excluded.

Gifts to Each Other

My awareness of God's mysterious presence within me
helps me become more aware
of the same presence within others.

Matthew's Gospel reminds us that to serve Christ the King is to serve the least of our sisters and brothers. But Jesus is not merely suggesting that we be charitable. Jesus is asking us to abandon our love of self and to embrace our own weakness and vulnerability. Jesus is saying we cannot enter into the universe of God without relinquishing everything that binds us to the false security of our own imagined self-sufficiency. God demands absolute allegiance. Jesus is asking us to give ourselves entirely over to him every day of our lives. And this we find terrifying.

It is not enough to pray.
One must be prayer incarnate.

When we have felt the embrace of God's love, we are no longer unwilling to embrace others. When we are filled with God's boundless love, we have no other choice but to be endless mercy to all. Cloaked in God's protective and nourishing love, we are free to live a life of childlike vulnerability.

God's love is universal.
It is for all.

We need to recognize the inalienable dignity of every human being, regardless of race, religion, or nationality. The inclusivity of the gospel requires us to love everyone, especially those living on the margins of society, the poor, the outcasts, the neglected, and the abandoned.

We need to make ourselves poor with the poor, to identify with their misery, their grief, their sickness, and even their death. Only then will the poor feel loved and, as a result, strengthened. Only when we enter into this kind of relationship with the poor is it possible for them and others to detect the divine-human solidarity of the God-man, Jesus Christ, with all men and women. Our lives need to reflect the reality that God gave us as gifts to each other.

Soulmates

Love of God requires us to reach out to the poor, to tend to their basic needs.

Prayer and charity are soulmates.

Charity is the art of knowing how to do the will of God. In prayer, we learn what to do, how to respond to the poor, the persecuted, and the suffering. It is prayer that sustains and guides what we do for them.

Jesus asks us to love as God loves—without counting the cost or holding anything back. Love gives all away. Love frees us to act for the good of another rather than for ourselves. God's love is unbiased and all-embracing. It does not ask who we are or how successful we are at what we do.

Every living thing should cause us
to praise the Creator of all living things.

Every event of our lives is open to God; prayer reveals how. The whole world, including every aspect of humanity, is sacred and a gateway to God. Wherever you are, whatever you are doing, God is there. Strive to feel God's presence and warmth in the ordinary moments of the day. The commonplace is also a divine place.

The sacred is not here or there but everywhere.

God is rarely where I think God should be. God is in the quiet whispers of the olive trees in Assisi and in the harsh noises of a subway train in Rome. The challenge is to become aware of it.

We need to spend less time
trying to understand God
and more time adoring God.

When we are freed from merely mouthing petitions, prayer expands our self-knowledge and consciousness. Once the clouds of self-deception have been blown away by prayer, the need for repentance becomes clear: we are not who, or how, we once thought we were. When an understanding of who we are and where we came from permeates our entire being, we are truly on the road to redemption.

Thank You

Each day I must open myself up to the splendor of God.

The two most important words of any prayer are: thank you. Gratitude to God unleashes enough energy to move mountains.

A grateful heart is a joyful heart.
A joyful heart is a creative heart,
finding new ways to give itself away.

Plant a seed of gratefulness in your heart, so that day by day you grow more thankful to God for the overflowing goodness and mercy God has lavished on you.

If you greet the sunrise with God in your heart and a prayer on your lips, your day stands a better chance of reflecting God's love, mercy, and justice, and you will be better able to treat others the way God would, with unlimited kindness and compassion.

There is a candle in your heart . . . light it!

An Oasis of Silence

We each need to create our own sacred space, a space outside the rat race, an oasis of silence, a space dedicated to inwardness, a simple space of sanity and sanctity.

We can turn any space
into a sacred space.
A bedroom corner
can be a basilica,
a portal into
the mystery and meaning
of life.

Waiting, waiting, waiting. Our spiritual lives are a vigil of waiting. We wait with hope for the advent of God. Yet as we wait for God, God is already here with us. And we are with God, yet not fully so, and so we wait, living with paradox and expectancy.

Spiritual transformation
never ends . . .
it is always new,
forever beginning.

Each of us is on a lifelong journey to wholeness. We all want to overcome the fractures and divisions we feel within ourselves and among our circle of family and friends. Our lives are like puzzle parts and we can't see the full picture.

Wholeness and completeness are ultimately only found in intimacy with God.

Intimacy with God is only found through desire and surrender. When we desire God above all else and when we let go of our clinging egos, God is free to enter into intimate communion with us.

Flowers and Bird Songs

> *Christ does not provide his followers with a set of wings to flee into heaven, but with a weight to drag them into the deepest corners of the earth.*
> —Madeleine Delbrêl, *We, the Ordinary People of the Street*[14]

An encounter with God, as the mystics claimed, is not a gentle affair, filled with pretty flowers and chirping birds and all the right words. An encounter with God is like being woken up by an earthquake. It shakes us to the very core of our being, crushes our false self. To confront the transcendental is to lose control and be filled with trepidation and awe. Nothing is the same; everything changes after an earthquake. God topples the false temples of our lives, and when the dust settles God gives us the grace to rebuild on a firmer foundation. Yes, there are flowers, but many have thorns.

A genuine encounter with God is ineffable,
beyond concepts, images, and words.

Infinity and eternity take on clearer meaning, seem more real. Dualistic discourse becomes a thing of the past, replaced by mystical nonduality. All is One.

An Elephant and a Mouse

During a retreat at a Cistercian monastery, a monk told the retreatants an amusing story in order to make an astute point.

One day, an elephant was bathing in a pond. He was splashing around and having a grand time. A mouse walked up to the water's edge and demanded the elephant get out of the pond. The elephant ignored the mouse and continued bathing. The mouse became insistent, yelling at the top of his tiny lungs, "Get out of the water now!" The elephant's trunk dipped into the water, and he continued to playfully shower himself. The mouse became even more agitated, jumping up and down, demanding the elephant get out of the water immediately. Finally, the elephant had had enough. He slowly made his way from the deepest part of the pond to the water's edge. He stopped, looked down on the mouse, and said, "Who do you think you are, bossing me around? What is your problem?" The mouse responded, "I can't find my bathing suit and I wanted to make sure you were not wearing it."

The point: it is easier for the elephant to fit into the mouse's bathing suit than for God to fit into our human concepts. The monk was telling us to let go of everything, even our limited ideas of God, and enter into the silence of the monastery in order to hear from God.

We do not have to go to a monastery to find periods of silence in our lives. God is calling everyone to silence in order to talk with us. All we need to do is be still—interiorly and exteriorly—and listen, and we can do that anywhere.

If you stop talking, your hearing will improve.

Linguistic Limitation

We toss around the word *God* so freely and with such flourish that we deny the reality that the word names something that is beyond all naming, beyond all comprehension. We seem to easily dismiss (or not even understand) that the very word *God* is a linguistic limitation that imposes on the reality of the entity it is feebly attempting to name. God emerges out of primordial silence and is forever silent. We know nothing of the experience of God; we can only experience something of God living in us. God is in all things. God's relationship to all things is expressed in silence. Our experience of God is beyond words; we experience God in silence. Silence is the breath of God.

In stillness and silence, you can hear the notes of grace singing in the breeze.

Silence is a gift from God, to let us speak more intimately with God. If you are constantly talking, God will be unable to teach you anything. If you don't listen, you will never learn.

True silence is a garden enclosed, where alone the soul can meet its God.

You are who you are when you are alone. Who you are with others is mostly fiction.

The Salvation of the Day

Punctuate your day with thoughts of God, recalling God's unselfish, self-giving love for us. Do not be seduced by perishable things. Detachment reflects the realization that God alone matters. The world demands more and more from us. God only asks for empty hands.

Detachment from things not of God leads to a greater attachment to God.

We've become nonstop achievement machines, denying our inner need for leisure, intimacy, and communion. We are a result-orientated society. No matter what we are doing, it is the "doing" that is more important than the outcome. A wise person is not concerned with results, and therefore is unaffected by the outcome.

To live is to struggle, day in and day out, with all the foibles and failures that are part of being human. The salvation of the day depends on seeing whatever happens during the day as either a burden or a grace. On earth none of us escapes trouble, disappointment, and suffering; all we can do is endure it and allow it, through prayer, to transform us.

Life is mostly failure. Failure is not found in falling down, but in not getting up.

One Organic Whole

> Solitude has its own special work: a deepening awareness that
> the world needs. A struggle against alienation. True solitude
> is deeply aware of the world's needs. It does not hold the world
> at arm's length.
> —Thomas Merton, *Conjectures of a Guilty Bystander*[15]

Society is becoming increasingly divided and polarized, and this poses a great danger. In today's increasingly divisive, "us versus them" world, watching just an hour of news or reading just a few pages of a newspaper makes it painfully clear that most of us are not living a life of love and mercy, but of death and condemnation. We are in desperate need of a spirit of communion and compassion to wash afresh over all of us. We need to resurrect the lost art of conversation in which we truly listen to and share with each other. Through communion, compassion, and conversation we can find our common ground and work together for the common good of all, while at the same time realizing that we are all fumbling around in the dark of an infinite mystery that is beyond words and understanding. While God is beyond words and shrouded in silence, God nonetheless is in a perpetual conversation with each of us, even if most of us are rarely listening; our failure to recognize and appreciate this divine conversation has caused us to turn a deaf ear to the other, to anyone who does not believe as we do, and this in turn stifles communion and compassion.

Each of us is a different expression of the same divine energy, and we were created to be in communication with each other and the Other. Each of us is a part of one organic whole. Each of us is only a temporary and infinitesimal fraction of a gigantic universe, and our failure to humbly grasp our individual smallness allows us to assume a far greater importance than we deserve and causes us to be human-centered rather than God-centered. We are so centered on ourselves that we have failed to grasp the organic wholeness of life and the divine beauty of the entire universe.

We are drowning in words and shrouded in noise.

Silence was once a natural part of life. Max Picard, the famous Swiss philosopher, accurately observed, "Nothing has changed the nature of man so much as the loss of silence."[16] He wrote that long before such noisemaking devices, such as television, were invented. Today, it is normal for earphones to be almost permanently jammed into ears, earphones connected to iPods, iPads, iPhones that are channels for endless, pointless chatter. We watch life through little screens that distract us from the real life in front of us. We film our lives with our phones and then e-mail selected scenes from our self-centered lives to everybody we know. No one looks up anymore. We are all looking down at our iWhatevers and typing something that someone else needs to know. Writing has become "texting." We Twitter away the day and keep God at bay.

We seek to make connections. God calls us into communion.

The path to truth is paved by personal and communal experience and interpretation, aided by sparks of insight from our own personal stories and the life stories of members of our family, friends, and communities.

A Knapsack and Walking Stick

> *When the brothers go through the world,*
> *let them take nothing for the journey,*
> *neither knapsack nor purse, nor bread,*
> *nor money, nor walking stick.*
> —St. Francis of Assisi

I'm amazed how much people carry onto a plane. How do we make sense of such advice from St. Francis? Perhaps he is saying that it is good to realize we are on a journey. A journey to God. What are we taking with us? I'm lugging a lot of stuff, far more than can fit in a knapsack. Mostly, I'm carrying my sins. They wear me down, slow me down.

I'm learning to see that my sins do not erase from my soul the fundamental dignity that God stamped on it at my conception. God does not want to see my demise. God's mercy continuously desires to give me new life. Sin alienates me from God. But God does not reject me because of my sin. God simply wants me to refrain from sinning, because my sins prevent me from experiencing the love God wants to shower on me.

I thought my sins were beyond redemption. They had me bound so tightly it was impossible to free myself from their choking control. But I did not understand the power of grace. I underestimated the unlimited power of God.

I'm beginning to see that God can overcome my personal weakness. All I have to do is let him. But before God can work, I must wake up and admit

I need God's help. Genuine, sincere contrition is always fully embraced by God's tender loving mercy.

> *Lord Jesus Christ, have mercy on me a sinner.*

As I journey through life, that simple phrase is constantly on my lips. The more I repeat it, the more profound its truth.

> *Lord Jesus Christ, have mercy on me a sinner.*

Rules and Regulations

To renounce sin means to work at defeating our natural weaknesses and selfish passions. To sin is to refuse God's love. God is not interested in rules and regulations; God is interested in love and communion. Most of us have that backward, which is the problem.

To be human is to make mistakes. To be human is to be in constant need of forgiveness. God knows this.

> *We are all vulnerable and incomplete—and in need of*
> *God's love, grace, and mercy.*

God's mercy is always there to pick us up and dust us off. God pours his self-emptying love into unlimited acts of mercy wherein he eagerly shares in our sufferings. God's mercy heals and renews us, gives us new life. God's mercy is strong and steadfast in its embrace of sinners, absorbing our suffering and helping us the weight of our misdeeds.

Without God's mercy I would quickly wither and die. And if I do not share God's mercy with those around me, with all those in need of mercy and forgiveness, then I'm guilty of hoarding the transforming power of mercy for myself. Divine mercy must flow through one human toward other humans. The more of God's merciful love we receive, the more compelled we are to extend an offering of mercy to others.

> *The gift of mercy must be shared.*

God reveals my sinfulness to me, not to make me feel guilty but to offer me forgiveness and freedom from the bondage of destructive behavior. Penance paves the way for continual conversion.

Redemption isn't a ticket to heaven; it simply means a soul has been redeemed—set free—from self-interest.

God loves me because I'm weak and powerless,
not in spite of those qualities.
I'm poor and needy, and God lifts me up.

Original Goodness

Original sin did not eclipse original goodness. Original sin damaged and diminished original goodness. Deep inside us there is goodness that has been tarnished by selfishness.

Original goodness
contains a trace
of sacredness
that cannot be erased.

When it comes to following Christ without reservation, I know exactly what to do. What I lack is the courage and discipline to do it. Surrender is never easy. When Jesus was called to his final surrender, he sweat blood.

Virtue is attained only by hard work. We must struggle to grow in love, prayer, self-control, and compassion, which are the roots of all virtue.

Heart and Soul

God is humble. God lives in our poverty and weakness. Simplicity safeguards the spirit from distractions and leads it to God. Love and trust are the heart and soul of simplicity.

It is in our weakness that Christ's strength and power is able to reveal itself.

We experience God's love in proportion to our experience of our own weakness. Divine mercy is incarnated in human weakness.

Jesus chose to be poor. We wish he hadn't. We are embarrassed by his poverty. His poverty makes us uncomfortable. Jesus suggests that poverty is a privileged path, that the poor possess an eminent dignity. We don't get it. We do not choose to be poor. We run from poverty. We hide from poverty. Poverty makes us uneasy. For us, there is nothing "blessed" about being poor. But the truth is: I am poor. I am in constant need. I'm impoverished by my many weaknesses, my many bad habits. I'm at the age when each day I'm impoverished by the lack of time I have left to do the things I want to do.

> *To understand poverty,*
> *one must enter the poverty of another,*
> *as Jesus entered our poverty.*

The poverty of a homeless woman named Loretta in the Skid Row section of downtown Los Angeles, the poverty of a drug addict named Michael in the Kensington section of Philadelphia, is my poverty. Our poverty is blessed when we do not possess anyone and we are free to be possessed by everyone.

> *In my poverty, I can possess Jesus . . . and give Jesus away.*

A Life of Holiness

> *Holiness seems beyond our grasp, so we settle for mediocrity.*

God calls us to a life of holiness. Does holiness ever take a holiday? It does in my case. I still yield to temptations. There are temptations that still seem beyond my ability to resist. There are little pockets of resistance to holiness in my life that I have been unable to surrender. I am weak. I keep my unholy behavior hidden. But God sees, God knows . . . and God still loves. But in holding on to these unholy behaviors I'm keeping myself from the one thing I really want the most: God.

How ironic: I have devoted my life for the last twenty years to fighting the cruel impact of poverty, and yet I do almost nothing to combat my own inner poverty. My poverty exists in my weakness to resist certain temptations, even though after continually succumbing to temptations I feel dreadful and loathsome.

Because God is holy, I want to be holy. God's holiness never takes a holiday. God is always working on behalf of my salvation, my wholeness. My salvation lies in forgetting myself and yielding to God. Even when I resist God's grace to overcome temptation, God does not look at my rejection, but at my heart, which truly wants to beat with love.

All that I can give God, who has everything, is my nothingness, my emptiness, my inability to overcome my own inner poverty.

My Heart's Desire

What is my heart's desire? It seems to desire so many things, some good, some bad. How do I know the difference between a desire that is good and one that is bad? Maybe I shouldn't think in terms of good and bad, but in terms of healthy and unhealthy.

> *If the desire is self-centered,*
> *then it is unhealthy,*
> *because it deflects me*
> *from the self-emptying love*
> *that is the one and only path*
> *to God.*

Sin is a failure to love; sin is wanting my own way instead of God's way. God's way is paved with humility. God gives God away.

A good and healthy desire is one that longs for God. When I desire God more than anything else, all my other desires will bow to that one true, most noble desire: a desire for God and God alone.

> *A desire for God*
> *is nurtured in*
> *stillness and silence.*

A Gift of Love

> *Let there be a place somewhere in which you can breathe naturally,*
> *quietly, and not have to take your breath in continuous short gasps.*
> *A place where your mind can be idle, and forget its concerns,*
> *descend into silence, and worship the Father in secret.*
> —Thomas Merton, *New Seeds of Contemplation*[17]

Prayer is a gift of Love, and a means of living our whole life as a communion with the Lord who, through the Incarnation, came to share in our human condition. As we encounter God in the depths of ourselves, we are no longer astonished by the darkness of God's mystery, but we merely accept it, living by faith. We no longer belong to ourselves but to Love, the giver of the gift. When we enter fully in the Presence, we experience spontaneous joy . . . even during trials, hardships, and suffering. Even when we are weak, empty, and hurting, we know the Lord is present. Trusting in this Presence, we are compelled to accept everything as coming from God.

Everlasting Love

> *"Give thanks to the LORD for he is good,*
> *for his steadfast love endures forever!"*
> —Psalm 118:1 NRSV

At the heart of love is a desire (eros) to be one with the beloved. This passionate desire for unity is so strong it feels the absence of the beloved. Love wants what it is missing so badly it hurts. But while love desires the love of its beloved, love also wants to give itself away to its beloved. This gift of love (agape) exists side by side with the desire for love (eros) within our hearts. It is in the very union of eros and agape that love reaches its fulfillment.

God loves us, wants to be one with us. But we shunned that love, turned our backs on God. God's passionate desire for us, even after feeling the pain of our rejection, is joined with God's gratuitous gift of endless love to us in the person of Jesus. In Christ, humanity and divinity are wedded in everlasting love. As we desire the one we love and want to give ourselves completely to that person, so too does God love us, wants to be with us, and wants to fully share God's divinity with us. It is not enough to simply desire God. We need to give ourselves to God.

A Prayer: First and Foremost

O Lord, my mind and heart
are centered on so many things
other than you.
Mostly good things,
but not you.
Help me this day
to desire you
first and foremost,
and not to be distracted
by all the things
that pull me
this way and that way,
fragmenting my being.
Teach me this day, O Lord,
how to forget
my fears and anxieties,
and put all my trust and hope
in you alone.

Painting by Paolo Grimaldi

PART THREE

CONTEMPLATIVE PRAYER

No Idea

"My Lord God, I have no idea where I am going." Thus began Merton's most famous prayer, now printed on countless cards that often end up taped to mirrors or refrigerators. His acknowledged ignorance in the prayer resonates deeply with anyone who reads it. As the prayer continues, Merton moves hopefully forward in his darkness.

> *I do not see the road ahead of me. I cannot know for certain where it will end. Nor do I really know myself, and the fact that I think I am following Your will does not mean that I am actually doing so. But I believe that the desire to please You does in fact please You. And I hope that I have that desire in all that I am doing. I hope that I will never do anything apart from that desire.*[18]

So many things flash before my mind as I read the words of that prayer. I have no idea of God's will for my life, but whatever it is, I know I've done many things that cannot possibly be in harmony with God's will, countless little acts of selfishness, endless moments of unloving behavior. Mine has been a messy, imperfect life, littered with missteps and mistakes.

Merton's prayer goes on to say that if he continues to strive to do God's will, no matter how often he fails, God will lead him down the right road, even if he knows nothing about it. Merton prays, "I will trust You always though I may seem to be lost and in the shadow of death. I will not fear, for You are ever with me, and You will never leave me to face my perils alone."

Oh, what comfort I've taken from those honest words. But more than comfort, in the last few years, especially during one densely dark period of my life, I came to feel and know the truth of those words: I am never alone; God is always with me, no matter how dark, no matter how bad any situation is.

Merton knew it was in darkness that we find the Light.

"The only unhappiness," Merton wrote, "is not to love God." Loving God requires prayer. Prayer for Merton was a matter of awareness, an alertness to the possibilities of the hour, what he called "the grip of the present." Most of us are stuck either in the past or the future, making the present moment lost time. We're too busy to be present . . . present to each other, present to the poor, present to God.

During his twenty-seven years behind the monastery walls, Merton learned the art of attentiveness. The monastic stability of being rooted in one place freed Merton to delve ever more deeply by reflection and prayer into the meaning of his unfolding life in the unfolding history of his times. He steadfastly honed his writing craft, which became an instrument of confession and witness in a prolific outpouring of poetry, journals, letters, and books on a wide range of interests, everything from civil rights, to war, to Zen Buddhism. From his perch in a rural forest of Kentucky, Merton explored a galaxy of ideas in an effort to become a better, more Godlike, human being. In the darkness of humanity, he discovered the light of God.

Merton learned that waiting for a "word" he could not speak to himself was the essence of prayer. In our age of instant communication and instant gratification, waiting has become intolerable. Stillness, poverty of spirit, keeping vigil, guarding thoughts, and fasting from one's own selfishness were essential attributes of Merton's practice of monastic humanism. He wrote that contemplation was "essentially a listening in silence." According to Merton this listening in silence should have an air of "expectancy" to it, but not an expectancy that "even anticipates a special kind of transformation." Merton learned how to sit in the darkness . . . and wait—even if answers never came. Answers rarely do come.

In 1941, after being at Gethsemani for less than two weeks, a young Merton penned this prayer: "Your brightness is my darkness. I know nothing of You and, by myself, I cannot even imagine how to go about knowing You. If I imagine You, I am mistaken. If I understand You, I am deluded. If I am conscious and certain I know You, I am crazy. The darkness is enough."[19]

In honestly communicating the darkness that became his rite of passage into God's presence, Merton freely admitted the complexity and the paradoxes of his own life. Merton saw the contemplative life as a life of relationships informed by love in search of freedom.

The hallmark of Merton's prayer life was his ability to keep vigil in silence with his heart's eye on the horizon of the next moment. The next moment could reveal in light or in shadow the presence of the Beloved he so eagerly awaited. He kept his mind's eye open for the unexpected epiphany. Waiting without projecting his own needs into the next moment became a dark form of hope for him. Down through the ages, mystics of all faiths understood that silence is the place where time and eternity embrace.

Like us, Merton had no idea where he was going on his journey to God. Unlike most of us, he simply followed where he thought God was leading him, trusting that if he was mistaken, God would gently give him a course correction . . . and all would be well in the end, no matter where he ended up. Not to know where his life was going was always to begin again in Merton's journey to love learning and desire God. Ignorance acknowledged was a stimulus to new experience. Awareness of the darkness kept Merton sober and watchful, though never perfectly, so that he might miss a gate to the rose garden. He didn't just see things—he saw God in everything.

It does not matter where I am going if I am not going to heaven.

From Darkness to Shadows

I once was in deep darkness. Then came a shocking revelation in an empty church in Rome. In a flash, the God whose existence I denied became undeniably real. Not only was God real, but even more amazing, God loved me. Suddenly, everything I held to be true was upended. All props and crutches on which I relied were kicked out from under me. Nearly twenty-five years after that giant spiritual light bulb was lit, I now live not in darkness but in the shadows. I long to live in the fullness of God, in the fullness of grace.

By grace I transitioned from darkness to the shadows. I'm in a permanent time just minutes before sunrise . . . that normally brief period when the darkness of night is slowly being vanquished and the air is filled with the expectation of an explosion of light and warmth from Brother Sun.

We cannot control the setting of the sun, nor its rising. It just happens. We either see it and experience it . . . or we don't. Really seeing the sunrise or sunset, taking the time to be present to it, springs from an appreciation of it.

Disarming Our Inner Wars

> *Without great solitude no serious work is possible.*
> —Pablo Picasso

Contemplation takes us out of the world so we may see the world better, more clearly. Hidden from the sight and influence of others, in solitude we are to encounter our true selves. Solitude gives me the space and opportunity to be alone with God.

> *Settle yourself in solitude, and you will come upon Him in yourself.*
> —St. Teresa of Avila

Every month I travel back and forth between Haiti and Florida. After three weeks in Haiti, I need a week of solitude in Florida. Going from garbage burning in the streets to miles of beautiful beaches is a jarring transition to make. The biggest transition is going from constant noise in Haiti to the total silence of my small apartment on a sparsely populated island off the coast of central Florida. In Haiti, I'm always surrounded by kids and staff; in Florida I enter deeply into a sense of aloneness. In that aloneness, my need for God is more clearly manifested.

My aloneness, however, is not loneliness. There was a time in my life when my loneliness was so acute it caused me to seek relief from empty things that offered no contentment or satisfaction. Material things such as alcohol, sex, or extravagant possessions do not eradicate our existential loneliness. Some of us, including me, sought relief in other people: please validate me, tell me I am lovable, make me feel worthy.

If we truly and honestly face our inner pain, our loneliness, our sense of desperation, our failures, our sense of hopelessness, those harmful feelings can become agents of change. In facing these feelings head-on instead of running from them or burying them, we can arrive at a point where we see clearly our need for God. Only God can offer true fulfillment, genuine hope, and lasting transformation. It is in our darkest moments, if we turn to God and follow God's lead, that we can put an end to the dysfunctional patterns in our lives. I'm still trying to do this. I have more to surrender to God. Change, especially radical change, is never easy or even completed.

Being Present

Since before my teenage years, I've been strongly attracted to Jesus. But as a teenager growing up in New York City, I looked at life in my little slice of the Big Apple, which at the time was slowly and reluctantly becoming racially integrated, and saw that most Christians did not really take Jesus seriously, did not act according to his way of life. The same lips that proclaimed Jesus was Lord also uttered disgraceful racial epithets.

My entire adult life confirmed the truth I saw then, that we don't really take Jesus seriously. We don't love our enemies. We don't turn the other cheek. We don't forgive seventy times seven times. We don't bless those who curse us. We don't share what we have with the poor. We don't put all our hope and trust in God. We say: I am not a saint. We say: This Gospel stuff can't be meant for everybody. We say: The Gospel is an ideal. But the Gospel is not merely an ideal.

For the followers of Christ, the Gospel is the Way.

Yet we more readily embrace war, embrace works of death, than we do peace, works of life. Why? Because the Gospel has not become flesh within us. We have not incarnated God's Word. We trust in the ways of the world, not in the ways of the Word.

Solitude gives us the time and space for the difficult work of self-examination.

In solitude we have the chance to reflect on just how far we have strayed from the Way. Jesus asks us to empty ourselves of everything, but we seem to only want to acquire more and more. Jesus was and is a truly countercultural figure. Christ is not asking us to be successful or productive. Christ is looking for us to be present . . . present to God (in prayer), and present to each other, present to each other in acts of love and mercy, especially present to the poor and the suffering.

When I look into the sad face of a starving child living on the margins of a slum, I find myself looking into the very mystery of life. Chronic poverty with its desperate and endless struggle for survival fills me with grief. Yet these dreadful and hopeless slums can be sacraments of transcendence that can unlock our unconsciousness and lead us to a place of solidarity with the poor.

> *The mystery*
> *of poverty and pain,*
> *the very mystery*
> *of life and death,*
> *is too deep,*
> *too sensitive,*
> *too fragile*
> *to be understood or solved by*
> *one person,*
> *one church,*
> *one religion,*
> *one system of thought.*

But in these places of desperation I often catch fleeting glimpses of hope and the feeling that life is truly magnificent and precious. The Cross is clearly visible in these nightmarish slums, but so is the joy of Easter.

A Land of Plenty

After each trip to places of crushing suffering, such as Kenya, Uganda, and Haiti, coming home is always a difficult transition for me to make. Going from extreme need to stunning abundance is jarring and mystifying. We have so much of everything. Yet we want more.

The pandemic of consumerism and busyness deadens our capacity for contemplation and stillness and causes a deterioration of our interior lives.

> *In a land of plenty*
> *we hunger for more.*
> *We have turned greed*
> *into a virtue.*

Our lives are fragmented and disconnected. Television and the internet have turned our interior dwellings into shantytowns. Instead of looking in, they prompt us to look outward, and we become what we gaze on.

> *When praying, we turn away from ourselves*
> *and turn toward God.*

Long ago, in a remote village in the South of France, St. John Marie Vianney, known as the Curé of Ars, noticed an old farmer who used to sit for hours in the humble, empty church. When the priest asked the farmer what he was doing, the farmer replied, "He looks at me and I look at him." It really is that simple, but modern life is so connected to so much we are easily disconnected from the All. Contemplation cannot be relegated to some secluded corner of our life, dualistically existing apart from other tasks.

> *Contemplation lives and breathes*
> *in the recognition of*
> *the divine possibility*
> *of the present moment.*

How Two Poor Kids Changed My Prayer Life

Sustaining a life of prayer is not easy in our culture, where we are constantly bombarded with some many scintillating distractions. Our ever-increasingly pampered lifestyles actually tend to erode our faith and our prayer life. While social justice was central to life of Christ, it makes little inroad into our busy lives. Modern culture is so alluring it consumes us. We are being entertained to death. Even politics has become a theater of the absurd, more an entertaining horse race than a serious discussion of public policies that address the common good.

Our indulgent, coddled lifestyle is not conducive to deepening our faith. We can't fully embrace or emulate the self-emptying love of Christ without compassion. I know that my own mediocre prayer life was improved when I began to come into regular contact with the chronically poor on the peripheries of life around the world. According to the Gospel (Matthew 25), to feed the poor is to feed Christ. We don't see the poor, and as a result, we don't see Christ in his distressing disguise. Everything in our culture blinds us to the reality of the poor . . . and hinders the deepening of our prayer lives.

When I returned to the church in 1995 and made a sustained effort to renew and increase my faith, prayer wasn't easy for me. But, a few years later, when I began to film in horrific slums around the world, not only were my eyes opened to the dreadful plight of the poor and their endless suffering, but I was also forced to my knees in order to try understand what I was capturing on film. In the early years of filming I encountered displaced people in refugee camps in Africa, lepers in India and Brazil, and the homeless in Philadelphia and Los Angeles. When I returned home from Africa or South America, it was hard to readjust to our pampered culture. But slowly, the poor and infirm I had encountered (Little Moses in El Salvador, Loretta in Skid Row, George in Jamaica, Victor in Peru) would slowly fade from my consciousness. I still carried them within me, and whenever I would see them in a film clip or in a photograph, I could quickly reconnect with the emotions I felt when I was with them. But they had no tangible impact on my daily life. My prayer life was still dry and mechanical . . . and didn't really change my behavior. Sin still played a far too active role in my life.

But in July of 2007, in a remote section of the sparsely populated bush in northern Uganda, things began to change when I happened to come across two little children named Sam and Esther who were lying face down in the dirt. Naked from the waist down, they were motionless. They wore only tattered, dirty T-shirts. Flies were in their eyes and in the snot from their runny noses. Their bellies were bloated. Their behinds were shriveled and laced with deep lines left by their shrinking body mass. Their legs were tiny bones covered in dried-out skin. It was clear to me that starvation had pushed these helpless kids to the verge of death.

Slowly, some people approached me and my film crew and we began to piece together the story. We were shocked to learn that Sam was about seven years old and Esther was about five years old. Based on their body size, we would have guessed Sam to be four years old at best and Esther perhaps three years old. Severe malnutrition is horrible: it stunts growth and forces the body to turn on itself for food. Sam was under three feet tall and weighed under twenty pounds.

Both Sam and Esther were also afflicted with polio. Neither of them could walk. I could not imagine why they were abandoned, left starving, lying hopelessly in the dirt. As I tried to absorb the nightmare before me, a little girl emerged from the bush. It was Sam and Esther's older sister, Jane, a very small eight-year-old. She had on a threadbare, poorly fitting, dirty white dress. She had walked miles to fetch water in order to bathe her brother and sister. In utter fascination, I filmed this little, determined girl bathing her siblings. She poured the water into a small basin. Then she rolled out a small piece of black tarp and placed Sam on it and began bathing the boy. He screamed throughout the procedure. And with good cause. Jane was too small to handle the boy with any degree of delicacy. After bathing Sam, Jane moved him to a small mat made of grass and dried him off with a rag. She then repeated the process with little Esther, who seemed more dispirited and traumatized than Sam.

While most eight-year-olds are busy playing, Jane faced a life-or-death situation—alone. She could not feed her hungry brother and sister, but she could see how dirty they were, and it was within her power to take a long walk for some water, lug it back, and bathe the kids. Little Jane, a hungry child herself, assumed the awesome duties of a parent.

It was then and there that I really first saw Christ in the poor . . . but I had no way to understand what that really meant. The film I made in Uganda, *The Fragrant Spirit of Life*, featured a scene with Jane bathing Sam and Esther. Without question, it is the most compelling scene in any of my twenty-five films. The scene was put on YouTube, and it attracted nearly a million viewers. The scene literally saved the ministry of a Baptist woman who still cares for orphaned children in Uganda. It also saved and forever changed the lives of those three kids.

Sam, Esther, and Jane changed my life. I knew I had encountered Christ in a profound way. Here are a few lines of narration that I spoke in the film over footage of Jane bathing Sam and Esther:

> *To look into the face of a suffering child*
> *is to see the depth of humanity*
> *and the heart of God*
> *and we are able to drop all vestiges of our selfishness*
> *and desire nothing more*
> *than to see another experience relief and joy.*

> *Most organized religions, sadly,*
> *devote much of their time and energy*
> *to defending dogma*
> *or destroying dissidents.*

*When kneeling before
a fragile, little boy like Sam,
that kind of petty and immature
religious practices
dissolve into a sea of insignificance.
Love is all that matters.
And love compels us
to reach out
to Sam and Esther.*

I've seen that scene at least five hundred times. I end every presentation I give with it. People never forget it. Often as the scene is playing in a church or school auditorium, I'm moved to tears. I always speak with uncanny power and conviction following it.

Those three kids, who live outside the global village, in a dark, electrically starved world of hunger and disease, entered so deeply into my heart, soul, and spirit that they are virtually always a profound part of my life. They changed my entire perspective on life. I saw more clearly that what modern culture offers us is truly empty—and easier to resist than ever before. My eyes had been opened, not in prayer, but in communion with two powerless, crippled, starving kids. To touch those who have no place within our culture is to give ourselves a perspective far beyond our culture.

While filming we continued to collect facts and tried to form a response. The mother had long ago abandoned the family for unclear reasons, but spousal abuse seems likely; before running away, she tried to drown the children in a pit latrine, but the hole was too small. The father was a drunk who spent his days in the village. Sam and Esther contracted polio when he was just learning to walk and she was still an infant. Care for the three children had fallen on the shoulders of their grandmother, who provided care for eight children. They all slept in a tiny hut on a dirt floor with only a few blankets. Two days before we happened on the scene, the grandmother had left for a distant village in order to do "digging"—that is, to dig up root plants that form the basis of the diets of most of the poor in the region. The grandmother left because the kids were starving. She left the kids in the care of some neighboring adults, but they clearly had not fulfilled their obligation, most likely because they could not care for their own overwhelming needs. And so, little Jane, a hungry child herself, assumed the awesome duties of a parent.

We scoured our van for any snacks we had with us. We usually carried a few cookies and health bars and some fruit with us because we never knew when we would be able to eat. We gave Jane some crackers with peanut butter filling. Amazingly, though starving herself, she first offered the crackers to Sam and Esther. Only after her brother and sister devoured a few crackers each did Jane take one for herself. I was astounded at how this little girl embodied the self-emptying love of Jesus and the Gospel, a love that always puts others first.

In late January 2016 I was working on a new film titled *One Human Family*, which consisted of scenes from many previous films that I hoped would be a visual meditation on global poverty. (The film was not completed.) When we came to the scene of Sam and Esther, the film editor and I decided to look at original raw footage that was shot in 1997. I was astounded by how much compelling footage never was used in the original scene. I think perhaps at the time we edited the film, I felt it was just too hard to watch. The Sam and Esther scene we edited for *One Human Family* is really far more interesting and more powerful, as we let the footage play pretty much the way I filmed it. We trimmed the narration down to the bare minimum to convey the story . . . and we let the images speak for themselves. It was very intense.

As I watched over and over again Jane tenderly caring for Sam and Esther, I could not help but draw a parallel to Lovna in Haiti, the little eight-year-old girl who cares for her one-year-old twin brothers, Carlo and Carlos. Jane and Lovna, separated by an ocean but united in dire poverty, show me that mercy is the holiness of God made manifest, it is God's love in action. Mercy and God are inseparable, one and the same. Mercy is an act of creation, springing forth from unconditional love. "Whatever you do to the least of my brothers and sisters, you do to me," Christ assures us. Christ is telling us that in the poor, God is ever-present in our world, waiting for us to reach out to God in love. God is present in those we do not value: the destitute, the dying, the displaced. The power of God is mysteriously hidden in the powerless. The voice of God is heard in the voiceless. In the bush in northern Uganda, God and love entered my being in such a way that I was forever changed. I realized that my safe, secure, comfortable life amounted to less than a pile of beans because I had not learned how to pray, how to love. I'm still learning.

Now that I spend most of my time in Haiti, I know that my prayer life is much richer than ever before. In Haiti, prayer seems to always be on my breath. In Haiti, I make time for prayer and I enter into prayer more easily. Life in Haiti becomes a prayer. In Haiti, I'm instantly aware of any unloving action I take. In Haiti I'm more aware of my own weaknesses and my own need for mercy. In Haiti, I become more of a man of prayer and a man of mercy.

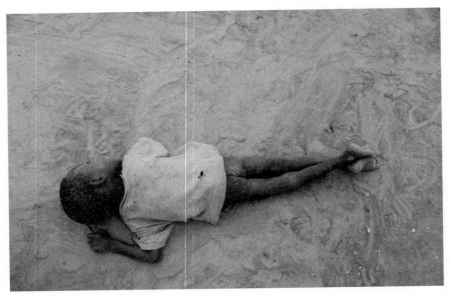

Sam

We were able to get Sam and Esther to a German medical missionary who treated their malnutrition. In time, the Baptist woman was able to get them to a hospital in Kampala to treat them for the polio.

For many years, I've been pondering the deeper meaning of my encounter with Sam and Esther. In an odd way, while I was trying to help Sam, Sam in fact was helping me. The lesson he has taught me is: let go of everything. God's grace guided us down an uncharted path to an arid patch of dirt that was the bed on which two feeble, helpless children of God lay awaiting a fate unknown. Life or death were their only options, but they were powerless to choose. We are all lying on a bed of dirt, half naked, crippled and starving. We need God. We need each other.

I always end my "Poverty and Prayer" presentations that I have given over the years at some 250 Catholic schools and churches with these words:

> Being with Sam and Esther forced me to face my own poverty, my own weakness, my insecurity, and my own brokenness. And by doing so, I slowly learned that Christ is not asking us to be successful or productive. Christ is looking for us to be present . . . present to God (in prayer), and present to each other, present to each other in acts of love and mercy, especially present to the poor and the suffering. But we don't really take Jesus seriously. We don't love our enemies. We don't turn the other cheek. We don't forgive seventy times seven times. We don't bless those who curse us. We don't share what we have with the poor. We don't put all our hope and trust in God. We say: I am not a saint. We say: This gospel stuff can't be meant for everybody. We say: The gospel is an ideal. But the gospel is not merely an ideal. The gospel is the Way.
>
> Maybe it is a time to recognize that we have strayed from the Way. Maybe it is time for us to take a good look at our lives, and to turn away from our self-centeredness, turn away from things that block us from being more fully united with God. Maybe it's time to take Jesus seriously.

Making Sense of Suffering

Whether implicitly or explicitly, we all seek security and consolation. Yet even when we find some level of security, some degree of consolation, it isn't enough. For many, security and consolation are beyond their reach. Far beyond. Jesus claimed that true security and consolation could only be found in God.

In Uganda, seeing so much intense, unfathomable suffering shook my notions of security and unmasked my true helplessness and inability to control anything in life. When you look, really look, at the suffering on full display in Uganda, you are forced to clearly see that life is unfair, often brutally unfair. In the midst of so much suffering, our flimsy ideas of God are blown to pieces. God's seeming silence in the face of such widespread suffering and violence is baffling. Yet, as St. Francis discovered, Jesus is found and encountered at the foot of the cross. The mystery of love and the mystery of the cross are one and the same. The inflowing of God's love purges and transforms . . . and it hurts.

We must die to our self-centeredness, must divest our ego and put on the mind of Christ and grow in love for all of humanity and give our lives, as Jesus gave his life, so that others may live . . . even our enemies. Jesus wants to shatter our complacency toward the suffering poor, wants us to see and feel their suffering; he wants us to renounce our own security and share our love and material possessions with those who have nothing. When we let go of our own security and put our trust in God alone, the kingdom of God shall expand and suffering shall decrease.

A Shimmering Ocean of Love

A small empty begging bowl holds the great void of life. Flowing along with birth and death, so many people hauling water and carrying firewood. So many people walking so far for the basics of life, being so far from the elixir of hope. If the human species could reach a place where there was neither lack nor excess, we would be entering a place of inexpressible light, we would be entering a place of lasting peace, we would be entering a place of immeasurable grace, we would be entering the kingdom of God. But we seem unable to discard greed and anger, unable to live without grasping, unwilling to embrace the other. So, we are unable to sail on the shimmering ocean of love that is God.

A Life of Prayer and Adoration

In the summer of 2009, I spent a week in Paray-le-Monial, France, where I spoke and showed film clips to a gathering of 4,500 Catholic young people from all over Europe. Centuries earlier, a nun from Paray, which is located in the heart of Burgundy, had a remarkable vision that gave birth to deep devotion to Jesus. She was a simple nun. She lived in a small, rural town surrounded by lush fields and rolling hills far from the centers of human power. She lived the hidden life of a cloistered nun, a dedicated life of prayer and adoration. Yet she saw something no one else had seen. What she saw is still touching and transforming lives more than 335 years after her first vision.

In so many ways our sophisticated, modern world is vastly different from hers; yet, in the most essential ways, life today is still very much the same as it was for this obscure, humble, veiled sister living long ago and far away in a monastery in the 1670s. We still all seek communion, all need something beyond ourselves. We need to know the heart of God, to give our hearts to God and to each other.

In a series of visions, Jesus revealed his most precious heart to Sr. Margaret Mary Alacoque, a divine heart beating and overflowing with endless love for humanity, a human heart bowed and broken by the suffering endured by countless humans around the world because of poverty and violence, unjust and chronic poverty, unwarranted and brutal violence.

In the nine years before going to France, I had made more than a dozen films on chronic poverty, films that had taken me to the worst slums in India, Uganda, Kenya, India, Brazil, Peru, El Salvador, Mexico, Jamaica, and the Philippines. In those dreadful slums, I had witnessed an unfathomable amount of misery, suffering, and death; I was physically, emotionally, and spiritually drained.

During my time in France and learning about St. Margaret Mary Alacoque (as well as visiting Ars, the hometown of St. John Marie Vianney), I felt led to intensify my relationship with the Lord through deepening my prayer life and to more firmly commit myself to being a voice for the voiceless poor around the world. The commitment to prayer waned, as it bumped up against periods of spiritual dryness and sinfulness. By God's unmerited grace, I kept being drawn back to prayer, back to an authentic life that had no need for idle diversions manufactured by a culture obsessed with trivial entertainment and mindless gossip. But it is a constant struggle.

St. Margaret Mary Alacoque and St. John Marie Vianney knew that God was found in stillness and silence. In contemplation, God gives new hearts, new eyes.

In stillness we feel the movement of God's Spirit transforming our hearts.

Heal Me

"Jesus have pity on me," the blind man cried out as Jesus passed by. Touched by the blind man's faith, Jesus healed him. We may not be physically blind or hurting, but we are all blind and injured, all in need of Jesus's healing touch or word. Life is an ever-flowing stream of injuries, and frequently the injuries are inner or spiritual wounds that can cripple us. Melancholy, depression, abuse, betrayals, and bitter disappointments can blind us to the fullness of life, can trap us in a dark corner of despair. The inner injuries that we accumulate and allow to go unhealed can rip apart the fabric of our existence. Our spiritual maladies become who we are. These injuries can prevent us from seeing Jesus, from reaching out our hand to him for healing. The power to heal still resides within the risen Lord. Jesus can still turn to us and say, "Have sight; your faith has saved you." But first, we must reach out to him.

Jesus, heal me of all the inner hurts that I do not even recognize, buried hurts that have influenced me in ways I cannot even imagine. Heal me, sweet Jesus, of the destructive behavior that allows me to choose poorly as I navigate my way through the day. Lord Jesus, heal me . . . heal me of all bitterness, all resentment, all anger, all impurity, all unloving tendencies, all behavior that does not reflect the love, compassion, and mercy that is ever-flowing from your Sacred Heart. Come, Lord Jesus, heal me, make me whole, help me love.

New Eyes, New Hearts

God does not bomb us to get us to change our behavior. God whispers words of love. We may resort to "shock and awe" to show our power to get others to bend to our will, but that's not God's way.

> *God gives us*
> *space and freedom*
> *to accept or reject*
> *his gentle overtures of love.*

God seeks a response from us that emerges from a transformed inner life that allows us to acknowledge God's power and our need for God. God seeks a deep emotional response from us. It is our response to God that allows us to subdue our ego and permits our true self to emerge.

This transformational change leads to a radical reorientation of our outlook on life. We will see the world and all of creation with new eyes and we will love with new hearts. Badness shall be transformed into goodness.

> *Grace changes everything,*
> *makes everything beautiful.*
> *We simply need*
> *stillness and silence*
> *and ears to hear.*

Moments of Grace

Thomas Merton felt that the more contemplative a person became, the better they would be able to recognize moments of grace in their lives and respond in a manner most pleasing to God. I think grace is happening all the time, but we are usually totally unaware of it. For most of us, moments of grace are only seen in retrospection, when we see how one seemingly small event in our life actually contained the seed that had, in time, a major impact on our life, perhaps even a life-altering change as when a chance meeting turned into a lifelong friendship.

> *Grace is the breath of Love.*

A Dizzying Merry-Go-Round

> *Be still, and know that I am God.*
> —Psalm 46:10 NRSV

Modern life has become a dizzying merry-go-round of nonstop activity, where it seems most of us are doing many things all at once, where people are working longer hours and their lives are increasingly fragmented by an endless array of demands, where multitasking and instant messaging are the norm in the consumer-crazed, computer-driven, cell-phone-crazy world of ours that has virtually no room for stillness and silence.

Our lives have become frantic, frenetic, frazzled, and frustrating. We ache to know how to become whole, to find meaning in and for our lives. The world is growing ever more falsely sophisticated, yet is unable to find its God and largely incapable of experiencing the simple joys of living. While we haphazardly chase after a spiritual brass ring, we continue to make bad choices that take us further away from an authentic spiritual life, a life shimmering with meaning and purpose. We feel lost, and the light of hope grows dimmer with each passing year.

We live in dark times, in an age of global anxiety and deep despair. Everyone feels threatened and concerned about the future, which looks more and more bleak for more and more people. Fear and uncertainty, along with a sense of isolation and emptiness, have skyrocketed.

Over the years, there were times in my work among the chronically poor of the world that I was left with a feeling of hopelessness. I was in Haiti immediately after the earthquake and was nearly crushed by a staggering sense of hopelessness. Without an inner sense of depth and freedom we easily become oppressed by the darkness and despair, victims of our circumstances. With God, we can see and move beyond our limitations. God created us for growth, for an ever-expanding realization of the divinity within us.

In God, there is true freedom. Outside of God, there is only bondage.

For me, seeing so much suffering in the massive slums of the world forced me to forget myself, my own limitations, and to hear the silent voice of God calling me to respond, not only to the shameful injustice, but also to God's infinite mercy and love. In seeing so many starving kids with bloated bellies and the overwhelming need of the poor, I prayed often and became less concerned with my own subjective needs and harmful compulsions, and more aware of the self-emptying love of Christ, which I needed to imitate to the best of my puny ability.

But the noise of life sometimes distracted me and rendered me deaf to God and capable of only hearing my own confused and rambling voice. By the fall of 2018, before being invited to give a retreat on prayer, "often" had become "sometimes." I'd failed to practice what I'd preached.

Without the stillness and silence of occasional solitude,
into the mediocrity of a comfortable Christianity that is no
gun-toting, hopeless nihilism of postmodern life where everything
to a commodity for sale, where unbridled greed has caused a catas
global economic recession, where materialism without qualification and
without love are affirmed and championed, where mainstream corporations
distribute pornography without shame or reproach, where dialogue has
given way to vitriolic hate speech, where alleged Christians threaten to burn
Muslim scriptures, where conflicts are settled by violence, where barbarous
acts of terrorism threaten all, where loneliness has reached epidemic
proportions and suicide is on the rise, where blind religious fundamentalism
passes for true faith, where drug addiction and alcoholism are rampant,
where opioid use is off the charts, where thousands of kids die every day
from hunger, and where selfishness and individualism have created prisons
of poverty and are destroying the earth.

In stillness and silence, we are able to catch a glimmer of the
interconnectivity of all life, to see the sun as our brother and the moon as
our sister, to see that all of humanity and all of creation as part of our family.
We are truly human when we live in harmony with God—and each other.

By hating another human being, a person is denying the existence of God.

Connecting the Dots

For a writer, solitude is essential. Solitude helps me create a state of
mindfulness. Or perhaps, better put, mindfulness is best cultivated in
solitude. But time alone is also good for my own personal and spiritual
growth. It is in solitude that I truly see and understand my deepest needs,
feelings, and impulses. Spending occasional time alone is essential to
achieving self-discovery and self-realization.

During the alone time spent while working on this book, I was able to
connect the dots of my life. During my solitary time, I saw patterns and
tendencies in my life that needed serious adjustments. I confronted the fact
that while I desired Jesus, I often defied him. I think we often cling to negative
things in our lives because without them we would feel empty. Periods of
aloneness help me refocus and renew my spirit; it is a time of learning and

nger periods of solitary time, I need to feed
ach day, taking a moment to breathe deeply
ks or praise.

ert, you must nonetheless "make some
′ and then leaving men and looking for
ed silence and prayer, the stuff of your
desert" in your spiritual life. One has
to be courageous not to let oneself be carried along by the world's
march; one needs faith and willpower to go cross-current towards
the Eucharist, to stop, to be silent, to worship.
—Carlo Carretto, *Letters from the Desert* [20]

The Desert Within

According to the Gospel of Mark, the Spirit drove Jesus into the wilderness.
Is the Spirit driving me into the desert? Seems like lots of things are driving
me, but I rarely feel the Spirit driving me. Lent is a time the church makes
space for the Spirit, a time to move away from the normal distractions of
life and be renewed by the Spirit of life. Lent is a time to look at what drives
me, what excites me, and see if those things actually drive me away from the
reality of God. Lent is about empty spaces, desert places, that give me the
opportunity to feel the Spirit drive me into the desert of my heart and mind
in order to purge them of all those desires that are not healthy. We don't have
to wait for Lent because we can enter the spirit of Lent anytime.

In the wilderness for forty days, Jesus was tempted by Satan. The desert,
with its lack of clutter and people, has endless stretches of time to look closely
at the wasteland of my life. The desert challenges me to come back to my true
self, the self that was made in the image of God, an image I have tarnished
by my self-destructive behavior, my yielding to the drives and desires that do
not reveal the beauty of God.

The desert reveals my essential neediness and vulnerability. But the
desert, with its vast horizon of empty space, is a place where I learn that I am
not alone. In the desert, you find the Spirit who shows you how to be your
true self.

In the Desert

At some point in time God calls each of us into the desert. The desert is a place of discipline, which we need but don't want, and so we avoid it. In the desert, under the blazing sun, all our weaknesses are made clear. We look around and see the vastness of nothing. We do not know which way to go. In the desert, our need for God is also made clear.

In the desert, we grow weary, we lose hope. We can't quench our own thirst. We know no pleasure. All around is only a void that stretches out beyond our sight. The day turns to night.

The arid, parched landscape can only be watered by God. God's water is sweet; God's manna is tasty. In the desert, God's love is our only comfort. In the desert, God's spirit transcends the bleakness in the depths of our souls and we can see beauty and tenderness. In the desert, ideas about God give way to God.

O Lord, help me
not evade the desert,
not flee the pain of life,
the suffering that not even
your beloved Son avoided.
Help me enter
the desert of silence,
the desert of surrender,
the desert of doubt,
the desert of sorrow and loneliness
so I can be nourished
by your loving Word alone,
which is the only source of
true refreshment
and lasting peace.

solitude is not something outside you, not an absence of
sound around you; it is an abyss opening up in the center
of your soul.
—Thomas Merton, *Seeds of Contemplation*[21]

Every year, life becomes faster and noisier. And crueler. The ever-multiplying pressures of modern life cut us off from the healing influence of nature. In Haiti, every day I watch the sunrise and the sunset from our second-floor balcony. I'm often joined by one or more kids. It is a better show than anything I could find on television—if we had a television in Haiti.

In his book *Thoughts in Solitude*, Thomas Merton wrote, "The solitary life, being silent, clears away the smokescreen of words that man has laid down between his mind and things. In solitude, we remain face to face with the naked being of things."[22]

Early monastics withdrew from society to escape the distractions of life. Solitude allowed the ancient monks to find inner peace and see more clearly the self-deceptions we all employ. Silence keeps us in touch with our soul. Quiet time is getting harder to find in our fast-paced society. When I look at the chaos in Washington, DC, at the moment, I see a bunch of people who have probably never experienced tranquility and concentration of spirit because they were busy pursuing power, fame, and fortune.

Without authentic silence, it is hard to truly listen
to what is really going on inside ourselves.

We can't live without air, water, food, and sleep—but the need of occasional periods of silence is almost as important. Even Jesus thought so: he set the example by retreating to the wilderness to pray and reflect. Solitude has transformational power. When we are alone and quiet unexpected insights often arise.

I spend one week a month in Florida in order to handle administrative chores and to beg for funding—and to sit alone in silence. When I'm in Florida and I need to go to the bank, post office, or shopping, I don't take my cell phone with me. A long line at the post office goes from being an annoyance to a time of silent prayer.

In his book *The Power of Now*, Eckhart Tolle writes, "You cannot pay attention to silence without simultaneously becoming still within: silence without, stillness within."[23] While silence and solitude are essential to our well-being, they are nonetheless uncomfortable states because we must face unpleasant truths about ourselves.

Who I am is often in conflict with who I want to be.

We each have dark sides we want to hide or ignore. Thomas Merton suggested that in quiet alone time we confront a harsh reality not with terror or shame but with tender acceptance. I've found that to be true for myself. Merton said that the harsh realities we confront in solitude are "clothed in the friendly communication of silence, and this silence is related to love."[24]

The silence of God is the silence of love.

Hidden in the Ordinary

In the incubator of silence, wisdom and tolerance are born. Life emerges in the darkness and silence of the womb.

Silence is the soil of renewal.

We shout. God whispers. God works in silence. Without voice, God silently speaks in and through everything . . . even the hopelessness of Haiti.

Silence is the language of God.

Keep Hope Alive

In Haiti, hope is always delayed and often betrayed. To effectively serve the kids in my care, I must constantly struggle against the temptation to think my work is hopeless. The only way to disarm the destructive sense of hopelessness is prayer. My search for God has pulled me strongly in two opposite directions: to the impoverished kids in Haiti and to solitude. Balancing action and contemplation is essential in our humble, often flawed efforts at following Christ and living the Gospel more fully.

Nurture hope to stay alive.

Our singular aim as individuals, as communities, and as a church is living out and being true to the Gospel. All of us, including the institutional church, are not yet fully converted to Jesus, and we all remain in constant need of conversion. I believe the Beatitudes are the core of the teachings of Jesus and the primary pathway to authentic Christian discipleship that gives birth to a spirit of peace and nonviolence in which we extend mercy and compassion to all.

Hope is the wind in the sail of spirituality.

Where Is God?

The terrible suffering of the people in Haiti is a result of centuries of man's inhumanity to man that cumulatively resulted in Haiti ending up with no infrastructure, no support system, nothing to help them when the earth shook their homes down on them, killing more than 300,000 people and leaving more than a million people homeless. On that dreadful Tuesday afternoon in January 2010, Port-au-Prince was, in a blink of an eye, pushed off a cliff into an abyss of despair. The monumental size and scope of the devastation left me speechless and disorientated.

When, in the face of such destruction, we ask, "Where is God?," we are in essence screaming into the darkness, "Why?" Why has the life been so painfully snuffed out of so many? Why are so many enduring the excruciating pain of severe crush injuries? Why are so many kids instantly orphans?

In our grief-stricken hearts, we cannot comprehend so much death, so much pain, so much sadness, and so we are shocked out of our innocence, and into the stark-naked reality that humanity is vulnerable and that centuries of greed and abuse of power by those who have banished a loving and merciful God from the equation of their lives, has left them free to rape and pillage innocent souls and fertile land. These godless, power-hungry men (including men from the United States government and commerce) have stripped countless peasants of their God-given dignity and left them absolutely powerless and imprisoned in a modern form of slavery, unable even to feed themselves.

Sadly, during much of Haiti's history, some of it rather recent, the church turned its back on the poor and sided with the rich and powerful elite. And when and where the church does not side with the poor and powerless, it is no longer the church of Jesus. It is nothing more than a social club for people pretending to be religious.

If we love God, we should try to emulate God's behavior, but for the most part we don't. God gathers. We scatter. God unites. We divide. God embraces. We exclude. And so we get Haiti. It really is that simple. The reality of so much suffering should deeply disturb us and render us mute. The slums of Port-au-Prince should bring us to our knees and keep us there for a long time before we speak.

The "why" of suffering is a question that is unanswerable. For reasons beyond our comprehension, God created a world where affliction exists, and the affliction seems random and arbitrary. We prefer seeking a supernatural remedy for suffering, while the life of Christ indicates we should be seeking a supernatural use for suffering.

The depth of our affliction is where we encounter the immensity of God's love.

Love and Goodness

Within everyone we meet there is an inherent goodness.
It is our duty to shine a light on that goodness.

In the face of such massive destruction and monstrous loss of life in Haiti, it is easy to lose faith, to begin to doubt and even succumb to hopelessness. The misery is inescapable and indescribable. Haitians and well-intentioned outsiders are quick to offer an array of social, economic, and political solutions to the problem of widespread suffering, but nothing changes and the misery goes on virtually unabated. The only way that Haiti will recover, rebuild, and renew itself is with love and goodness, and huge amounts of both for a long period of time.

It really is time we rebuild our lives, our communities, and our world on the eternal principles that cannot be destroyed by brutal dictators, gangs, terrorists, or earthquakes.

We need to see God in each other. We need to turn away from hatred and more fully embrace love. We need to make compassion the foundation of our lives and actions. Tolstoy said that our great duty as humans is to sow the seed of compassion in each other's heart. It is only compassion that will change and save the world. Anne Frank reminds us, "How wonderful it is that nobody needs wait a single moment before starting to improve the world."

Easter beckons us to build bridges to unity, bridges to a distant shore where common ground is found and peace prevails. Easter is a time of healing, a time for us to embody Christ's work of reconciliation. Our very woundedness is waiting to be transformed into compassion. Our emotional and physical pain helps us understand and respond to the suffering of another.

Compassion is as elegant as any cathedral.

At Easter, we proclaim in song that "Christ is risen." And he truly has. But yet, when we look at the reality of the world around us, we see death and destruction, revenge and retaliation. Our culture of death dominates our spirit of life. We have lost our prophetic voice, and we no longer defend the stranger, the widow, and the orphan, those who are hurting and have no voice.

Cité Soleil, the largest and worst slum in Haiti, and places like it exist because we as the human family have forgotten God and turned our backs on God's children. We need to share our time, our treasure, our love with the chronically poor. Jesus wants us to give our lives away. This is Gospel giving. In our giving of ourselves, Christ is truly risen.

> *Life and death, words and silence, are given us because of Christ. In Christ we die to the flesh and live to the spirit. In Him we die to illusion and live to truth. We speak to confess Him, and we are silent in order to meditate on Him and enter deeper into His silence, which is at once the silence of death and of eternal life—the silence of Good Friday night and the peace of Easter morning.*
> —Thomas Merton, *No Man is an Island*[25]

A Different Perspective

Within three months of the earthquake, the world pretty much moved on, moved on to other crises and disasters around the world. Ordinary Haitians struggled along pretty much on their own, pretty much forgotten.

The long stretch of time, some thirty weeks, between the liturgical seasons of Lent and Easter and the year-end weeks of Advent and Christmas is known as Ordinary Time. In Ordinary Time we descend from the mountain peaks of Christmas and Easter to the more ordered pastures and vast mundane meadows of everyday life where we live out our vocation to love. Day by day during the long stretches of the year not marked by major holidays we are called to become active vessels of divine grace by responding to the needs of our neighbors and opening our hearts to them.

As the months rolled by after my third visit to Haiti, during Holy Week 2010, I could not shake Haiti from my consciousness. It was ever on my mind. I had to return, had to go deeper into the suffering, deeper into the bloated belly of poverty. I returned to Haiti in August for two weeks, and again in October for ten days. I did not stay in a hotel. I lived in a large slum known as Girardoville. I lived without electricity and running water . . . and with mice and rats. I've filmed poverty like this all over the world. But to actually live in it is another story altogether.

To live in a slum, even for a short period of time, is to see Haiti from a different perspective, to see it through the eyes of the outcast and oppressed, the eyes of the hungry and powerless. To see Haiti from the point of view of those who are suffering changes everything. Suddenly, the cross of Christ and solidarity with the oppressed are linked in a bond of tangible holiness. In this bond, the sufferings of others become as important as our own sufferings . . . or in truth, they are one and the same, all united in the mystery of Christ's painful death on the cross.

To contemplate the naked and rejected Christ on the cross as we share in the ordinary lives of the suffering poor helps us see our own weakness, vulnerability, and failure. In recognizing my true nakedness, I see more clearly how we are all in need of God's loving and merciful embrace. In Girardoville, I'm no different from nor any better than anyone else. In Girardoville, I faced my worst fears and they were slowly overcome, and from their death new life was born.

On the cross, violence ended . . . and death was no longer repaid by death.

It is in Ordinary Time, in the ordinary days of our lives, we the ordinary disciples of Christ live out our calling to be more and more like Jesus.

The Road to Holiness

> *There is only one journey. Going inside you.*
> —Rainer Maria Rilke

Shortly after the above-mentioned two-week trip to Haiti in August 2010, I began writing about the experience in a very long book that, even after more than 257,326 words, I never completed. It was titled On Becoming Mystical Mirrors of Mercy. *Here is the prologue from the book, which I read for the first time in over six years as I was finishing* The Sunrise of the Soul. *Reading it had a profound impact on me and I knew I needed to incorporate it in this book. Forgive me.*

It happened in Haiti. After five full days, I was ready to give up. Life in the slum was just too damn hard, too harsh. I was emotionally and physically drained. I didn't think I could survive another day. I've filmed in slums like this all over the world, but to live in one is another story—a horror story teeming with rodents, roaches, ants, and mosquitoes. Life without running water and electricity was exhausting and brutally difficult. The stench of human waste and rotting garbage was inescapable and nauseating. Violence and corruption were commonplace. The slum that had been my home is in the earthquake-devastated city of Port-au-Prince, in a profoundly impoverished area known as Girardoville. Access to the heart of the slum is limited to one unpaved, bumpy, downhill road that is almost impassable. The grueling physical journey out of the slum is symbolic of the even more challenging journey out of the hopelessness of the place and a city where the toxic air reeks of death.

On August 16, 2010, during the night of my sixth day in the slum, I became very sick. I awoke in the middle of the night and was shivering even though the night air was still very warm. I was running a fever and was wet from perspiration. Worse, I could not stop coughing. I became anxious when I realized I was trapped, that there was no way out of the slum at night. When people get sick here, especially at night, they die. It is that simple. Residents of this slum have nowhere to go for help; even if they did, they would have no money to pay for medical treatment. Curable illnesses, such as malaria and pneumonia—even a simple infection—quickly turn into death sentences. I was more fortunate. My fever ran its course within two days, and I was able to find a pharmacy outside the slum and purchase medication for what I assumed was a bronchial or lung infection that dogged me for the rest of trip.

In this place of overwhelming need, I faced my own emptiness and limitations.

In a sea of black faces, I faced my own dark side, my own deep poverty and loneliness, my own weaknesses and doubts. Before leaving on this two-week-long immersion into the life of the poor I told family and friends that I would be living with the poor so I could be one with them in a more tangible way than ever before. In essence I was saying I wanted to go deeper into the bloated belly of poverty, deeper than I was able to go in any of my films. Of almost equal importance, I saw the trip as a way to try to discern God's will for the balance of my life, whose days, at my age (sixty-three at the time), are certainly numbered. Of course, the ultimate truth we seek is always beyond our grasp. How do we make sense of an earthquake that killed more than 300,000 Haitians or the tsunami in the Indian Ocean that killed nearly 250,000 people in 2004? How can we ever begin to understand, despite all our metaphysical musings, the mystery and paradox of creation and destruction? Before the mystery and meaning of life, we are all extremely poor.

We cannot grasp the transcendent; we can only be present, albeit weakly, to it.

In this deeply dysfunctional capital city of Haiti, where extreme chaos and suffering are woven into the fabric of daily life, I found beauty, grace, and a new way to look at life. I saw the futility of my own self-centeredness. In a broken place, I saw my own brokenness, and I caught a fleeting glimpse of wholeness where there is no division between body and soul, faith and actions, where there is unity of being. In the harshness of daily life I came to see how hauling water could become an act of love that bound me to myself, to a neighbor, and to God. In this slum, my understanding of myself, my life, and God was stretched way beyond the boundaries I'd previously experienced. This slum became a place of personal transfiguration and a way through a dreadful personal crisis.

Mysticism and mercy help us learn to love beyond our present capacity. The mystic is simply a person who has experiential knowledge that God dwells within, in the deep recesses of the soul, hidden but truly present. Mercy is a ray of light and love in the midst of darkness and despair.

Mysticism and mercy form the bridal chamber of love.

I believe my spiritual life is essentially a journey in which I move from what I am to what I will become. I'm just beginning to learn that life is a journey to weakness. The saints truly learned to live when they began to explore their own weaknesses. By God's unmerited grace, every experience of weakness is an opportunity of growth and renewed life. St. Catherine of Genoa made a stunning statement: "My deepest me is God." On the contrary, during most of my life I felt within me a dreadful emptiness. I've come to believe that sense of barrenness stemmed from not realizing I was created for communion with God. Thomas Merton said, "We all exist solely for this—to be the human place God has chosen for his presence, his manifestation, his epiphany."[26] If I'm not growing toward unity with God, then I'm growing apart from God. I need to be inwardly still and humble in order to move into a greater union with God. I need to bring to Christ what I am so that in time I might become more like what he is. To become more like Christ requires me to divest all traces of ungodly behavior, and this is not an easy task.

The spiritual life, for Christians, is a grinding process
where we eventually are ground into God.

In following Christ, I've seen with my own eyes in so many unrelentingly bleak places around the world how life is filled to overflowing with pain and struggle. Following Christ leads to the cross, and it doesn't offer an easy way around it. It's all about surrender. To become a disciple of Christ, to become fully human, means accepting a spirituality of the cross and renouncing a spirituality of glory. Christ humbled himself in order to love me. He gave of himself to love me. In turn, I must give of myself in order to love Christ and all of creation.

I've filled up many frames and minutes of my films, many chapters and pages of my books, with words about poverty. So much of what I had written was merely empty rhetoric because I really was far removed from the brutal reality of chronic poverty, experiencing it from behind the safety of a camera and the shelter of a hotel. Even living for two weeks fully immersed in the life of the poor in a Haitian slum was not a true experience of poverty because I had a plane ticket to Los Angeles in my pocket and a credit card in my wallet; I could go home or to a hotel whenever I wanted to escape the misery and protracted trauma. But it did give me a much clearer idea of just how terrible the lives of the poor are.

Life in the slums and tent cities of Haiti is saturated with violence and boredom.

Basic human dignity is snuffed out by the constant struggle to survive each day. It's hard to imagine living a life without hope, and having to face on a daily basis absolute insecurity and complete vulnerability. How can we truly know and understand what it is like to live with constant degradation, desperation, uncertainty, and hopelessness? After being home for only three days, I had already begun to slip back into my comfortable and orderly world where I do not have to give a thought to food and water—even though, by the standards of my society, I am a poor man. The mere fact that I had options places me far above the Haitians with whom I was living.

Haiti was born and bred in hatred, oppression, deprivation, and despair. Empires came and went, flourished off that small island parcel, once paradise, today hell. The long history of violence and neglect has left Haiti so expended, so exhausted, so completely without any resources, that truly impoverished Haitians have barely a glimmer of hope of how to change their sorrowful plight. The poor of Haiti have been maligned and neglected for so long it seems it took nothing short of a cataclysmic earthquake claiming tens upon tens of thousands of lives for the world to focus on this tormented sliver of humanity and become aware of the torturous conditions so many endured before the earthquake. And then the world quickly forgot Haiti.

Today the necessities of life are far beyond the reach of most Haitians, and the consequences of this reality are dire. Humans have a need to work. Combined with love, the need to work is essential. Work gives us a creative release and helps us feel valued and useful. Ideally our work should help us make the world a better place. It should connect us to the world beyond ourselves and contribute constructively to the well-being of our neighbors.

Through our work we become co-creators
with the evolving world in which we dwell.

For the poor, there is no meaningful work in Haiti. Deprived of the deep need for fulfilling work that will liberate their creative potential, many poor Haitians have become apathetic. The menial work they do find does not validate them or bring them any satisfaction or joy. The work is pure drudgery performed solely for a sinfully meager amount of money that can barely purchase the bare basics for survival. Their dignity and giftedness have been stripped from them. Life in the slums slowly sinks into a state of total dysfunction, despair, and anomie—and the slum becomes a womb that gives birth to an array of deviant behavior and violence. In similar massive slums around the world, people suffer from a deep sense of alienation, as they are cut off from any form of connectedness to the world and the society surrounding them. Escape is not possible; hope is dead.

During my fourteen-day trip, I took about a thousand still photographs as I documented life not only in the slum where I lived but also in two small tent cities. From my perspective, after three previous trips to Haiti, including one just a few days after the earthquake that demolished Port-au-Prince, and two subsequent trips (October and December 2010), the situation in Haiti seemed to be getting worse. One year after the earthquake, there were still a million homeless people in Port-au-Prince. Tents were everywhere. They lined the streets, filled the fields, and were jammed into every open space. Many tents had become frayed from the intensity of the sun and the nightly rain storms. Infectious diseases were spreading like wildfire. Violence against women was rising steadily; rapes were commonplace. Many people were forced to bathe in the streets without the benefit of any privacy. The poorest of the poor ate cakes made of mud and polluted water. At night, kids chased the rats away with sticks. The rubble from the collapsed buildings was everywhere. Traffic was a nightmare thanks to roads cluttered with potholes and debris from fallen buildings.

By simply being in Haiti without any agenda, without the pressure of trying to make a film, I gained a clearer sense of perspective—of myself and life. In the slum, I saw how defenseless and vulnerable we all are, how precarious the human situation is. Every day people die from the icy cold of indifference and loneliness. But poverty is more than a lack of food, work, and options. Poverty is a destructive force that destroys the unity of the human family by dividing us into camps of those who have and those who don't have.

Between the rich and the poor, there is an impenetrable wall that separates us. That scandalous wall must come down.

Old Testament scholar Walter Brueggemann says, "It is the vocation of the prophet to keep alive the ministry of imagination, to keep on conjuring and proposing alternative futures to the single one the king wants to urge as the only thinkable one."[27] The king today—that is, the rich—is the soulless corporation that fuels insatiable desire for endless consumption without any concern for the common good. Sadly, daily life in our day is ruled by competition instead of cooperation and by conflicting interests instead of collaboration. In order for the poor to elevate themselves they need a basic level of security that safeguards and satisfies their essential survival needs.

Contemporary society, with its ever-accelerating pace of life, is becoming increasingly fragmented and superficial. We're in such a hurry we don't take time for simple acts of kindness. For the most part, sadly, people worship on the altar of self-interest. The structures of poverty and oppression are so deeply ingrained that it will take more than random acts of kindness to uproot them. Unless there is a global movement toward working in solidarity for the common good of all, we are doomed. But that kind of shift in understanding and consciousness is extremely difficult in our current environment because politics has become so riddled with rancor and divisiveness that a union of hearts working together for the good of all is virtually impossible, the mission of a fool. Moreover, thoughtless religious fundamentalism is fueling hatred and violence and reducing the wisdom of loving your neighbor to just the person living next door to you, as long as that person doesn't subscribe to a faith you consider evil. Our definition of neighbor has been far too narrowly defined.

Our neighbor includes everyone, and loving our neighbor excludes no one.

Extending compassion to all people, even our enemies, is the very heart of the Christian faith. It is, I believe, the path to holiness. Jesus makes it abundantly clear that compassion is to be our central spiritual practice. And through compassion, we are better able to control greed and work together for the equitable distribution of the resources of God's creation so that one day soon there will be no hunger on planet Earth, and that everyone will be able to fulfill the basic human desire to live fruitfully. The lives of the saints clearly show that compassion is the fruit of holiness. For St. Francis of Assisi, whose life never fails to inspire me, mysticism and mercy became a single, seamless garment that comforted and protected him on his unique journey to God.

Somewhere deep inside of each of us, there is, I believe, a desire to be holy. We can quibble about what being holy means, but essentially it means being really, really good . . . even when no one is watching. For a Christian, the essential meaning of holiness is more precise: it means being like Christ. But the manifest goodness on full display in the lives of the saints grows out of love. Their love of God is so strong, so deep, that their lives pulsate with God's love and goodness.

Saints are icons of holiness.

Saints make holiness real; they show us holiness is possible. Saints are also fully human. They make mistakes and have their share of failures. They cry and they laugh. They endure illnesses and disappointments. They fight long and hard to overcome doubts and insecurities. They often experience rejection and scorn from family and friends. They struggle with spiritual growth as they attempt to follow a path they hope and pray leads to God. Saints are ordinary people whose passion to emulate the self-emptying love of Christ is extraordinary. Saints are flesh and blood, not pious plastic statues. They are not perfect; but they allow the love of Christ to transform their weaknesses and imperfections into something beautiful.

To study the lives of the saints arouses within us a response, a desire to imitate real examples of holiness. The good news is we don't have to be another St. Francis of Assisi. We simply need to become the saints we were uniquely created to be. And in a hundred years, it will not matter if we are in a book of "official" saints. Even today, there are countless everyday saints living holy lives of prayer and service who are virtually invisible. But God sees them, sees all of them. I've met a few of them: men and women living the Gospel, sacrificing everything as they serve the poor; they too have truly inspired me as I filmed their work.

Each of us is called to become a saint in our own quiet way.

The road to holiness, I firmly believe, is paved with mysticism and mercy, which is the true way back to ourselves and back to God.

Genesis

We live in a constant state of genesis, always changing, always evolving, always being born anew.

Today we begin again. This very moment is pregnant with new possibilities for growing in God, with God, through God.

Today is a new creation.

A Field of Poppies

Our spirits need time to rest, to wander in a field of poppies, to soar with the sunrise, to swing in a hammock. Our spirits need time to simply do nothing, which, oddly enough, will give us the ability to do everything better.

Solitude gives us insight into our deepest needs and feelings.

Tranquility of heart and mind springs naturally from the well of solitude.

God speaks in silence.

Bird-Watching

Our senses have become dulled to the wonder of creation, which we take for granted. We don't see the beauty before us. Beauty is everywhere. Every landscape we love is the landscape of our soul. Pay attention to the lilies, watch the birds.

Celebrate life . . . instead of trying to control it.

Technical skill and tangible results, high priests of our age, are of little worth in the spiritual life. The spiritual life places a premium on integrity and integration.

The mystery of life cannot be solved with scientific or psychological answers. The key to the solution, if there even is one, is mystical.

The eternal confounds everything we say and do.

Life is littered with conflicts that cannot be resolved. Moreover, we can't escape conflict in our lives. Conflicts are a part of life. But we do have a choice in how we respond to a conflict. And fighting is always a bad choice.

So much of life is contradiction and chaos.
Only in stillness and prayer
can harmony emerge from the confusion.

A Luminous Creation

Asceticism plays a part in the spiritual life just as discomfort plays a part in the natural life. We do what we need to do in order to fight cold and heat; so also we need to fight sin and weakness. But compulsive asceticism is of no use.

At the very least, asceticism can be an effective self-management tool. However, extreme asceticism can be detrimental.

When asceticism and mysticism wed, the saints tell us they give birth to a luminous creation . . . as long as both are hidden with Christ in God.

Out of nothing comes everything.
Out of darkness comes light.
Out of desolation comes consolation.

Creating Beauty

In the act of creation, we begin to approach ever so dimly the divine imagination. It is important for each of us to create something, our own creative expression, that is a mere fragment of the creative explosion birthed in the boundless imagination of God.

Our very lives can create beauty by our very presence.

We Are All Fragments

A fragment is a part of something that has broken away from the whole. It is detached, isolated, an incomplete part of something larger. We are all fragments, part of the fullness of God, thousands of little bits of colored tile in the vast mosaic that is the divine face, each of us a tiny part of the infinite reality that is the face of God. As the great fifteenth-century German mystic Nicholas of Cusa said, "Every face you encounter in life is a face of the Faceless One." The face of God is so vast it is faceless from our limited perspective.

I like the metaphor of a road, that we are on a journey to our real home, a home in a faraway place that will cloak us in love and mercy, kindness, and forgiveness, and allow us to heal our fragmentary selves and blend in to the safety and unity of a truly Holy Family, where God our Mother and Father watches over us, protects us, nourishes us, and loves us into and through all eternity.

Each morning we are awakened to the presence of God. When our hearts and minds are awakened by God, each morning becomes a silent symphony, each day is orchestrated according to the ways of harmony and peace, and each moment becomes a sacramental moment where heaven and earth have the potential to meet. Our journey to God begins afresh each morning. If we begin the day in prayer, in God, then the day will flow out from God and lead us home to God.

Be the fragment of God you were meant to be.

The Still Point

The super-excited, overstimulated pace of life today is way out of sync with the way God operates. God works without rush or noise in stillness and silence.

While our lives are lived in fast-forward, Christ invites us to press pause and to "come apart and rest awhile."

> *We need to stop running and find the still point*
> *where God waits to embrace us.*

God's love does not shout, it whispers. Be still and hear God whisper soft words of fondest love. Listen . . . don't think.

> *Love radiates, not dominates.*

Every facet of our lives needs to be permeated by love in order to grow closer to God. Any portion of our lives that we have not surrendered to love becomes an obstacle to reaching God.

Mystical Eyes

Each day brings its share of sweetness and bitterness, of joy and misery, of comfort and pain, of laughter and tears, of hopes and disappointments.

Each day brings rejection and acceptance, loneliness and communion. Each day brings moments of fear and despair and courage and delight. Each day brings a flood of words and a desert of silence.

Each day we have moments of transparency and deception, moments of faithfulness and infidelity, moments of strength and weakness, moments of purity and lust, moments of beauty and cruelty, moments of abundance and famine, moments of peace and turmoil.

> *Each day*
> *God is present*
> *in all these things,*
> *in all the ups and downs,*
> *in the heartache and elation,*
> *in the victories and the defeats.*

But God's presence is hidden and silent. It is only through faith that we can see and hear God, even though our seeing and hearing are gravely impaired and far from perfect. We really don't know God, yet we do know God. In our not knowing is the beginning of our knowing. But the fullness of knowing will always be beyond us, yet hidden within us.

> To see God
> in all things
> each day,
> is the mysticism
> of everyday life,
> the ordinary mysticism
> that sees the extraordinary
> work of God
> even in the mundane events
> of everyday life.

With everyday mystical eyes we are able to see God in both the cries of the poor and the laughter of a child, in both a tender kiss and in a deadly disease.

Mystical Possibilities

God speaks to us even in the smallest and most ordinary events of daily life. Even the most ordinary moments of the day are charged with mystical possibilities. To see the mystical in the ordinary, we need to pause often during the day and be attentive to what is really happening all around us and inside us.

As soon as you open your heart to God you are in the mystical world.

Mystical hope does not look for miracles, does not depend on external circumstances. Mystical hope wells up from within, springs from a deep sense of presence and intimate communion. Not tied to good fortune, mystical hope can smile in the face of the harshest of hardships. We, on our own, cannot generate mystical hope even though it comes from within us rather than from outside us.

The Difficult Journey

Everyone experiences heartbreak; everyone is in need of tenderness and compassion. At some point in our lives, we all have to face the difficult journey of coming to terms with feelings of rejection, humiliation, and fear. These very real and very painful feelings, which I know all too well, in time and in prayer, become an authentic path from despair to hope. Tragedies and disasters become places of courage, of perseverance, places where we learn to plumb the depths of our inner life, our true essence, and are able, by God's grace, to move from rejection and terror to healing and hope.

> *Love grows from that deep-rooted pain*
> *within the universe where God is present,*
> *and ever-willing to embrace us and bless us.*

A by-product of our fast-paced modern life is that most of us are so fully engaged in an endless stream of activities and endeavors that we have lost the aptitude for deep listening and as a result have alienated ourselves from the very source of our being. We have forgotten the clear biblical instruction: *Be still and know I am God.* By periodically, perhaps even on a daily basis, silencing our intellect and senses, we are not briefly fleeing the world but attempting to experience the essential reality of a full life in God. The "life in abundance" that Jesus promises is blocked by our whirlwind of activity that only leaves us feeling tired and impoverished.

> *The universal lack of an interior life is a key element*
> *behind the rash of violent political and religious conflicts*
> *that plague so many nations.*

Man is exiled from God and from his inmost self. He is tempted to seek God, and happiness, outside himself. So his quest for happiness becomes, in fact, a flight from God and from himself: a flight that takes him further and further away from reality. In the end, he has to dwell in the "region of unlikeness"—having lost his inner resemblance to God in losing his freedom to enter his own home, which is the sanctuary of God.
—Thomas Merton, *The Inner Experience: Notes on Contemplation*[28]

The Streets of Life

The spiritual life does not lift us above the human condition—its misery, problems, confrontations, pain, and difficulties. Spiritual life plunges us deeply into our humanity. It would be nice to sit in church all day, hands clasped in prayer, drinking the ecstasy of the Lord. But that is unrealistic; we must enter into the marketplace, walk the alleys of commerce. We must help each other out of the ditches into which we fall. In the streets of life, we encounter God. Everything human is divine.

Strive to live the present moment as it truly is: a gift from God.

Every living thing should cause us to praise the Creator of all living things. Every event of our lives is open to God; prayer reveals how. The whole world, including every aspect of humanity, is sacred and a gateway to God. Wherever you are, whatever you are doing, God is there. Strive to feel God's presence and warmth in the ordinary moments of the day. The commonplace is also a divine place.

The sacred is not here or there but everywhere. The challenge is to become aware of it. God is rarely where I think God should be. God is on a crowded tap-tap in Port-au-Prince. God is in the stillness of the early morning dew. Everything speaks of God. Thank God.

In stillness we detect the movement of God.

St. Francis of Assisi found God not in pomp and glory, but in infirmity and foolishness. He found God in what we throw away. Francis found the God of endless light hiding in the shadows, on the margin of society.

Everything human is divine.

Merton's Hermitage

In 2000, I spent the first week of Advent alone in Thomas Merton's hermitage on the grounds of Our Lady of Gethsemani Abbey in Kentucky.

Wednesday, December 6, 2000—10:40 AM, Merton's Hermitage. After breakfast, I sat quietly in front of the fireplace. The house was really cold and I had not started the furnace, thinking I would wait until later this afternoon. After I meditated for about twenty minutes, a picture flashed across my mind: the interior of an abandoned building in the Kensington section of Philadelphia, where squatters had set fire to the staircase to keep warm during a bitterly cold night. I had been in the building—and many more like it—while making the documentary on the St. Francis Inn.

Fr. Francis Pompei, OFM, found a young man in the abandoned building. He was bundled up against the cold night. His name was Efrem, and he had been homeless for about a month. He said, "It's rough." A towering example of an understatement. Sitting alone in Merton's hermitage—living in "rough" conditions—I'm reminded of the plight of the poor who live in far, far worse conditions because of injustice and not out of seeking a "spiritual" experience. We cannot walk toward God and turn our backs on our suffering brothers and sisters at the same time. If you are reading these words in the comfort of a home, put the book down and go show God's mercy and love to someone who does not have a home. To forget the poor is to forget God.

It is the hour for prayer; if you hear the poor calling you, mortify yourself and leave God for God, although you must do everything you can not to omit your prayer, for that is what keeps you united to God; and as long as this union lasts you have nothing to fear.
—St. Vincent de Paul

In My Brokenness

At the heart of every life there is a deep, mysterious pain. No one can avoid it or cure it. My faith tells me that God loves me in my brokenness. God loves me fully and unconditionally, without a hint of reservation, even in my darkest, most sinful, most unloving moments. God does not demand perfection; God gives love.

The essence of faith is trust . . .
trusting in God's undivided, unmerited love.

Sadly, life today tends to teach us not to trust anyone.

You must walk down the road of forgiveness if you want to reach peace.

Our brokenness is part of human life. There are times we will be unlovable, irritating, incompetent, and inconsistent. But it is okay. We must recognize who we are in word and deed and accept who we are and then work to change who we truly are. We can forgive ourselves for our faults and failures. The key thing to know, understand, and truly believe is that our sins cannot keep us from God. God's grace never stops flowing toward us. When, by God's grace, we repent and sincerely turn our lives around, we begin to live as a forgiven person, armed with the ability to forgive others and to live in peace with all. Being beloved by God becomes central to our identity. When we believe deep down to the core of our being that we are the beloved son or daughter of God, everything changes . . . because we see God everywhere and in all of creation.

In our brokenness
Jesus makes us strong.

God sees our broken parts, missing parts, and God loves us anyway.

Spiritual perfection is not measured by our piety. It is measured by our relationship with others, treating others with mercy and kindness. Satan lives in the spirit of divisiveness. God lives in the spirit of unity. We can't get rid of all our imperfections. We need to use our imperfections as a path to holiness.

In This Darkness

The horrific and senseless murder of fifty Muslims in Christchurch, New Zealand, in 2019 reveals the deepening fissures of divisiveness around the world. We are lost. All is hopeless. Look around, the evidence is clear. War, hatred, violence, lying, cheating, stealing, and corruption abound. Greed and lust are secular virtues. Morality has been tossed out the window. There can be no doubt: we are lost, all is hopeless. We are powerless to change anything.

But in this darkness, God sheds a light. What was impossible for us to see—love, mercy, compassion, kindness, hope—is possible with God. God has the infinite power to change everything. But we have the on/off switch to that unlimited power. That switch is surrender and obedience. To have access to God's power, we must first surrender our own will and then submit to the will of God. The switch is in our hands. We choose not to see it. We mask our blindness and hopelessness with an array of illusions and deceptions. So, the darkness remains because without God we are lost and all is hopeless.

What do I want? is the question we strive to answer. Jesus would have us ask a different question: What can I give?

A Journey Toward Understanding

> *Diversity is not the cause of disunity.*
> *A garden consists of many plants but is still one garden.*

Interfaith dialogue requires that people of differing faiths avoid dogmatic assertions when speaking with each other. Theological arrogance and rigidity stifle any authentic exchange. Nor will dialogue succeed if our aim is selling our theological perspective. True dialogue requires an honest mutual exploration of our respective theologies and felt experiences of God; it is a journey toward understanding, not convincing.

> *Perhaps people of differing faiths*
> *can each grow closer to God*
> *by drawing closer to each other.*

The path of peace is dialogue. Dialogue transforms a stranger into a friend. Friends can unite in the struggle against poverty and evil.

> *The world's faiths speak*
> *in uniquely different tongues*
> *of a transcendent reality*
> *common to them all.*

To be a Christian does not require me to deny the truth and reality of other faiths. To be a Christian allows me to honor the holiness and goodness of other faiths. We need faith without fanaticism; we need belief that admits ambiguity.

I confess to having a hard time understanding the quantum theory in physics. But the quantum principle of a complementarity that tolerates ambiguity, approximation, probability, and paradox greatly appeals to me. Inflexible certitudes turn me off and worry me.

Searching for Truth

The universe is clothed in diversity, yet humankind seeks and religion claims one truth. It would be nice to meet someone who had faith without having answers. Is it possible to learn enough to erase doubt? If only for a day I could take refuge in the comfort of certainty. But on the flip side, certitude is followed by repose.

We humans want to possess the truth, yet it is only in searching for truth that we can expand our abilities to be more human, more thoughtful, more loving. Unless your beliefs have never been questioned, or have hardened into ritualistic dogma, it is their nature to change as you change or your circumstances change.

People instinctively protect themselves, by any means necessary, from questions whose answers they cannot bear. Most people don't think, they simply secrete clichés. Humans are moved by falsehoods just as fiercely as by truths. There is never any need to dress up the truth. Truth travels best unadorned.

I saw the following message on a billboard in front of a church: "Faith sees things that are out of sight." To the believer, that statement is profound; to the unbeliever, it is profoundly stupid. Most people, most of the time, are not governed by reason or faith, but by habit and urges.

We fear the unknown . . . fear what we don't know. We worry about not being in control. We dread uncertainty. Yet the stuff we know about God, all our certainties about God, all our clinging to traditions, need to be held very loosely and even dropped if real spiritual growth, real transformation, is to be possible.

The truth of your faith is pointless unless it animates your heart.

Spiritual Friendships

We really need interreligious dialogue; in fact, our very survival depends on it. There is a Buddhist story in which a disciple once told the Buddha that he felt friendship constituted half of the spiritual life. Buddha corrected the monk by saying friendship was the whole of spiritual life. Friendship between religions is not optional; and that friendship must be based on mutual respect. Only in friendship can we begin to experience unity, and in that unity, we may come to realize that our collective understanding will lead to peace and harmony . . . and God. No religion has a monopoly on truth and wisdom. Even if I truly believe that Christianity, and even more specifically Catholicism, contains all the truth I need to help me find my way to God (and I do), it nonetheless is imperative that I be open to the truth found in other religions and be willing to learn from them. Many Christians have claimed that their faith has grown stronger through dialogue with Buddhists. I know my Christian faith has been made stronger by reading the spiritual works of great Buddhist and Jewish writers, such as Thich Nhat Hanh and Abraham Joshua Heschel. I'm greatly moved by the celebrated Muslim mystic and poet Rumi.

Hidden and Waiting

The innermost essence of God is hidden from us, totally separated from the created world. We can see only hints of God's love, which is enduring and incomprehensible.

> God is utterly transcendent
> and lovingly immanent.

The call to holiness is an invitation to enter fully into a committed relationship with God. As we respond, God graciously nurtures growth in the relationship, by using events, circumstances, and people in our lives as instruments to hasten a contemplative outlook on life. Prayer becomes a vital part of our day; and, in prayer, we encounter more fully the Author of our life.

This personal encounter with the Creator slowly transforms us into a divine likeness, as it gently erases all traces of the ungodlike substance within us. Of course, ridding ourselves of all ungodlike behavior is a goal most of us will never reach. But success is not the point. Persistent effort is what matters.

In prayer, we unlock
the vault to our deepest self
and allow light to shine on God,
who is already abiding
at the very core of our being,
hidden from us
yet patiently
waiting for us.

In a Fog

Let yourself be loved; let yourself be acted on by God.

There is nothing so steady and relentless, so committed and enduring, so firm and unwavering as God's love for us. Over and over again, in story after story, Jesus tells us that the defining characteristic of God is not anger but love.

Yet we stumble around in a fog of misplaced guilt and wrong attachments. As children of God, we are called to be people of love, people who accept God's love and people who transmit God's love.

Authentic Transformation

Outside the inevitable suffering caused by death and accidents, most suffering bubbles up out of our craving for transitory things and our worldly attachments. There are other forms of harmful attachments. For instance, it is easy to become attached to the kind of secure certainty peddled by religious fundamentalism. But this kind of "knowing" is a roadblock to true knowing. Clinging to the comfort of certainty is just as bad as all our other addictions. It is difficult for God's Word to enter our inner temple because its entrance is blocked by our endless array of attachments.

In order to be heard, God requires us to be silent and detached.

Without daily contemplative silence it is impossible to have a true encounter with God's Word within us, where authentic transformation begins.

Prayer is waiting, intending, desiring God. Prayer, we might
say, is a holding on to God, until waiting, waiting, waiting, we
move into the knowledge that we are being held.
—Robert Llewelyn, *Why Pray?*[29]

Human Weakness

In weakness the power of Christ is made perfect.

Prayer consists of becoming aware. The more you pray, the more you will become poor, plain, and empty . . . and ready for God. We experience God's love in proportion to our experience of our own weakness. Day in and day out, God the divine Sower liberally plants seeds in the soil of our lives. Prayer tills the soil, making it receptive to the flowering power of the seed. But far too often the soil is hardened by sin, worries, and an unhealthy pre-occupation with money, power, and success, and so the seed is trampled on or blown away.

We talk a lot about love, but the concrete experience of love is a rare thing indeed. We claim God's love created the earth and that the same love appeared on earth in Christ. But we do not see it or feel it. God's love goes unnoticed. To make visible the hidden love of God, to feel more intensely the inexpressible marvel of God, we need to spend time in prayer and time with the poor.

Because each of us is a child of God,
each of us possesses the eminent dignity
of a child of God.

Divine mercy is incarnated in human weakness.

The Heart of Darkness

I cannot learn about God. I can only unlearn the things that are keeping me from a full awareness of God. To find Christ you must make a pilgrimage to the center of your being, to the place where the human and the divine meet. The key to being a pilgrim is to remain still interiorly as you journey. Without interior stillness, you are just a wanderer.

To pray is to embark on a journey without end—a journey deep into the heart of darkness, of paradox, of mystery. The journey to God is slow. Each day, we inch our way along a steep, winding road. The pace of spiritual transformation moves about as quickly as traffic in Port-au-Prince. Spirituality is essentially a journey in which we move from what we are to what we will be; it is a journey to weakness. We truly learn to live when we begin to explore our weaknesses. Every experience of weakness is an opportunity for growth and renewed life.

Weaknesses transformed
by the reality of Christ
become life-giving virtues.

I think that as followers of Jesus we need to adopt the spirituality of a pilgrim, being on a journey, a spirituality of questing. Such a spirituality is expressed on the road as we journey through life, pressing on to new horizons, new understandings. It is an unfinished, far-from-perfect spirituality of striving to do better, to be holier.

Dryness, darkness, and doubt are natural parts of the spiritual life.

Paperback Reader

December 7, 2000, during my week in Thomas Merton's hermitage, I wrote the following in my journal:

> I spent a few hours today reading Merton's *No Man Is an Island*. I bought the paperback edition a long time ago: it has a sticker price of $4.95 on it. What I found interesting were the passages I had highlighted with a yellow marking pen when I first read it, perhaps a dozen years ago in 1988. Back then, I caught a glimpse of what Merton was saying, but not enough of it to have any real impact on my life. Today as I read it, Merton's thoughts were jumping off the pages and I was able to catch hold of them and apply them to my life. And that is not to say that by next week, when I'm home in North Hollywood, I will not have forgotten. It simply means that progress along the spiritual road is slow, deliberate, and cannot be rushed. Each day, each season of our lives, hopefully adds a little more to our understanding and our ability to surrender more and

more to God. This stuff is actually very simple, yet, somehow, we've made it complicated. There seem to be so many options, so many ways to God—yet it all comes down to one basic truth which each of us needs to discover, embrace, and live.

Reading that eighteen years later, I more fully realized just how painfully slow progress along the spiritual road truly is. I've only been crawling for two decades. In truth, I've been resisting the changes the Gospel requires of me, unwilling or unable to make the sacrifices required in order to give up or let go of things I know are not good for me.

> *A lamp cannot be kept burning without oil; nor can the light of spiritual gifts continue to shine unless one inwardly sustains it with actions and thoughts consonant with it. For every spiritual gift requires a corresponding inner quality in the recipient to feed it spiritually as though with oil, thus preserving its presence.*
> —St. Maximus the Confessor

Radical Transformation

> *The eyes with which we look back at God are the very same eyes with which God first looked at us.*
> —Meister Eckhart

In his book *Radical Grace*, Richard Rohr, OFM, writes, "We really need to be saved from the tyranny of our own judgments, opinions and feelings about everything, the 'undisciplined squads of emotions' that T. S. Eliot criticizes in his poetry."[30] I certainly am keenly aware of my wild and unpredictable emotions. So much of our trouble comes from thinking we are the focal point of reality, that the world revolves around us, and that we can pass judgment on everything that touches us. Because of this egocentric thinking, everything in the world becomes an object that exists for our personal benefit. We even turn God into an object, another tool in our arsenal of weapons of destruction and survival.

But I am not just another individual object in a world of objects. I am, as the mystics of all faiths came to see, a "no-thing." Not "nothing" but "no-thing." That means I am more than my body, and reality is more than my consciousness. When I become aware of my true reality, that is my "no-thing*ness*," I suddenly have room for "some-thing" else—namely, God. This kind of transformation of reality changes everything. We see goodness and unity. We see as God sees. We are no longer chained to our unruly emotions, no longer prisoners of our exalted feelings, opinions, and judgments. We have room for the other. The great twelfth-century Sufi philosopher and mystic Ibn 'Arabi said, "The hero is he who smashes idols, and the idol of every man is his ego."

The ego's need to control reality is as determined and uncontrollable as a wild bronco. It must be tamed.

An egocentric search for self-fulfillment is doomed to failure.

A Crowded Subway

> *The story of God's inner being is written everywhere,*
> *strewn around us like pearls in a parking lot . . .*
> *like treasure hidden in every field . . .*
> *All we ask for is the grace to notice and*
> *Believe in this extravagance,*
> *To identify . . . the grace place.*
> *This is the work of contemplation.*
> —Daniel O'Leary[31]

Individual holiness allows God to appear in our midst, on our streets, in our homes, on a crowded subway, in a factory, in an office, at the beach or a ballpark—anywhere humans are. Holiness makes God visible. Make each new day holy.

The Gospel asks us to live without embellishment or pretense, to live without anxiety and to live free from all illusions of success. Ambition should be confined to topping yourself.

Seek wonder, not success.

A Faint Echo

We were created in, by, and through Love. We were made for intimacy with God. Intimacy with God is at the heart of all our searching for human friendship and intimacy. We become more fully human only in relationship to our ever-deepening consciousness of and abandonment to God, the true source of fulfillment and love.

> *Happiness and peace*
> *are found*
> *in a self-emptying love*
> *that is made tangible*
> *in a relationship*
> *with another.*

Happiness and peace are not found in isolation. We are communal beings, the fruit of communal love made tangible within the loving exchange found in the triune God.

> *Human love is merely*
> *a faint echo*
> *of divine love.*

> *Human love is*
> *weak, imperfect, and*
> *prone to failure*
> *because of human love's*
> *ingrained selfishness.*

But every loving human relationship, no matter how flawed, teaches us—if we are open and willing to learn—about the constantly beckoning, always giving, ever deepening, perpetually self-emptying love of God.

> *Love is not merely*
> *romance.*
> *Love is a school*
> *where you learn*
> *to let go*

of all that is not God
so you can be filled
with God.

When we begin to take feeble steps toward the true self-emptying intimacy for which each of us was created, we'll begin to sense the beautiful unity of God.

We have turned
the words
"I love you"
into a trite expression
—spoken today, forgotten tomorrow—
but they are the most
powerful words
we can ever utter.
We long to hear those words,
words that God whispers
every day.

Regular Meals

Hunger and starvation have reached epidemic proportions in many parts of the earth. While widespread physical hunger is disgraceful and lamentable (not to mention preventable), the real global hunger is the inner famine of the experience of God. Many of us who believe in God are lacking an integration of our expressed belief and our daily lives. We hunger for a prayerful spiritual experience at the core of our beings. This unfulfilled hunger is the cause of deep frustration and longing. Our spiritual lives are underdeveloped and overly restricted, resulting in crippling neuroses and an unhealthy pursuit of money, power, and pleasure. Regular meals of prayer feed our hunger for God.

Prayer moves you into the presence of God. God is a consuming fire. To live a life of prayer will cost you your life as you have known it. This is frightening.

At its deepest level, prayer is perpetual surrender to God.

Prayer prepares and purifies us for the never-ending yielding to the will of God and the life we were created to live.

Through the Eyes of Faith

Perseverance in prayer grows out of a spirit of humility. I pray because I know I'm powerless without God. Faith is always accompanied by humility. There was a time in my life, back in my thirties, when I was always on the verge of despondency, because, I see now, the folly of my pride made me think my own counsel contained all the answers.

It's in the recognition of our true powerlessness and vulnerability that the seeds of faith are planted. Faith grows out of a profound loneliness and desperate longing. Through the eyes of faith, we see the emptiness of our perishable lives, and see how we were created for union and communion, with God, our true selves, and each other.

Faith is an endless exodus to the heart . . . our own heart and the heart of God.

Faith is more than clinging to a belief or a dogma or merely obeying God. Faith is approaching God and getting to know God and giving yourself to God. And that takes time. And prayer. Faith is an ever-deepening desire to taste God more fully . . . which primarily happens in the stillness and silence of prayer. Unfortunately, our frenetic busyness deadens our capacity for contemplation.

> *Faith moves us beyond*
> *the superficial and trivial.*
> *Faith gives us the eyes to see*
> *the beauty and interconnectedness*
> *of all of creation.*

God is not beyond the clouds, hiding in heaven. God is on the ground, down in the gutter with us. God is hidden in the endless stream of busy, messy, mundane moments of everyday life, and in the many tragedies that dot the vast landscape of humanity.

My faith tells me that God loves me in my brokenness.

Moreover, God loves me fully and unconditionally, even in my darkest, most sinful, most unloving moments. I repeat: God does not demand perfection; God gives love.

The Broken Christ

You can meet the spirit of the broken Christ in the harsh, barren landscape of unjust poverty, in dark places where Christ still has no home.

Jesus lives outside
the city of conventional thought,
beyond the bounds of conventional wisdom.

Poverty isn't just a matter of not having sufficient income to live. Poverty isn't just living with hunger. The poor also experience a total lack of a sense of well-being and peace of mind, which so many of us take for granted. Poverty isn't about the lack of food, shelter, and security; poverty is the rage one feels when you can't do anything about it. Poverty is the sense of hopelessness that kills the spirit.

While God's love embraces all people, God has clearly demonstrated deep concern for the poor and the needy, the helpless, and the oppressed. God demands that we side with the poor, the powerless, and victims of injustice. To walk with the poor is to be in harmony with the will of God.

Mother Teresa and the Zen Master

A Zen master was asked, "What is the path?" He answered, without hesitation, "Everyday life is the path."

The dreary and commonplace events of our everyday life
are where we discover God.

Mother Teresa said, "You can and you must expect suffering." None of us has any choice when it comes to pain. Pain and suffering catches us all.

The only choice we have in the matter is what we do with it. Christ hopes we transform our pain, that we go from the cross to the resurrection.

God's Vulnerability

Divine love is not fickle. It has only one desire: total self-giving.

God became vulnerable for us. God's vulnerability is a supreme expression of divine love. The psalmist once said that God's love is better than life itself. More to the point: God's love is life.

> *Without God,*
> *I am nothing,*
> *have no life.*
> *With God,*
> *I lack nothing,*
> *have the fullness of life.*
> *Love is life.*
> *Jesus is a lover.*

Love cannot be conditional. Love cannot be purchased. Love cannot be used for our gain, cannot be self-centered.

You can give without loving. But you can't love without giving.

Love is liberating. Love is self-emptying, is to be given away. Love is only known from within, as an experience that changes everything, even changing bread and wine into the very substance of God.

Love is all-powerful, all-merciful, all-compassionate, all-forgiving, always giving. The source of love is God the creator and sustainer of everything. Love animates all life. Through love all life is connected.

> *Love does not build walls.*
> *Love builds bridges.*
> *Love does not*
> *throw stones.*

Love tosses
bouquets of kindness.
Love does not
judge or condemn others.
Love only gives and shares,
everything, always.

Falling Down

Everyone experiences heartbreak; everyone is in need of tenderness and compassion. At some point in our lives, we all have to face the difficult journey of coming to terms with feelings of rejection and humiliation and fear. These very real and painful feelings can, in time and in prayer, become an authentic path from despair to hope. Tragedies and disasters become places of courage, of perseverance, places where we learn to plumb the depths of our inner life, our true essence, and are able, by God's grace, to move from rejection and terror to healing and hope.

Love grows from that deep-rooted pain within the universe
where God is present,
and ever-willing to embrace us and bless us.

I believe the mystery of God is buried in solidarity with those who suffer. In the midst of suffering, divine compassion is revealed as a loyal companion that transforms pain into praise, discomfort into consolation. Love needs the need of another. In our need we find God's love, which heals and renews us.

In Haiti, the heartbreak of the crucifixion is very real. In Haiti, I can see more clearly that the way of Christ, the way to God, is by way of the wound, the way of surrender and sacrifice.

Christianity is a spirituality of imperfection. It is the folly of the cross of Christ, the paradoxical realization that in dying we rise to new life. St. Paul understood this when he wrote, "For when I am weak, then I am strong. " (2 Corinthians 12:10 NABRE). When we are in a place of woundedness or weakness we see more clearly our insufficiency, our incompleteness, our need for God.

Jesus said that the first shall be last and the last shall be first. That sounds silly. We strive to be first, to win at all costs. Last place is for losers. We want to be seen as winners. But the hidden wisdom of Christ says that in falling, in failing, in dying, we are in a place where change is possible, where growth can happen. But the downward mobility of the Gospel is a message our ego, in its blind love of the status quo, does not want to hear. The path of human imperfection leads to the perfection of God. Simply following all the rules and regulations of any religion, as noble and necessary as that may be, won't guarantee we'll find our way to God.

God hides in our imperfections.

It's in seeing and embracing my mistakes that I learn what doesn't work. In seeing and acknowledging my imperfections, I become more tolerant and understanding of the imperfections of others, which makes it easier to forgive . . . and to love.

In life, bad things will happen. Pain, sooner or later, will visit all of us. No one can avoid or escape suffering. Suffering and death are a vital part of the mystery of life. Our money, power, and status are of no use in helping us avoid suffering. Suffering does not discriminate between the good and the bad; it befalls all, without exception. But within the pain of suffering the hidden comfort of consciousness is discovered.

The medieval mystic Julian of Norwich boldly proclaimed not only that sin is unavoidable because of our inherent imperfections but also that sin is necessary and even good. It is in our recognition of our sin that we find the forgiveness, mercy, and love of God.

Jesus said the very rich and the very religious will find the road to God a very steep and rocky climb. Perfection is not the path to holiness. We rise to holiness by falling down on our knees in recognition of our imperfection. We rise only after falling.

To plumb our spiritual depths is the only way to reach our spiritual heights.

From Darkness to Wholeness

We each have a dark side. My dark side scares me. The more I actively engage in the difficult work of self-knowledge, the more I see how I've been a prisoner of my own blind instincts, compulsions, and illusions. In prayer, my dark side has been illuminated and I'm slowly learning to act from my true center, not from the shadows. What we need to become whole is hidden in our brokenness.

Humility increases with self-knowledge.

Amazing Grace

Sin is saying no to grace. Sin closes my eyes to the truth. Sin erodes the will and renders it impossible to stand against the tyranny of lust in all its alluring manifestations. Sin weakens us, then kills us.

Christ's resurrection turned disgrace into grace. Grace opens the door to the possibility of change. Grace changes a person. Conversion is about being changed.

Beg for the grace of prayer. Hail Mary, full of grace, help me to pray.

The Possibility of Changing

When you pray you are opening yourself up to the possibility of changing, of becoming more loving. Yet we resist changing, so we downplay praying, leave it to chance, or give it a minimal amount of our time or attention.

Grace is really not so amazing; grace is happening all the time, all around us, because God is always present. God is always offering us the grace of renewal, always inviting us to come home, to feel the embrace of divine love and forgiveness.

God's love and mercy are far greater
than my countless infidelities
and my inability to totally surrender my will.
Thank God.

God's Gaze

Often in the Rule of St. Benedict, I run across statements and language that make me uncomfortable, such as,

> *Yearn for everlasting life with holy desire. Day by day remind yourself that you are going to die. Hour by hour keep careful watch over all you do, aware that God's gaze is upon you, wherever you may be.*

I don't think "God's gaze" is on me all the time, wherever I am, in the sense that God is waiting for me to screw up, so he can dole out some excessively cruel punishment (which is what I was taught as a child). God is with me always, waiting for me to turn more fully toward him. Conversion is about dying to yourself in order to live in Christ. Conversion is the work of a lifetime, slowly turning over more and more of our lives to God, surrendering everything that diverts us from full unity with God. It means slamming shut the door on selfishness and sin.

St. Benedict is trying to tell us we have a lot of work to do, and we have only a limited amount of time to do it. He knows that conversion is hard, serious work, and he does not want death to catch us not having completed the job. He knows how easily we humans get distracted from the task at hand.

As for me, I know there are changes I need to make. I just can't seem to make them on my own. I have left a few doors slightly ajar. I stumble and fall. Often. I need a hand. God's gaze is always on me, waiting for me to reach out for help.

Help me, Lord. Please.

The Cost of Following Jesus

Jesus challenged the religious orthodoxy of his day, and the orthodox leaders in turn opposed his practice of amnesty and inclusion. The good news of the nonviolent, self-giving divine love preached by Jesus fell on deaf ears—as it still does today.

The cost of following Jesus is nothing less than everything: one must abandon self to imitate the self-transcendence of the Cross and the Resurrection. The cross symbolizes the extremity of helplessness more than the extremity of suffering. The cross rejects power and accepts surrender. When we have little or no worldly power to rely on, we are able to offer unambiguous love and service.

The chasm between Christ and Christianity is so great as to be virtually immeasurable.

To walk on the path God wishes us to take requires a paradigm shift in which worry becomes trust, doubt becomes faith, despair becomes hope, sadness becomes joy, unwelcomed becomes embraced, ugliness becomes beauty, the mother of Jesus becomes the mother of all, the earth becomes Eucharist, Good Friday becomes Easter Sunday, every state of death becomes a state of resurrection.

May God Bless You

May God bless you with discontent with easy answers,
half-truths, and superficial relationships,
so that you live from deep within your heart.

May God bless you with anger at injustice, oppression,
abuse, and exploitation of people.
so that you will work for justice, equality, and peace.

May God bless you with tears to shed for those who suffer
from pain, rejection, starvation, and war,
so that you will reach out your hand to comfort them
and change their pain to joy.

May God bless you with the foolishness to think you can
make a difference in the world,
so that you will do the things which others tell you
cannot be done . . . .
—Sr. Ruth Fox[32]

In My Nothingness

Only through humble eyes can God be seen. I am nothing; God is everything. But in my nothingness, God gives me everything. Humility helps shatter illusions. Humility is the truest form of honesty. It sees our weaknesses and vulnerabilities. Humility allows God to transform our weaknesses into strengths.

Humility is a pathway to prayer.

Prayer is the doorway to the heart, the center of our being, the place where we can let go, let go of pretense, pride, ego, and a host of things blocking us from the true source of life, the true source of love, God. In the innermost chamber of the heart we see the dissonance between the Spirit of God and our spirit; it is here we struggle to dissolve that difference. In the safety of the heart we can let go of fear and we can risk change. In the heart, conflict gives way to harmony. In the heart, what's mine becomes God's. In the heart, humility becomes holiness.

An Act of Surrender

The purpose of authentic prayer is to lead human beings to experience the unconditional love beyond love that is God's presence within us and to have that love lead us to respect and befriend and love one another. During a retreat, the late Trappist monk Fr. Thomas Keating said, "Holiness does not consist in any practice but in a disposition of heart . . . trusting to audacity in God's unconditional love. Only that can bring us into full emotional or spiritual maturity."[33]

Prayer is an act of surrender, an act of presence, an act of love.

Prayer should nurture a heart that prompts us to love and respect one another. Prayer needs the calm and presence and silence that will diminish the toxicity pumped into the air by our corrupted, soulless society bent on pursuing power and pleasure, so that we can become more present to the gentleness and goodness within each of us. Prayer helps us realize that we are all part of something beautiful beyond our wildest imagination; when we begin to see that beauty, we will begin to heal.

Prayer is hanging on to God,
stubbornly clinging to God.

It is good to contemplate the unconditional trust that made it possible for Mary to allow God's love to take over her life. Mary is the perfect model of trusting in God. It takes a bit of audacity to trust that we all belong to God. When we embrace that truth, that we are all one in God, we will begin to heal the divisions within ourselves and within our society.

The universal lack of an interior life
is a key element behind the rash
of violent political and religious conflicts
that plague so many nations.

Political language has become more and more aggressive if not outright incendiary. Americans scream at one another in an inferno of partisan rancor and mutual contempt. Outside the circus in Washington, DC, everybody feels aggrieved and nobody feels safe. A sense of danger is infiltrating every part of life.

Today a grand total of forty-two individuals control as much wealth as 3.7 billion of the world's poorest people. Suffering is real; but in this increasingly unequal and ecologically besieged world, vulnerability is also something that more and more people share.

The truth has been reduced to whatever happens to be your preference, to whatever an individual believes to be true.

One Word

Love casts out the darkness of hate and division. From love flows understanding, compassion, mercy, forgiveness, and peace. Love unites. Love is One. Christ loved every human being, without exception, without limits. Can we do otherwise? Thomas Merton said, "The whole idea of compassion . . . is based on a keen awareness of the interdependence of all these living beings, which are all part of one another and all involved in one another."[34] Communion needs to be a significant part of our spiritual language. To isolate ourselves from the world stifles our ability to sense the dignity of the divine image in human beings.

The road to salvation is a journey to wholeness. When people lack the basic necessities to sustain life—clean water, adequate nutrition, electricity, and sanitation—it is hard to become whole. Survival is struggle enough. For the people in the slums of Port-au-Prince, their every waking moment is directed toward meeting their basic physical needs. To see a woman squatting in the rotting rubbish to urinate or defecate is an unthinkable indignity. In love, through love, and with love we must unite and eradicate such indignity wherever it is found. We are called to incarnate God's love.

We need to connect to our deepest passions to the needs of others.

A Tangle of Contradictions

Our incapacity to love is rooted in pride and our false notion that everything must have a tangible benefit toward increasing our status and security. What's in it for me? is not a question love asks. Love seeks no remuneration, knows nothing about the market economy or cost-benefit analysis.

Love is a gift to be freely given and freely received. We do not merit nor can we earn God's love. Yet, in every moment, in every place, in every situation, God's love is there reaching out to us, calling us by name.

But most of the time we are deaf; we do not hear the silent voice of God. The wordless voice of God can only be heard in the heart. God's heart speaks to our hearts. Our hearts are a tangle of contradictions, fragmented and overwhelmed by disappointments, struggles, worries, and doubts; in the noise and chaos of our cluttered hearts we cannot hear God, cannot know God, cannot feel God's love.

Come, Holy Spirit, fill the hearts of Your faithful
and kindle in them the fire of Your Love.

The Heartbeat of God

Our hearts are broken, wounded by a thousand little cuts and bruises. Jesus came to heal our hearts. Through his sacred heart the heart of God is revealed.

To contemplate and imitate the Sacred Heart of Jesus is to contemplate and imitate the love of God. Through Jesus's heart God loves us and shows us how to relate to the divine and to all of humanity.

Jesus is the heartbeat of God.

The heart is the center, the core of our bodies, spirits, and souls. The heart is the home of our deepest thoughts, our deepest desires, our deepest longings. It is in and through our hearts that we come to understand ourselves and learn how to relate to others. The heart is fundamental to physical and spiritual life.

In the physical heart of Jesus, the spiritual heart of God was incarnated and made flesh. Jesus loves with a human heart, a human heart that beats with divine love. Our human hearts need to be transformed into sacred hearts, divine hearts that beat with human love.

We were created
for relationship.
Love is the doorway
to authentic, life-giving
relationships.

Symphony of Life

Love is
the symphony of life.
It needs to be
practiced and played
every day.

God is
the composer,
Christ is
the conductor,
and we are
the performers.

A More Suitable Chamber

O Lord, help me to renew
my innermost being.
I stumble and fall often.
My many failures

disappoint me.
But you never treat me
as I deserve.
You close your eyes
to my faults.
I trust in your endless
mercy and compassion.
But I need your help
to truly purify
my deepest being,
to create there
a more suitable chamber
for your spirit to reside.

A Silent Symphony

Before bed at night, I try to surrender the anxieties of the day into the tender hands of God's love. Rest in peace; arise in hope. To bring to a new day yesterday's pain and failures is the easiest way to darken the new day.

Every sunrise is accompanied by
a silent symphony
of hope and peace
that can only be heard
by a surrendered heart.

As each new day dawns, God's light gives us a renewed pledge of God's love, a fresh beginning that is pure gift, a gift meant to be given away during the day.

In the silence between night and day, I feel God's grace and peace and am commissioned to become an instrument of that very same grace and peace. In the splendor of new light, God's love and mercy are revealed.

O God help me to see
the radiance of your light
and show me this day
how to be a servant of your peace.
Help me, O God, to share

the delicate, intoxicating fragrance
of Your mercy and love
with those whose lives
are lived on the shadowy
and dismal margins,
with those whose days
see no happiness,
with those whose days
end without hope.

God Provides

One day a few years ago, I was left feeling scattered and a bit perplexed after my morning prayer time. I felt unnourished. I wanted to "hear" something, something that would feed me. Instead I endured a noisy silence, hearing nothing but my own scattered thoughts, most of which reflected my concern about my inability to raise sufficient funds to effectively operate my ministry. We seem always on the brink of extinction.

Then, as I pushed myself away from my desk, I spotted a little book I had not looked at in years. The book featured selected readings from the works of Ruth Burrows, an English Carmelite nun. I opened the book randomly and slowly read the following passage:

> We must submit our whole being to the discipline of the desert and not seek to avoid it. Like the Israelites of old we must press forward along a way we know not, trusting ourselves to God's guidance, relying on him to supply all our needs.
>
> Alas! Like them we grow weary of the wilderness, but let us not lose hope. Let us leave it to God to give us sufficient pleasure and comfort to sustain us. He will send us manna and make sweet water spring from the rock in due time, when we really need it.
>
> We learn by experience that there is beauty and tenderness even in the desert, but it must be of God's providing. Let us accept with humble love all the comforts both material and spiritual which he provides for us but let us not seek them for ourselves.

Oftentimes the silence and bleakness of the desert seems to penetrate into the depths of our souls, a desert of loneliness and aridity. We must not try to evade suffering; just trust in God to see us through, putting a seal on our lips, letting the silent peace of the desert enfold us.[35]

Suddenly and unexpectedly, I had been nourished. God provides.

Present Moment

"I Am," says God. God did not say, "I Was," or "I Will Be." In saying "I Am," God is saying, "I am present."

Am I present? Or do I live in the past, replaying old scenes, clinging to old wounds?

Am I present? Or do I live in the future, chained to useless fantasies and baseless fears?

God is beyond time and always present. But we look away. We look back and are hurt. We look ahead and are terrorized.

In this present moment, God is facing us. In this present moment, we will no longer be victims of the past or be paralyzed by the future.

In this present moment we can face God. In this present moment we can encounter God.

> *O God, help me*
> *be*
> *in this present moment.*
> *O God, help me*
> *see*
> *in this present moment*
> *You.*
> *O God, help me*
> *see you*
> *in all I do,*
> *in all my encounters,*
> *in all the people I meet,*
> *in all of creation.*

Frazzled and Fatigued

The health of our interior life rests on our attentiveness. We need to be able truly to pay attention in order to hear the wordless voice of God that is continually drawing us into Oneness. To be attentive, we need to be awake and alert to the boundless grace of the present moment, the eternal now. Our lives have become so splintered, divided among so many responsibilities, so many demands on our time, that most of us feel frazzled and fatigued. So much of modern technology, designed to make things easier for us, has in fact increased the things that tug for our attention. The internet, cell phones, laptop computers, iPhones, iPods, iPads, and the ever-expanding world of cable television all squeeze every ounce of stillness and silence out of life. Life has become a blur, a dervish of enticements and anxieties. Entering into our interior life, where we can encounter the love and mercy of God, is becoming increasingly more difficult.

For me, writing *The Sunrise of the Soul* has become an avenue into that interior empty space where the fullness of God resides. The very act of writing demands attentiveness. Simone Weil claimed that all study and serious reading, with its required concentrated focus, is in essence an excellent preparation for prayer.

The Buddhist road to enlightenment is paved with attentiveness. Thomas Merton's encounter with Buddhism helped him embrace a freer, more experimental form of writing. His thoughts flowed out onto the page in clear, simple words that expressed the openness of his heart and spirit. It also helped him see the entire world in a more positive light. Buddhist meditation practices drew him into a deeper silence, which helped him to be more aware of his true self. Merton's interior journey helped him affirm and deepen his Christian understanding that (as he wrote) "Christ alone is the way."

The way of Christ is all-embracing love and peace.

The human heart is drawn to God. The language of the heart is love. Not soft, wimpy, fleeting Hollywood-style love, but a bold, deep, penetrating love that requires openness and transformation, a love that perpetually gives itself away. We live in a world of hearts. Sadly, most hearts are broken, unloved, and unable to love. God wants to give us new hearts, mystical hearts throbbing

:o be loved. If you can imagine a world of divinely transformed
will see a world at peace, a world of plenty where no one goes
ich a world begins within each of us, if we are able to shake off the
counu⸳⸳ distractions of modern life and pay attention to the silent voice of God.

There is a mystic within everyone.

In Front of the Television

Spend one week watching television, thoughtfully observing what is being
presented, and you'll see how we have evolved into a culture of violence, how
we have sunk into a sea of hopelessness, how quick and easy gratification,
no matter how fleeting its pleasure, has become acceptable, how gratuitous
sex and explicit nudity has become commonplace, how infidelity is a strictly
private affair, how any relationship is disposable, how politicians offer
expedient solutions to difficult problems, and how preachers of all faiths
offer shallow answers to deep questions. One week in front of the television
will illustrate how far our society has drifted from the innate dignity God
endows to every human being.

Before television and the ascendancy of mass advertising, kids formed
their understanding of life and the world, their personal cosmology of the
world's meaning, in their homes, from their parents and older relatives.
Today, before a child enters the first grade or has any serious exposure to
religious ceremonies, he or she has already absorbed about thirty thousand
advertisements. They will spend less time in high school. Whatever spiritual
and moral truths a parent tries to transmit to their child cannot possibly
compete with the onslaught of sophisticated advertisements.

The effect of the nonstop advertisement blitzkrieg aimed at the young
all day, all week long, cannot be undone in an hour at church on Sunday.
Corporations pay big bucks to attract the brightest, cleverest people to
create their dazzlingly deceptive ad campaigns, employing every artistic and
psychological trick in the bag. No kid can withstand the onslaught. Sadly,
grown-ups increasingly seem to be unable to resist the hard sell. As a result,
consumerism has become the dominant faith in America—and Christmas
is its major feast day. On the day we celebrate God entering our poverty, we
equate desire and delight with shiny things we find in a mall. Jesus asked us

to give everything away to the poor and follow him. But we give each other iPods and rush back to the mall for after-Christmas sales.

The Messiness of Life

We live in a world that is filled with pain. The planet is covered with people who are overwhelmed by suffering. Wars, monstrous acts of terrorism, famines, economic injustice, chronic poverty, drug addiction, diseases, and natural disasters are killing people every day. We are impotent when it comes to making the pain go away.

Life is hard and messy and painful.
Hurt abounds
and hope is in short supply.

Jesus did not clean up every mess or relieve all the pain he encountered. Jesus simply told us to take the pain and the mess of our lives and place them before God. Even then, the answers to the riddles of our lives are not always perceivable or even obtainable. Jesus teaches us to live with the questions, to live with the pain. Peace, he suggests, is found in faith.

God is bigger than we are; and we, in our weakness, need to lean on the strong arm of God. Cures and answers may not come to light, but faith, hope, and love change who we are and how we deal with the messiness and pain of life.

Faith, hope, and love,
the triptych of the spiritual life,
are nurtured in stillness.

Without solitude,
finding sanity and sanctity
is virtually impossible.

Give Us This Day Our Daily Bread

Part of the Lord's Prayer is a request for the bread we need to sustain life. Even though we work to obtain the bread we need daily, our daily bread is a gift and a grace. For many people, having bread every day is not something they even have to think about or pray for: their cupboards are full. But for countless millions of people, having bread every day is a rarity: they live with hunger, with barren cupboards.

Bread is about relationship.

It comes from the earth and from work and is for everyone. The earth produces the grain, we harvest and produce the bread, the bread is distributed, we give thanks for it and consume it. Bread is meant to be shared, to give life to all. The earth sustains humanity, is in a life-giving relationship with us. We need to respect and protect "our sister, mother earth," as St. Francis so poetically called her, so she can continue to produce our daily bread, bread meant to sustain the kingdom of God.

In his book *Three Prayers*, Olivier Clément prays, "Give us—all of us— the bread we need, and may it also be the bread of the Kingdom, the bread of fraternal benevolence and of beauty." He goes on to say:

> If we want to make a conscious and honest request for this bread, we must assume another obligation: that of sharing. Eucharistic communion is sharing. As St. John Chrysostom would say, the sacrament of "one's neighbor" cannot be separated from the sacrament of "the altar." Socialist atheism and oppressive communism came about because Christians were unable to share; because they retained the sacrament of "the altar" and forgot that of "the neighbor." The tragedy, as we now can see, continues to worsen on a worldwide level.[36]

Part of the very Eucharistic mystery is the fact that the consecrated bread already contained the sacred before the words of consecration were uttered. Nurtured by the sun and watered by the rain, the unconsecrated bread is the fruit of the earth and the work of human hands. Bread is the gift of God's benevolence, and like all of life it is therefore sacred and a manifestation of God's presence and love.

Change comes slowly; hunger will not be wiped out in a heartbeat. But if more and more people's hearts beat with love and mercy for the poor, hunger will slowly disappear. Each of us might consider consuming our daily bread in moderation so we can share more of it with those who have none of it.

No Hunger

Around the world and in our own cities, hunger and malnutrition are on the rise due to the disastrous escalation in basic commodity prices during the recent global recession. We urgently need to guarantee regular access to sufficient amounts of food and water for those who face hunger on a daily basis.

Today, more than one billion people are undernourished, and one child dies every six seconds because of malnutrition. In light of such an overwhelming (and underreported) disaster, we are compelled to put the common good ahead of greed and profits. Food production cannot be geared solely toward consumption; food is not like any other commodity. Every human has a right to enough food to sustain life. We must practice compassion and ensure that no child will die due to a lack of adequate food.

Extending compassion to all people, even our enemies, is the very heart of the Christian faith. You can't receive what you don't give. Jesus said, "Give and it will be given to you. Good measure, pressed down, shaken together, running over, will be put in your lap" (Luke 6:38 ESV). In other words, in the jargon of today, outflow determines inflow. Jesus makes it abundantly clear that compassion is to be our central spiritual practice.

Through compassion our moral blindness will be healed and a new world will be possible. We must control greed and work together for the equitable distribution of the resources of God's creation through the fullest utilization of humanity's creative ingenuity so that one day soon there will be no hunger on planet Earth.

We are called to realize the unity of creation.

The Collection Basket

Most of the poor at Santa Catarina de Sena Church in Manaus, Brazil, located in the heart of the Amazon region, do not have any money to place in the collection basket during the offertory of the Mass. But they are still able to give something. While making my film *Embracing the Leper*, I attended Mass at the church. Rather than passing a plate or basket down each pew, two altar servers, both young girls, stood in front of the altar, each holding a wicker basket. The congregation walked up and placed their offering in the basket. A friend whispered to me that those who have no money to give are invited to come to the altar servers and offer themselves in silent prayer. Many did.

I had no money with me. Still, I walked up to one of the little girls who was holding a nearly empty basket. I placed my hands, palms down, over the basket and offered myself to Jesus. The symbolic gesture so moved me I began to cry as I walked back to my seat. It felt better offering myself than it would have if I had been able to put a $1,000 into the basket. I loved the symbolism of the poor being able to offer something of great value—themselves—when they have no money. I later learned that when a person does offer themselves, they pray that God would give them an opportunity to perform an act of kindness after the liturgy has ended.

The poor around the world have taught me a great deal. Over and over again I was astounded by their generosity, kindness, and mercy to others, more often than not rendered while they themselves were in a state of absolute insufficiency. It is so easy for me to give from my excess, from what I really don't need. But Christ desires that we do much more than simply share our "leftovers." I think Christ truly rejoices when he sees a poor woman in Manaus offering herself when she has no money to give. Even those who drop a small coin in the basket are giving out of their want, and perhaps the coin they drop in the basket is the only coin they have. And yet they give it or give themselves.

O Lord, help me be more like the poor I have been privileged to meet while making films. And please, Lord, help me to continually realize that I am totally dependent on you, no matter how much money I have in my pocket.

Small Drops of Love

Mother Teresa said, "We cannot do great things on this earth; we can only do small things with great love." She urged us to be "faithful in small things because it is in them that your strength lies. . . . Do not think that love, in order to be genuine, has to be extraordinary. What we need is to love without getting tired."[37]

What the saint was saying is that the formula for becoming more fully united with God is to love, beginning with small acts of love that will not exhaust us, and that the easiest way to do this is by concentrating on the small, everyday things of our daily life and being open to manifesting small acts of love in every person and situation we encounter. In time, our small acts of love will increase, both in number and size, as love becomes more self-emptying and more inclusive.

Mother Teresa told her sisters that one small act of loving after another begins to make a difference. "How does a lamp burn?" she asks. She answers, "Through the continuous input of small drops of oil. . . . My daughters, what are these drops of oil in our lamps? They are the small things of daily life: faithfulness, punctuality, small words of kindness, a thought for others, our way of being silent, of looking, of speaking, and of acting. These are the true drops of love."[38]

> Each of us can bring light into the world through
> our tiny but continuous drops of love.

There is no other way for the darkness to be defeated.

The Power of an Act of Kindness

The following comes from the last paragraph of a letter to me written by Fr. John Navone, SJ, dated January 28, 1996. He was a professor of theology at the Pontifical Gregorian University in Rome.

Watch out for any form of religiosity without cheerfulness/ joy. People living in the spirit of the Beatitudes are joyful. The first fruit of the Holy Spirit is joy. The Spirit is where it acts, and cheerfulness/joy is evidence of its active presence. "Beatitudes" means happiness. Each one begins with "Happy" are . . . because they enjoy God's delight in doing what God does for others. In John's Gospel, Jesus says that he is eager to give his life so that the joy that he and his Father share might be ours. That joy is their

Holy Spirit (of joy/love). Our radical joy consists in knowing that we are beloved of God, independently of our success or failure, long or short life, health or sickness. The joy that this world can neither give nor take from us is evidence in our lives that we have welcomed the Spirit of Jesus and his Father, *joy itself.* As Thomas Aquinas put it: "God is Happiness Itself."

Without debating the merits of his closing thesis, what the full letter showed me was that this celebrated Jesuit priest and renowned theologian saw my earnestness in seeking God and he took the time to offer me some of his acquired wisdom and insight. As I wrote in Part One, the thrust of the letter was Fr. Navone's suggestion that I throw out the novel I was writing (*The Canvas of the Soul*) that he graciously agreed to read, and write a book on St. Francis of Assisi. At first, I was reluctant to follow his advice, but thankfully in time I saw the wisdom in it and began writing *The Sun and Moon Over Assisi*, which dramatically altered the course of my life and in time led me to numerous slums around the world and eventually to living in Haiti. One man, one letter, changed everything in my life. We cannot overestimate how any act of kindness can have a life-changing impact on the recipient of that kindness.

Our Fruitfulness

We are not loved by God because we did something good. We are simply beloved by God.

I found "home" in Haiti. My family in Haiti, the kids and the staff, had no knowledge of or interest in my accomplishments, the television shows I produced, the films I made, the books I wrote. What they liked, what they needed, was my presence. I was there for them, and that was all that mattered. What we achieve in life is not important. It passes. What is important is our fruitfulness, which will last.

We were made to be loved and to love.

Life always has been and continues to be a paradox: every human being is rich, and every human being is poor. How we live boils down to a matter of point of view . . . how we see ourselves and how we see others.

Our thoughts and words are a powerful force in our lives, and in the lives of those we encounter; they can be a force for healing or hurting, for building or destroying. Our thoughts and words can be a source of resurrection or they can cause a crucifixion, both for us and others. Our thoughts and words can create and they can kill. And we determine the outcome.

The day you come to know, believe, and accept that you are a beloved child of God is the day you begin to live in true freedom, beyond all praise and blame. On that day, no one else can define, manipulate, or control you, because your true identity is rooted in God and cannot be taken from you. *I am a child of God; I am free.* Free to love and to be loved.

We are all beloved by God, simply because we are children of God.

A Follower of Jesus

To be a follower of Jesus
is to prefer life over death.
To be a follower of Jesus
is to prefer peace over war.
To be a follower of Jesus
is to prefer freedom over oppression.
To be a follower of Jesus
is to prefer forgiveness over revenge.

To be a follower of Jesus
is to prefer reconciliation over alienation.
To be a follower of Jesus
is to prefer contrition over excuses.
To be a follower of Jesus
is to prefer helping over hurting.
To be a follower of Jesus
is to celebrate the tenderness of God.

To be a follower of Jesus
is to prefer humility over pride.
To be a follower of Jesus
is to prefer vulnerability over power.

To be a follower of Jesus
is to prefer weakness over strength.
To be a follower of Jesus
is to prefer letting go over acquiring.
To be a follower of Jesus
is to prefer mysticism over materialism.
To be a follower of Jesus
is to prefer silence over noise.
To be a follower of Jesus
is to prefer prayer over idle chatter.

Downward Mobility

Christ climbed down from divinity to be a human being. He then climbed further down to become a slave. Christ's movement was always downward. We strive to move upward, to climb higher and higher on the ladder of success. Henri Nouwen called it "downward nobility." We have to let go of our need for prestige and privilege. It is on the margins of society, among the weakest and most vulnerable, among the suffering and destitute, among the migrants and refugees, that we will find Jesus.

How do we relate to Jesus? is a question we need to constantly ask ourselves.

One day, near the end of a long, dusty journey, Jesus was tired and thirsty when he spotted a well. At the well, he asked a Samaritan woman for a cup of water. The woman was surprised by the request because a Jew would never speak to a Samaritan. She was burdened by her past. She had five failed marriages and was currently living in shame with a man. She was truly marginalized and disorientated. She had come to the well at noon, because she knew few people would be there during the hottest time of the day. She was so embarrassed by her messed-up life that she wanted to avoid meeting anyone. But Jesus met her where she was. Jesus did not judge her or reject her. After asking her for a drink of water, he offered her the living water that would renew her by the power of grace from above. She was born again, renewed in spirit in order to live a new life in God. It is such a beautiful story illustrating that divine assistance is always trying to break through our pain and discouragement. Jesus was thirsty, not just for water, but for peace for the woman. He approached her and began a conversation. We are thirsty, and Jesus comes to the well to give us a drink, because God thirsts for us and wants to give us hope and strength. Amazing. Truly amazing.

Henri Nouwen wrote,

> Jesus' compassion is characterized by a downward pull. That is what disturbs us. We cannot even think about ourselves in terms other than an upward pull, upward mobility in which we strive for better lives, higher salaries, and more prestigious positions. Thus, we are deeply disturbed by a God who embodies a downward movement. Jesus' whole life and mission involved accepting powerlessness and revealing in this powerlessness the limitless love of God. Here we see what compassion means. It is not bending toward the underprivileged from a privileged position; compassion means going directly to those people and places where suffering is most acute and building a home there.[39]

The Incarnation was downward mobility at its zenith. God became the child of a refugee couple forced to give birth in a barn surrounded by animals. Christ was born in a world where there was no room for him. His parents were homeless and powerless. Christ belonged to people who did not belong. And so, with people for whom there is no room in our world, Christ is present. And Christ calls us to make our home among them, to be one with them, to love them as he does. Not all of us literally need to make our home among the rejected, but all of us need "to be at home" with them—that is, to be comfortable among them, to spend time with them, to laugh with them, to cry with them, to embrace them, to be bound in fraternity with them, to have them present within us, always mindful of their needs. To be one with God is to be one with all. We are called to realize the unity of creation.

Christ always approached people in a gentle, humble manner, seeking only to refresh them with a tender touch, a kind word. He always personified the love to which he called others. He gave himself fully to everyone. He saw everyone as a brother and sister, a child of God. He broke down the walls that separate humans from each other. If we are to be the incarnate body of Christ we too must love, must give ourselves away, must be with the poor. Our individual welfare cannot be separated from the welfare of those around us. So much of what passes for compassion these days is little more than condescending piety. Such demeaning compassion often comes dressed as pity, which only shames rather than restores. True compassion stems from fellowship and interdependence. We need to recognize our common humanity and realize that God sets a banquet before all of us.

The drawback to all of our technological advances is that much of humanity is attempting to have absolute control over nature and all the functions of human society. In the process we have become trapped in a system that requires ever more extreme forms of control. Rather than cooperating with the tendencies of the natural world and going with the flow, we use technical force to overcome nature. We are thus uncomfortable with mystery and surprise, preferring the way of power rather than the way of wisdom. If you did actually manage the impossible and acquire complete control of everything in your life, you would be condemning yourself to a life of eternal boredom. In contrast, the natural universe employs an infinite number of variables interacting simultaneously in a fashion whose outcome is unpredictable, amazingly intricate, and beautiful.

The common good,
which is the breath of freedom
and the social bond between people,
is being choked by the iron fist of individualism.

A Prayer: A Soothing Ray of Light

O God, help me let go of
everything in my life
and all that I expect and wish for.
I know that you have
the best plan for me,
and I'm trying
to give you everything:
my life, my time, my possessions,
and my aspirations.
Help me to wait upon you
and not take matters
into my own hands.

I want to give you my all,
and I believe
with all my heart and strength
that you will take care of me,
far and above anything I could ever do.
I love you, Lord,
and I want all of my life
to be my gift to you.
Help me, please, dear Lord,
let go of everything
that keeps me from being
more fully united to you.

Lord, help me grow
in humility,
help me confess
my own brokenness.
Help me move out of my world
of illusion and self-created desires
and into your universe
of love, joy, and peace.

Lord, I cry out for healing.
Transform my brokenness,
I beg you,
into a new life in you,
the true source
of strength and wholeness.

Help me, Lord, remove everything
that blocks me from joyfully living
the good news of the paschal mystery.
O awesome and transcendent God,
free me from the slavery of my sinfulness.

In my prison of darkness,
your unmerited grace
is a soothing ray of light.

The Carceri, Assisi

PART FOUR

THE SPIRIT OF ST. FRANCIS OF ASSISI

A Very Lonely Road

My global poverty films all present excruciating suffering. The suffering I've filmed around the world was caused by severe, unjust, chronic poverty. Following St. Francis led me to the worst slums on earth, where I witnessed the deepest and most profound levels of poverty imaginable. In these horrific slums I discovered what radical dependence on God truly means.

Following Francis into the depths of unjust poverty has been a long, lonely journey, during which I've struggled with periods of doubt and intense spiritual dryness. Too often, sadly, my longing for God has waned and I've thirsted for things other than God.

But during those times of doubt and dryness I renewed myself by following Francis into stillness and silence. We know of St. Francis's profound love of poverty, but he had an equal love for solitude. The saint spent half of his adult life in solitary prayer, often in hermitages that were little more than caves where a rock was his pillow. It was in stillness and silence that St. Francis entered deeply into unity with God, and, as a result, into unity with all of creation.

The story of St. Francis of Assisi is an authentically human drama with universal appeal, a story of an ordinary man who accomplished extraordinary things while transcending his time and place on his way to becoming a universally beloved true saint. His life was a visible manifestation of the conversion process that was going on inside of him. His life was his sermon. And his sermon still has something important to say to us today.

St. Francis of Assisi longed for God beyond all measure. His soul longed for God even in the night; from early morning and throughout the day, he kept watch, looking and longing for God and God alone. His intense longing took him to places deep within himself and places far from Assisi. On his journey to God he traveled down a very lonely road.

Each of us is, ultimately, alone on our inner journey through life. Each of us longs for something beyond what can be found on earth. Within each of us there is a loneliness and a longing. St. Francis understood that while finding God in the world is essential, we must always remember that social action needs to be tempered and nurtured by contemplation.

St. Francis belongs to all humanity, and we are sorely in need of his insights, insights garnered from a life of prayer and poverty. Francis had only one desire: the reconciliation of humanity with God, with experiencing the human condition, and nature.

What follows is a meditation on the spiritual world of the saint and how his discoveries of the sacred dimension of his experience can help us as we move toward God in our own way, in our own day. The story of St. Francis is the timeless story of transformation, a dramatic tale of epic proportions, filled with triumphs and failures, heroic deeds, and incredible acts of charity.

What does this saint from thirteenth-century Italy have to say to the world of the twenty-first century? He speaks to our growing interest in mysticism, our desire for simplicity, our concern for ecology, our search for alternatives to violence, our need for sincere interfaith dialogue, our anxiety over the harsh plight of the poor. The spirit of St. Francis speaks to our hunger for God.

A Mystical City on a Hill

In the heart of Italy, clinging to the side of a mountain, lies a walled medieval city where time appears to have stopped. The humble yet graceful city was the home of the world's most famous saint, a saint who gave up riches to live in poverty and complete dependence on God. Assisi is more than a city on a hill. It is both a symbol and the summit of humanity's deepest longing. Assisi is a living prayer that cries out to God, passionately expressing our hunger to be united to the heart of all creation. Assisi invites silence and awe.

In Assisi it is easy to see what Francis saw: that our being has nothing to do with having. Bathed in the serene Umbrian light, Assisi sings of the natural harmony between nature and humanity, a harmony that has been disrupted by our unrelenting greed and selfishness. In the ancient Etruscan soil of Umbria, a mystical Christianity bloomed and still flowers. Beauty abounds. Love resounds.

The silence of the Umbrian landscape conceals the vast presence and passion of God. In attentive silence, Francis heard God's instruction in the fields, streams, and hills; the wind and rain sang of joy and sorrow. Assisi is the wedding chamber of the divine.

There is a holy communion in Assisi. In a sacramental sense, the spirit of Assisi helps us transcend the appearance of things and to cross the threshold of our natural yearning for what lies beyond what we see. In Assisi, heaven gently kisses earth, and we long for a deeper embrace. In Assisi, there is a synthesis between poetry and prayer, between sanctity and song, between asceticism and aestheticism. Assisi taught me that simplicity, serenity, sincerity, silence, and song are the heart of the Franciscan spirit.

Assisi is an eternal shrine, in which Francis's candle still burns brightly.

The Breath of Life

For St. Francis of Assisi, prayer was the breath of life. Prayer was the simplest, most direct way for the saint to acknowledge his dependency on God for everything. Prayer enabled St. Francis to become more aware of God's presence, a presence that was at once far beyond him and deep within him. Prayer is communion with God. Prayer was the saint's safest haven, and he devoted himself to long periods of intense prayer, sometimes lasting throughout the night. He sought out solitary places where he could enter into communion with God.

For Francis, silence was the language of God; he knew the importance of being still and resting in God. Fully half his converted life was spent in contemplation and prayer. Prayer was part of the fabric of his life, and everything he did began with and grew out of prayer. Francis spent hours on his knees before the crucifix; adoration was the oxygen of his spiritual life.

St. Francis breathed deeply
the pure divine glory of Life itself.

Francis sacrificed everything in order to enter deeply into a life of prayer. For Francis, prayer was Reality, and it became the center of his life. He enlivened his soul with periods of solitude.

Daily Conversion

When St. Francis began to understand that his life was a gift of love, he desired nothing else than that his life become a loving gift to God and others. This shift in consciousness didn't happen all at once. The journey from the assumption of absolute autonomy and the false, egocentric notion that we are self-sufficient, to a posture of total surrender to God and the recognition of our genuine interconnectedness with all life takes time and requires daily conversion.

Day by day, step by step, prayer by prayer,
we inch our way along the Way back to God,
back to the fullness of life and love.

But we easily get distracted, sidetracked by false desires and empty illusions. This is why the discipline of prayer was important to Francis and he didn't want to leave it to chance. He carefully carved out time alone, time apart from the roar of the crowd, time for God alone.

It distresses me how often and how easily I succumb to things that are anathema to the Gospel principles I want to emulate and espouse. However, these ungodly diversions don't imprison me in guilt or self-loathing; they show me my true weakness and how I need God for the strength to more faithfully follow Jesus. In my weakness, God's grace is multiplied.

I have a weakness for cookies. God has a weakness for human beings.

For Love to Give Love

How tragically sad that we allow ourselves to be ruled and controlled by our illusions and fears. We live too many hours of our lives in a solitary confinement with falsity. This is not God's plan for any of us.

> *God wants us to know*
> *true peace and freedom.*

We were created in the image of God. We were created to mirror the love of the Trinity by giving ourselves away, for life to give life, for mercy to give mercy, for compassion to give compassion, for peace to give peace, for love to give love.

Because we do not know our real self, our true nature, we live in darkness and doubt. Conflicts haunt us. We feel threatened. We build walls around ourselves for protection, then we try to build walls across our southern border.

In the depths of our being we feel isolated, alone, naked. Joy is fleeting. Bitterness grows in our uncultivated garden starving for sunlight.

> *The goodness and creativity*
> *of God*
> *is unknown,*
> *hidden, in part, by*
> *our own brokenness,*
> *our own weakness.*

Oxygen for the Soul

On the road to God, words eventually dissolve into silence. Silence requires stillness; but everything today is about noise and speed. We have become perpetual-motion machines, constantly on the move. Today, most of us are drowning in a deafening sea of noise. There is no escaping the pounding, unrelenting drumbeat of noise. The need for silence in our lives is beyond measure.

Silence is essential to inner peace and growth.

Prayer quiets negative passions. Prayer helps restore our awareness of God. To neglect prayer is to neglect God.

Prayer is oxygen for the soul.

Prayer slows down the furious pace of life. Prayer prompts us to reach out in compassion to the suffering and weak, and helps us embrace all of humanity.

Contemplation takes us out of the world
so we may see the world better, more clearly.

The Deep Inner Voice

Talking is easy. Listening is hard. Talking is also exhausting. So much of our talking is pointless. Yet we chatter on, without end, even though we have little that is worth saying. But we dread silence and avoid it like the plague. Yet, the most essential element of prayer is silence, because it is in the silence of the heart that we can listen to God speaking. If we are constantly talking, God will be unable to teach us anything.

If we don't listen, we will never learn.

We don't need to be hermits to enter deeply into silence. Not all of us are called to be hermits. But as Thomas Merton suggested, all of us need enough silence and solitude in our lives to enable the deep inner voice of our own true self to be heard at least occasionally.

Only in silence can you hear
the vast, boundless depths of the Spirit
speaking more and more clearly
about the unlimited love and mercy of God.

Contemplation and Action

St. Francis of Assisi spent long, solitary stretches of time in prayer, in order to find out what God wanted him to do. He frequently left the busy, noisy marketplaces of Assisi and ascended the mountains in search of silence and solitude, where he could better hear the voice of God by deepening the vast reservoir of his prayer life.

Nothing distracted St. Francis from prayer; nothing diverted his love from God. Francis emptied his heart, leaving it undivided and available for God alone. "I have done what was mine to do," the saint said near the end of his life, urging his followers to "pray that God shows you what is yours to do." St. Francis of Assisi was unique. He was a mystic and a person of action. His actions flowed out of his contemplation, out of his longing glance at what is real.

For Francis, contemplation always led to action.

When we give ourselves to God in prayer, we begin to witness and experience the richness of divine love and mercy, and we are better able to respond by sharing that love and mercy with others.

In prayer, St. Francis was free from the complexities of thought (and figuring out what to do), and he discovered the simplicity of his own heart, which allowed his life to become a living commentary on the Gospel. His life was a performance of the text of the Gospels.

An Unquenchable Fire

Within St. Francis, there burned a voracious fire for God. He sought God, and God alone. At the core of his being, he longed for the embrace of God. This gnawing hunger, this relentless desire, energized every moment of his life and gave meaning to it, fashioning an inner strength and discipline to forge ahead on his quest for God no matter the obstacles.

Each of us has a fire within us, but unlike St. Francis most of us don't know how to direct and control that fire. We're either attached to or distracted by so many thoughts and things that draw us away from the presence of God. Our lives are so busy and disjointed that we have no time for prayer and contemplation. Without prayer, the fire for God that is within us slowly burns out and the process of internal transformation dies from the cold.

Two Steps

For repentance to be real and true it must be more than a fleeting twinge of remorse. Genuine repentance must lead to a transformation of our lives. Repentance involves two steps. Stop doing something bad. Start doing something good.

> *Contrition should evolve*
> *into acts of goodness.*

Humility is the cornerstone of repentance. Sadly, humility's stock has declined in our time. Instead, we value a sense of pride, a sense of self-glorification, a sense of self-righteousness. Today, many people view humility as a sign of weakness. How easily we forget the words of Christ: "Learn from me for I am meek and humble of heart" (Matthew 11:29 NABRE).

Repentance, deeply rooted in humility, is a return to the right order of things. Repentance is the path out of exile.

Repentance is more than "pleading guilty" to transgressions. Repentance needs to acknowledge our alienation from God, our failure to enter fully into the joy of communion with the divine. Repentance is not merely a response to a spiritual indictment; it must also be a response to the fact that we have strayed from the glory of God.

The Eyes of Christ

Following Jesus requires a lot more than learning abstract ethical and moral principles; it requires a change in heart, a change in the way we look at life. A heart transformed by the love of Christ is a patient heart, a heart that takes the time to be still and to listen.

To see
with the eyes of Christ,
is to see
the beauty of all creation,
to see
the beauty within ourselves
and within each other.

Christianity is not a moral code—it is a love affair. We are supposed to be human torches ignited by the furious, flaming love of God.

We're all in a hurry, rushing from here to there, from this to that, an endless treadmill of movement going nowhere. Anxiety is as common as a cold. We are anxious about the future, our jobs, our relationships . . . we are anxious about virtually everything. Our anxiety breeds a drive to acquire more and more of everything. Nothing is enough. We want more of everything. More money, more prestige, more clothing, more contacts, better cars, bigger houses, faster computers.

In our endless movement, our constant rushing, we don't see our own loneliness, our brokenness. We are all wounded. But as our hearts become more transformed by the presence of Christ, we're able, in our weakness, to feel the love of God and to trust in the abundance of God's love.

Our relentless drive to acquire more
is fueled by our deep-rooted
sense of scarcity,
our inability to trust
that God wants
to give us all that we need.

The Art of Remaining Still

Silence is a vital part of the natural cycle of creation;
it is a time of renewal, lying fallow, and gestation.

To be a contemplative is to be receptive to the divine Word. Contemplation requires tranquility and patience. The soul that waits on God, patiently and unhurriedly, will eventually be filled with the realization he or she is infinitely loved. The quest for God is a journey, a pilgrimage to the depths of the soul, the very seat of stillness.

> *The art of contemplating*
> *divine truths*
> *grows out of*
> *the art of remaining still.*

Prayer is being present. Transformation is a daily event. Every moment is a moment of grace—if my eyes and heart are open.

> *Humility is*
> *the heart of Christianity,*
> *and the gateway to prayer.*
> *Without prayer,*
> *God dies in our hearts.*

Within the tiny space of our cluttered hearts lies the infinite presence and love of the all-merciful God. To pray is simply to remain open to the inflowing of divine love. To pray is to be in a relationship with God. The more time we spend in prayer the deeper that relationship will become.

St. Francis spent a lot of time in prayer, often in remote caves, far from the chatter of people and the busyness of commerce. But he didn't need a cave or a cell to pray. In fact, he told his followers that wherever they went, wherever they were, they brought their cells with them.

Prayer was an inward journey for St. Francis, and he urged the friars to make a dwelling place within them where God could stay. In the midst of whatever he was doing, St. Francis knew how to quiet himself and enter deeply into his heart, his true cell, in order to find God waiting for him.

Clearing Our Inner Clutter

At the core of our being, in our very soul, we are one with God. The God we seek is the very ground of our being. In contemplation the false separation between God and us slowly dissolves, by grace, over time. Contemplation clears away our inner clutter and allows us to experience our unity with God.

We no longer see ourselves as separate from God and each other. We are all one. St. Francis and all the mystics down through the centuries came to realize the unity of all creation.

Decluttering is the work of continual contemplative practice. As our mental clutter dissolves, we experience a greater inner silence. We begin to forget the self and are more and more grounded in God. This takes discipline on our part and an outpouring of grace on God's part. Our inner stillness allows grace to operate and opens us up to be receptive to the inflowing grace.

Entering the stillness of contemplation is not an option. Without it, we are riddled with anxiety and fear.

Find the eternal space within your soul that neither time nor flesh can touch.

An Abundance of Fresh Grace

One day, Francis found a place for solitary prayer in the valley of Rieti, and stayed there for a long time. While he was praying for some sense of direction, his mind became preoccupied with the sins of his past. He began to repeat over and over again the words, "O Lord, have mercy on me a sinner."

Eventually the repetition of his plea gave way to a great joy. The depths of his heart were washed in a soothing sweetness; his spirit danced in the certainty that his sins had been forgiven. His soul was filled with an abundance of fresh grace.

Francis's compunction over his sins was not a simple matter of feeling sorrow about wrong actions. It was a sincere attempt to separate himself from those things within him that were harmful to his relationship with God. He no longer wanted any behavior from his past to have any power over his present, which was consumed by a love of God. God heard his cry and graced St. Francis with an unshakable peace and joy.

Lord Jesus, you are the good Samaritan; I beg you to pour your healing oil and wine into the half-dead moments of my life, those empty moments when I become vulnerable to temptations to seek comfort from things that can never satisfy, things that can only turn me away from you.

The Common Thread

Love is not something God does. Love is what God is.

God consistently showers undivided love on each of us, no matter our faith or lack of faith, no matter our holiness or sinfulness. We all need to find the common thread, to reveal the hidden wholeness, to see the inscape of the soul. We must do more than preach tolerance at a comfortable distance, without listening, without relationship, without growth.

We must open ourselves to one another.

We must risk learning something new and essential on the path to God, and thus risk altering the presumptions that have shaped our respective faiths. Perhaps all the various faiths embraced by people around the world need to be more lyrical and less dogmatic . . . so we can all live in peace and grow in unity as we strive to enter more fully into the mystery of life, the mystery of God.

We are made for community, made in the image of community.

Unity does not derive from a common background; it comes from an act of will by which each renounces individualism and strives to live in concord.
—Michael Casey, ocso, *Strangers to the City*[40]

Not Having, Not Knowing

It seems that lots of people today not only know God but also seem to possess God. They've got God in their pocket. I once rejected Christianity because, in part, Christians seemed to possess God. How is that possible? I mean, how can God be possessed? At best, all we can do, as Merton suggested, is wait for God. Once a year, during Advent, we're reminded of that simple reality.

I certainly feel as if "I have God" in my life. I can talk about God, share my experiences of God with friends and strangers alike, but I also must admit at the same time—and this is the really tough part—that "I do not have God," that I too am merely waiting for God. It's confusing. I have God, and at the same time I don't have God. I possess God, and I am waiting for God. I know God, and at the same time I don't know God. When it comes to God, there must be, as Paul Tillich suggests in *The Shaking of the Foundations*, "an element of not having and not knowing, and of waiting."[41]

Transformation is not possible where we, not God, are secretly in control, arrogantly pretending we "know it all." Prayer brings me face-to-face with the ultimate darkness. Prayer challenges me to enter the darkness or turn away from it. In the darkness I am able to see my own insecurity. In the darkness I learn I need light from Someone else. I cannot provide light for myself. Light is a gift that needs to be received.

For the most part, the life of prayer is lived in darkness.

The Help We Need

The proliferation of self-help books mostly proves to be of little help in dealing with the problems we face. It seems that every year our knowledge expands while at the same time our understanding shrinks. We chase after pseudo-formulas for happiness and cling to lifeless dogmas instead of entering into meaningful silence. Unplug the phone, turn off the computer, and just sit.

*The help you need is within you
if you take the time to listen.*

God spoke to St. Francis in the depths of his soul. His experience of God went beyond faith, beyond dogma and symbols. His experience of God gave birth to a spontaneous awe at the sacredness of life, of being. The invisible Source of Life touched Francis and he knew beyond all knowing that God was real. This deep knowing was beyond explanation, beyond discussion and debate, beyond himself, even beyond logic or reason.

God wants to touch each of us. God is always reaching out to us. God's invitation is perpetual. Sadly, for the most part, our response to God's invitation is timid and haphazard . . . at least mine is. We're not always aware of God's presence because we're too focused on ourselves, on our own wounds, our own ideas, our own selfish desires. The path to God's door and the fullness of life is straight and narrow, yet we keep veering off onto culs-de-sac of empty promises and phantom illusions.

*God knows all our doubts, all our confusions,
and the endless contradictions that spring from
our meager, parched inner life.*

God knows our weaknesses, our faults, and our many failures and sins. God knows we do not always act as we wish to act. Yet God still loves us and wants to heal all our inner wounds. It is impossible for God to withhold love from us. It is the one thing God can't do, for loving is the essence of God's being. God's unmerited grace is always present during our times of weakness and confusion. Thank God.

As we become more rooted in prayer
the more we will become aware of God's endless grace.

All God desires is for us to do as God does, to make ourselves invisible and silent, to make ourselves weak and poor, to give ourselves away, completely and without reservation, so that only God can shine within us, enabling us to love always, everywhere, everyone.

All Is Grace

One of my best friends, Jonathan Montaldo, is a committed student of the life and spirituality of Thomas Merton. In one of his retreats he spoke about how Merton learned the hard way that "no matter our ascetic practices and how much we pray, no matter how many books we read or books we publish, no matter our status as pope or international celebrity, we will eventually need to find that place in our restless hearts where we can kneel and wait for a mercy that we know we cannot give to ourselves (St. Augustine). We must eventually find that place in our restless hearts where we are deeply conscious that 'all is grace.' "[42]

My friend pointed out that Merton's private journals, which have been fully published in seven volumes, do not reveal his ascent to ever-higher stages of spiritual attainment; instead, they reveal his gradual descent into a spiritual poverty that fully turned him toward God's mercy. This is a very hard lesson to learn. Only over the course of ruminating over this book have I come dimly to see the truth in it. It is all about God's endless mercy and unmerited grace.

To the very end, according to Jonathan, Merton acknowledged that he was always stumbling forward and imperfect. I take comfort in knowing that, because on my own spiritual journey I'm forever stumbling around in the dark aware of only my own imperfections and weaknesses.

Jonathan gave one of the purposes Merton had in writing his journals: "to expose the fault lines between his ideals and his day-to-day struggles to achieve them, to mind the gap between his published pious rhetoric and his struggling practice, was a major motive that impelled Merton to write and publish his private journals."[43] In a sense, my life—and your life—is like Merton's in that all of our lives are riddled with contradictions and inconsistencies. And that is okay. Life is filled with ambiguity, failure, and false starts. And that is okay too, as long as we are aware of it and keep moving forward in the knowledge that we are nonetheless loved by God and completely dependent on God's mercy and compassion.

Imperfect People

As Christians, we do not need to be perfect. We simply need to be honest about our struggles, our darkness. The church is not a country club for saints. Rather, the church is a place for imperfect people to meet and fall in love with the perfect God and to help each other become more like the One we love and worship. Sadly, we often don't look or act like Christ. We seamlessly blend in with the rest of society that pays no attention to Christ.

A New Heart, a New Spirit

Prayer is about far more than asking for favors. The purpose of prayer is establishing a relationship with God who is in relationship with us always. Prayer helps us see our faults, purify our hearts, and center us in truth.

Prayer is the topsoil of love.

Prayer leads us to a deeper experience of conversion and a growing awareness of our constant need for repentance and renewal. Conversion, at its root, is a change of heart; it turns us away from the notion that we are the center of the universe. Conversion often means listening to the events in our lives that change our perspective. The fruit of conversion is a release from the burden of self-groundedness so we can enter into the freedom of being grounded in God, which will create a complete recentering of our passion and a complete realignment of our affections.

St. Francis tells us that we need to be given a new heart and new spirit; and that we need to be cleansed every day. Incarnation, for St. Francis, was a daily event.

A Sense of Balance

Life today demands that we be useful. Many people feel the need to at least have the appearance of being hard at work, even during their personal free time. It is as if we fear what lies beyond our usefulness. Our society views monks and hermits with suspicion because a life devoted to seeking God is incomprehensible to a materialistic culture.

Our drive for usefulness, for action, seems to far outweigh our desire to be still. We want to just plunge immediately into deep contemplation, but it doesn't happen. It takes a lot of time to still the restless movement within us. We are doers, performers who always have an itch to be acting. It is hard for us to simply sit before God and listen. How can we speak about God, or share God's love, when we haven't fully experienced it ourselves?

St. Francis knew he had to spend time listening to God
before he could speak to others about God.

In deep solitude, St. Francis transformed his loneliness into an interior empty space where he was able to hear the silent voice of God speaking about the necessity of love. Solitude became a place of engagement with God, a place of true peace.

St. Francis did not so much pray as he became a prayer. It was then that he experienced the spectacular greatness of God, which he shared with the world.

A Culture of Emptiness

For Francis, his interior life took precedence over all else. His primary desire was to have a mindful openness to God at all times. St. Bonaventure tells us that when Francis was deep in prayer he became "oblivious of all that went on about him" and that he often became "lost in ecstasy." That does not happen to many of us, and I suspect it doesn't because we don't give enough time to prayer. Our prayer is often hurried, squeezed in among other things.

Within himself, Francis created a culture of emptiness, an empty space for God to fill. To become empty, we need to do nothing, need to press the pause button on our society's addictive need to produce and consume, to always be doing something. So much of the crazy busyness that consumes modern life is an existential mask that hides our inner emptiness.

I think we need to create a culture of emptiness more than Francis did. Modern life is so filled with busyness, so cluttered with unfiltered and biased information tirelessly generated by the media and the internet, so overstimulated by a dizzying array of electronic gadgets, so pressured by the allure of nonstop advertising, and so driven by productiveness that we are almost incapable of stillness and can't tolerate silence. It was in stillness and silence that St. Francis forged his inner cloister of emptiness and flamed his desire for God.

St. Francis's form of monasticism had no walls; the world was his cloister. But he was diligent in periodically retreating to places of solitude where he could be inwardly renewed and find a clear sense of direction for his forays into the wider world of external activity and human commerce.

In time, God, who has no voice, spoke to Francis in everything. Francis became a word of God, echoing all he heard in the inmost center of his being during his prolonged periods of contemplation.

In Deep Silence

Listening to God requires silence. Silence is more than not speaking. There is within us a wordless noise that also needs to be muted. A silent listener tunes out all exterior and interior chatter in order to be totally attentive to the silent voice of God, actively listening and responding to the very Source of his or her being. It is only in deep silence that we can perceive the reality of God and the world around us.

Within the silence of our hearts lies a mystery beyond our hearts. In deep silence, we are fully awake, fully open and one with God.

To enter the silence of meditation is to enter our own poverty as we renounce our concepts and intellect and sit alert, waiting to hear from God, even if we must wait a lifetime. Prayer helps us transcend our preoccupation with the self and teaches us how to embrace the other.

Grace prompts us to pray, and praying opens us up to even more grace.

Visible Idols

We prefer the reality of this world to the mystery of the next world, and so we value what is expedient and useful instead of what is holy and creative. We erect visible idols to replace the invisible spirit of God. Our lives are consumed by competition, and our work is dedicated to producing a commercial commodity; and as a result, our spiritual fire has been all but snuffed out.

> *By serving the poor*
> *we are not only practicing Christian charity,*
> *we are also reforming ourselves.*

Every act of love, compassion, and sacrifice transforms our world in which hatred, cruelty, and avarice reign into a new world in which the kingdom of God blossoms.

You will not experience peace of mind if there is hatred in your heart. Hating just one person destroys your peace.

> *Compassion is the most effective response to hatred and violence.*

Summum Bonum

St. Francis's love of not only the poor but of poverty itself led me to explore the worst slums on earth in order to understand the saint's deeper meaning, his radical dependency on God.

For me, Franciscan spirituality rests on the foundation of poverty. St. Francis's concept of poverty was interconnected with his concept of God as the Supreme Good, and that Jesus Christ was the *summum bonum* of God given to humanity. Because of his great trust in the supreme goodness of God, St. Francis could give up everything and depend completely on God to supply every one of his needs in service of the poor from God's overflowing goodness.

Francis knew that even in his "poverty" he would be very rich, thanks to God's endless love and infinite goodness, which God wishes to shower on us. Francis wasn't interested in appropriating the things of God for himself. Francis was focused on expropriation, letting go of everything for God, who gives it back a hundred times more in return.

Franciscan poverty should not be equated with the experience of living in desperation. This is not what Francis or God wants from us. St. Francis wants us to let everything go and joyfully trust that God will supply every one of our needs. When St. Francis faced the end of his own resources, he was able to see the vastness of God's unlimited resources. St. Francis understood that a person's spiritual life will not prosper without an intense awareness of their own poverty and emptiness.

All growth begins in a womb of darkness.

Unity with God, Francis discovered, is obtained in only one way: total surrender. This is Franciscan poverty. This lesson is best learned by being one with the poor and helping to liberate them from the prison of unjust, immoral poverty that robs them of their human dignity, a dignity that flows from being sons and daughters of a loving and merciful God.

For St. Francis, voluntary poverty was a way for him to always be dependent on God for everything. When Francis experienced the self-emptying love of God, it awakened his desire to love God and God alone. He longed for nothing else but God. Moreover, Francis put his full trust in the grace of God, the overflowing goodness of God. Every moment was pregnant with the grace to see the boundless love of God in everyone, and to return that love by loving others and all of creation.

In Francis's eyes, everything that is good, every kind gesture, every act of mercy, every gentle touch, every gift of charity, every embrace of forgiveness, every moment of peace, flowed from God. Moreover, all loneliness, every disappointment, the very wounds of rejection, the bitter sadness of loss, and the times of suffering open us to the transcendent and allow us to experience the hidden closeness of God.

Without God Francis knew he was nothing.
With God he knew he lacked nothing.

A Fertile Garden

Voluntary poverty is rich in spiritual grace because it creates an emptiness where desire to be one with those unjustly imprisoned in chronic poverty is intensified. St. Clare of Assisi considered poverty her most prized possession.

A desire for poverty is synonymous with a desire for total surrender of the self, a desire for God alone. Voluntary poverty is a fertile garden where the imitation of Christ can flower.

The richer we are the harder it is
for us to see the poor,
and as a result, we lessen our opportunity
to experience an encounter with the crucified Christ.

An Ongoing Change of Perspective

St. Francis was willing to let God flip his world upside down. What an extraordinary act of faith. By listening to the events of his life, Francis slowly changed his perspective on life. Francis understood he had a need for an ongoing change of heart, an ongoing change of perspective that allowed him to see the way God saw and allowed him to see grace everywhere. That kind of faith seems beyond my reach, but it can't be, it isn't.

It was Francis's willingness to be "grasped" by God that made him unique. He approached each day with a simple, very childlike attitude: God, what do you have in store for me today! This outlook released him from the darkness of self-rootedness and into the light of being rooted in God, thus allowing himself to experience a realignment of his passion, and a complete recentering of his affections.

For Francis, conversion was a liberating experience,
freeing him from the prison of self-rule.
His ongoing conversion was rooted in prayer.

While St. Francis of Assisi was a man of action, he nonetheless spent fully half his adult life in prayer. It was prayer that prompted the action. St. Francis paved the way to a spirituality of contemplation and action.

Despite the importance of contemplation, it is vitally important to realize that contemplation without action is merely conceptualization. Likewise, it is equally important to realize that action without contemplation is merely busyness.

It was during this time of contemplation that the Lord spoke to St. Francis in the depths of his heart and he came to understand what course of action the Lord was asking him to undertake. The saint's quiet time gave direction to his outward ministry and gave him the strength and courage to complete it.

Allow God to turn your life upside down and inside out.
Allow God to topple your expectations.
Journey beyond your comfort zone.
Pursue true knowledge.

Broken and Incomplete

A desire to know God more deeply drew Francis into solitude. He felt broken and incomplete. He wanted to see God face-to-face. His only desire was to dwell with God alone. Like all of us, St. Francis needed God. The desire to be with God is planted deep within each of us. We seek to heal our own brokenness, our own incompleteness by desiring all kinds of things other than God.

Like St. Francis, we all need to surmount all unholy desire,
in order to be embraced by the Holy.

Who can begin to imagine the depths of yearning within the soul of St. Francis? I yearn for the Light of God to break through the darkness of my life. But how weak my yearning is. How much stronger is my yearning for things other than God. St. Francis's yearning for God permeated every fiber of his being. It animated everything he did. His intense, all-consuming yearning seems out of balance in our modern eyes.

Why doesn't the Gospel that so inspired Francis also knock us out of balance, upset and rearrange our lives? Can I surrender all yearning for things not of God? Can I rise out of the muck of my own "balanced" life and truly follow Jesus?

St. Francis embraced the crucified Christ. Do I?

Turning Around

The following is from my Haitian Journal of February 10, 2016.
Years later, I still fail to live the reality of the Resurrection.

Today is Ash Wednesday. I love Lent. Lent is a journey to Easter, a journey to resurrection. I need Lent because I get busy and I forget that Christ rose from the dead. In my fog of forgetfulness, I lose sight of how that unique event needs to have continual meaning for me, that this gift of new life still happens for me, even when I sink into despair over the suffering in Haiti.

But worse than forgetting, in the past I often failed to live the reality of the Resurrection, and in doing so I turned Easter into nothing more than an annual commemoration.

The gift of new life that the resurrection of Christ gives to each of us should dramatically change the way we view the world and the way we live life. But the reality of the end of death quickly fades into a dream. Yes, we will die, but Christ forever changed the nature of death. It is no longer an ending, but a passage—a Passover—to eternal life. Yet I forget, distracted by a thousand things, 995 of which are trivial. Christ made us partakers of his resurrection; that is the core of the Christian faith. But, sadly, it is not the core of my daily experience.

Living a life of faith, hope, and love seems virtually impossible because of our inherent weaknesses. God continually asks us to put him first, and seek him at all times and in all things. We want to put God first, but we are busy, engulfed in so many distractions and preoccupations that we forget and we fail to do it. Our forgetfulness makes it easy for sin to sneak back into our lives. Slowly, the new life of Christ recedes back into the old life of man. We become shallow and stingy. Joy loses its smile, and our faces turn dismal. Life loses its meaning; everything becomes pointless. God has left the building, or so we think. But no, God never leaves. It is we who turn our backs on God, and step by step walk further away. Until Lent rolls around, and prompts us to turn around and begin our journey back to God. The God we found but lost mercifully gives us an endless number of second chances to find him again. Lent helps me see and taste the new life in Christ I so easily betray. Lent is a time to repent and return to the Source and Sustainer of life.

I love Lent. Lent helps me find what I have lost. Lent helps me fall in love again.

The presence of God is found in the absence of things not of God.

A Thousand Things

St. Francis of Assisi said, "The truly clean of heart are those who look down upon earthly things, seek those of heaven, and, with a clean heart and spirit, never cease adoring and seeing the Lord God living and true."

My heart is not clean. Lord have mercy.

My heart is not clean. It is sullied by a thousand things, none of them dirty in themselves. It is sullied by my unhealthy desire for a thousand things that are merely distractions from the true longings of my soul.

I see and seek the things but not the Spring that animates everything. I often clutch what is not mine, what belongs to everyone. I often long for earthly things more than heavenly things.

The times I spend adoring God are weak, skimpy, fleeting episodes. Praising God is a low priority, usually left to the hands of fickle whim. It is no wonder I do not often see the wonder of the living and true God. My heart is busy, occupied with a thousand things.

My heart is not clean. Lord have mercy.

But a heart that is not clean is not cause for despair. For its very uncleanliness prompts a tidal wave of grace. Where sin abounds, grace is even more bountiful. Access to that overflowing grace requires an honest effort to look down on earthly things and seek those of heaven. The treasure we seek is within our hearts.

Our treasure is God,
and God alone.

Woven into the Mundane

St. Francis of Assisi was truly a vessel of spiritual renewal within the Catholic Church. He set Christian thinking on a new course. He opened windows that had been long closed; he let in fresh air and bright sunlight. Francis uprooted the gloom that pervaded Christianity, and supplanted it with joy.

When Francis was a child, the faithful were taught that their time on earth was brief and an insignificant prelude to eternity, and as they made their inexorable march toward this final reality, they did so alone. St. Francis did not believe the prospect of the next world should cloud humanity's vision of this world. He saw an inherent harmony between the realm of the spirit and the realm of physical reality.

For many in Francis's time, spirituality was otherworldly. But not for Francis. His spirituality was rooted right here on earth, and he never forgot that God humbly came to the earth he created. He understood that prayer was an act of humility stemming from a mindfulness of his own inadequacy. Prayer acknowledges our dependency on God.

For Francis, spirituality is found in relationships, work, attitudes, illness, and dreams. Simply put, spirituality is an essential part of ordinary everyday life, fully embracing our emotional, physical, and mental states of being. The difficulty lies in achieving the concentrated attention needed to observe what is going on, moment by moment, in ourselves and around us, to uncover that spiritual dimension. Prayer helps us see the divine intertwined in the commonplace events of our daily lives. Prayer helped Francis see the extraordinary hidden in the ordinary.

Francis loved nature and saw all creation as a gift from God that is meant to be enjoyed. Moreover, because God animates all creation, all of creation is in relationship. We are all brothers and sisters bound together by love and therefore all equal in the eyes of God. For Francis, Christ is not a cosmic ruler and judge to be feared and worshiped. For Francis, Christ lives in you and in your neighbor. Christ literally dwells in your flesh.

Francis loved the cross because the cross is a symbol of God's humility, poverty, and love. In meditating on the cross, Francis saw that God's love lacked nothing and nothing was held back.

To walk in the footsteps of St. Francis is, ultimately, to walk in the footsteps of Christ. In his own time and for all time, St. Francis is the tireless messenger of Love, continuously singing Incarnation's song. St. Francis reduced the entire Christian faith to one word: Love. As he neared the end of his earthly pilgrimage, St. Francis of Assisi did not judge, reject, hate, or condemn anyone or anything. He merely loved all, equally, passionately.

Merely—as if it were that simple.

A Sanctuary of the Spirit

> *All praise be yours, my Lord, through all that you made.*
> —St. Francis of Assisi

The life of St. Francis of Assisi is, for me, a sanctuary of the spirit that belongs to another time, a simpler time, a less complex and complicated time. To step into that sanctuary is to step out of our world and into that world. Francis felt most at home in nature. In nature, the divine became visible in the heart of Francis. Nature put Francis at ease and lightened the burdens of his heart.

The nature of the heart is that it is always dreaming of the beyond. Francis was a dreamer. His heart was imbued and enflamed with longing, which was the source of his creativity. Creativity derives from the disturbance of the longing within us. Faith is a helpless attraction to the divine. If you imagine God as an artist it changes your entire understanding of God.

After being alone with his God in nature, Francis was able to return to his society and bless those in need, including lepers. The hillside of Mount Subasio became the landscape of the future saint's soul. The landscape was alive and sacred, and had for Francis an actual resonance of the divine. All of creation became his brother and sister. Francis came to understand that every tree, every flower preexisted in the mind of God, who prepared a magnificent, bountiful world teeming with color, beauty, and wonder for us. God is present in the wind, the water, the sun, and all of creation. The saint did not separate compassion for all of humanity from compassion for all of creation.

Today, nature is property. It is real estate. God is absent. We abuse nature. Modern times are very difficult; problems abound and multiply. The turbulence of modern life prompts us to return to the stillness and presence of nature. In nature, the burdens of modern life dissolve. Walking in silence, in a contemplative spirit conscious of the elements, is healing. Walking along the oceanfront or climbing a mountain and doing so prayerfully is transformative and brings you to a place of inner peace. A long stroll in nature is the antidote to the toxic effect of spending hours in a room in front of a computer.

To step back into the rugged nature of Mount Subasio, which looms over Assisi below, is to enter into the spirit of St. Francis.

If you look closely, you'll see the presence of grace and divinity
in the natural world.

The Human Face of Jesus

St. Francis understood that we all are the human face of Jesus; he knew that all of humanity constitutes the divine face. God assumed flesh and was born into a world of oppression and persecution. Can we ever grasp the reality of the divine presence dwelling in a depraved humanity and that subsequently every man, woman, and child is uniquely precious, equal, and blessed, all brothers and sisters?

Jesus is hungry and naked. Yet we build and decorate elaborate churches in his name, but do not feed or clothe him. Every day, God comes to us in a distressing disguise, clothed in the rags of a tormented and neglected poor person, in hopes that the encounter will provide a place for healing and hurt to meet, for grace to embrace sin, for beauty to be restored.

Only with loving eyes can we see God's face in every face,
including our own.

We need to do good in a way that we are not above those we are helping. Our relationship with the poor is horizontal, not vertical. Still, to see the poor as if they were Jesus is hard. The poor are often unpleasant, hard to like. If I were in their shoes, I'd be filled with such hostility and anger; I would be highly disagreeable.

We Are All Mothers of Christ

In his *Letter to the Faithful* St. Francis writes, "We are mothers [of our Lord Jesus Christ] when we carry him in our heart and body through love and a pure and sincere conscience; we give birth to him by doing good."

So much of life today is deeply disturbing, especially our attitudes toward poverty and peace. I can't understand the irony of how we seek peace by going to war. Our impulse toward war uncovers our erroneous belief that some people are not important, that some lives, even the lives of some children (the children of our enemies), are expendable.

I cannot understand how we are undisturbed by the reality that more than twenty thousand children die every day from preventable diseases, most stemming from hunger. The recent economic downturn that has dramatically damaged the lives of the poor reveals the utter lack of moral and ethical constraints on capitalism and consumerism; the unbridled greed of commodity hucksters is nothing short of idolatry. We have become so numbed by the scope of poverty, as well as by our own self-interest, that we don't even feel the pain of the other, don't realize their misery is also our misery.

As a society we've failed to understand that our lives are both interior and relational, that we're designed for communion with God and each other. Our lives have become impoverished because we do not value simplicity, do not realize what is truly essential, and do not reach out to the chronically poor and rejected.

I think St. Francis came to see clearly that the fundamental principle of the Gospel requires that the weakest and least presentable people are indispensable to the church, that the followers of Christ must be in communion with the poor and must be willing to love our enemies. Each of us is wounded in some way; each of us is an enemy.

We need each other, and we need God.

The same tender mercy that sustains me sustains my enemy. To not love your enemies is to believe they are beyond the scope of God's power . . . and love.

Members of His Family

St. Francis gradually developed an ever-deepening attitude of reverence and respect for all of creation. He personalized the whole of creation, seeing the sun, the moon, the trees, the birds, the animals as his brothers and sisters. They were members of his family, and he spoke with them in the most intimate and lovely fashion.

Of course, from our rationalist point of view, it seems silly to preach to birds. But from the point of view of a mystic, Francis's dialogue with all of creation was profoundly wise and sanctifying at the same time. By personalizing creation Francis was able to put aside his adult prejudices and become like a little child and in the process discover a little sliver of the kingdom of heaven.

A Delicate Balance

In writing this book, I was preaching to myself. I desperately needed to slow down my physical work in Haiti and take more time to nurture my personal relationship with God. Whenever things in my life turned sour during the last twenty years it could be mostly blamed on my failure to maintain the delicate balance between contemplation and action.

How stupid it was of me to think that "my" work on behalf of the poor was more important than tending to my own inner poverty. It was never "my" work; it was work given to me by God. I was doing God's work. To perform at the highest level of effectiveness I needed to have the work be more fully rooted in the grace of God. It seemed the more my former ministry grew in size, the more I felt it was dependent on my tireless effort in order to sustain the growth. Whenever I became truly exhausted by the effort, I too frequently succumbed to my weaknesses instead of nourishing myself on the bounty of God's tender love and endless compassion. The demands of the ministry were overwhelming. Yet I didn't need to carry that burden by myself or think it all depended on me.

No film, no book is going to save the world. Only love will save the world. What I did on behalf of the poor—and what I'm doing—is not that important, nor will it make much of a difference. But God's work is not subject to a cost-benefit analysis; it freely gives itself away without counting the cost or expecting a reward.

My books and films, all rooted in Franciscan spirituality, no matter how many people they have touched, are irrelevant unless they become more real inside of me and continue to be written afresh in my heart. As I penned these humble, stumbling words, I realized I knew a lot about the life and spirituality of St. Francis. Big deal. What is important is that after nearly twenty-five years of immersion into the Franciscan charism I haven't yet allowed the saint's insights to truly enter deeply into my being and radically transform who I am; instead, I tinkered around the edges. It really does not matter if I write another book or make another film or feed another hungry kid. The only thing that matters is that I surrender my heart more fully to God and begin to really love. All the words and images in the world are all but useless if they are not animated by the Word that speaks of evolving life and increasing love.

When I speak or write about my inner spiritual journey, I know that I'm on unstable ground because my own spiritual life is still impoverished. There are days I feel truly lost. But those are the days when God's grace is most fervently present.

Sunflowers and Grasshoppers

Our lack of reverence is destroying the earth and crippling relationships.

Global warming is real, a measurable reality. By any honest measure planet Earth is in trouble, perhaps even in peril. Many think the fate of humanity is precarious. The Earth can't sustain our unrestrained greed and growth, our misguided philosophy of individualism. At the root of our common problem is a rampant spirit of disconnectedness. The survival of our fragile planet, our home, depends on our ability to rediscover the connectedness of all life. Every particle of nature is attached to the rest of creation. Even the least thing affects everything. When one part of creation is hurting, all of creation is hurting. We are abusing creation, plundering its resources; the earth is crying, dying, because of our failure to see the solidarity of all life.

Our spirit of individualism separates us from each other and all of creation. We have become the center of the universe. It is all about "me." And that self-centered attitude gave us our recent economic disaster. St. Francis was not self-centered. He was God-centered, which means he was also creation-centered, seeing all life as his brother or sister, seeing all life as connected by virtue of the fact that God created everything, permeates everything, is the Father and Mother of all, of the sunflower and the grasshopper.

The sixth-century-BCE Jewish prophet Isaiah saw God as a supreme landscape artist, carefully designing a garden of delights to support, sustain, and entertain all of life. By God's divine hand a mountain rose here and a lake formed there. With dirt below and sky above, our home sprung from nothing and contained everything. But it was not enough for us. We wanted more. Much more. We wanted to rule ourselves, each other, all of creation. We wanted to be God.

In the scope of the massive and magnificent creation, the poet-prophet Isaiah saw us mighty humans as mere grasshoppers. Funny yet insightful. If only we had acted like grasshoppers, as little slivers of life, instead of acting like lords, dominating all of life.

St. Francis saw himself with humble eyes, no better than a lowly worm. He also saw himself with exalted eyes as a son of God and hence connected to and equal with all of creation, a delicately interwoven tapestry of wonder and awe, lovingly stitched together by the Master Weaver.

He saw our original connectedness and desired nothing more than to restore it. Because we do not see the tapestry of unity created by God, we are slowly killing the poor and the weak. We are slowly destroying planet Earth because we don't realize that God entrusted the beauty and bounty of creation to us, to sustain us. God laid all of creation at our feet, gave us dominion over it. But instead of safeguarding this priceless treasure we choose to dominate and abuse it.

St. Francis of Assisi understood that the earth belongs to God and that God let us be temporarily in charge of creation. We betrayed that trust. Lord have mercy. St. Francis would say: It is not too late. God is a God of hope, a God of mercy. Turn back. Love life, all of life. Give praise and thanksgiving to the Author and Sustainer of life—God our Father and Mother—by embracing and protecting all of life, even the lives of our enemies. We are one.

Sing in unison a song of praise.

Our Father

The heresy of American Christianity is rugged individualism. We speak of "my rights" and "my relationship with God." We are self-centered and narcissistic. The great prayer of Christianity begins: "*Our* Father . . ." We are connected, our prayer is communal.

Know yourself and forget yourself.

Isn't it odd that we pray "thy kingdom come" yet we really love and cling to this world and its fleeting pleasures? Isn't odd that we pray "thy will be done" yet we cultivate and worship our own self-will?

I need to strive continually to make Christ present in every ambit of my life, in every encounter, every deed, every relationship. Of course, I all too frequently shut the door on Christ, or worse, set up a wall around some hidden area of my being that I want to keep all to myself. It's crazy how we seem to protect the very things or behaviors we should reject. The fact is, we pray . . . and we sin. But where there is sin, there too is grace, overflowing and abundant. But only in stillness can we see the movement of grace. My faith may be fickle at times, but God is always faithful. Alleluia. Alleluia. Alleluia.

Made for Communion

The emptiness we often feel stems from not realizing we are made for communion with God. If we are not growing toward unity with God, then we are growing apart from God. We need to bring to Christ what we are so that in time we become what he is. Wholeness is attained when we achieve freedom from the greedy tendencies of the ego and its insatiable hunger for possessiveness. A person becomes whole when the self learns how to be empty, willing to lose itself in order to enter into a deep and rich communion with others.

I need to escape from the distorting influences of society by refocusing my life with periodic times of solitude. Only solitude allows me to reconnect with the truth of my own nature and my relationship with God.

No one can see the depths of their own poverty. Without words or thoughts, I must force myself to stand naked before God. Only then can I learn to say truthfully: "Blessed are those who know that they are poor." Coming face-to-face with my own total poverty is the only way to come face-to-face with God and find true enlightenment.

Solitude is never alone time. It is time with yourself.

Poverty of Spirit

Poverty of spirit is a manger of gentle receptivity that allows the divine to be born within us. To be wholly present to God, with all of our heart, mind, and soul, we must be poor in spirit.

Poverty of spirit is far more than material poverty. While material poverty may help to facilitate poverty of spirit, it is nonetheless important to realize that a person without possessions can still be possessed by a craving for things. It is the craving that makes us restless, distracting our hearts and minds from being present to God alone.

Poverty of spirit frees us from being divided by false idols and uncurbed passions.

Poverty of spirit is a means of maintaining a continual attitude of dying to self without succumbing to self-hatred or causing a lack of self-esteem. We need to die to self because it is the only way to be fully alive to God.

A cluttered heart

is

a deaf heart.

Unsatisfied Hearts

We are all beggars. None of us is sufficient unto ourselves. All of us are plagued by unending doubts and restless, unsatisfied hearts. By ourselves, we are incomplete. Our needs are always beyond our capacities, and we only find ourselves when we lose ourselves. Prayer and contemplation free us from self-serving and prepare us to lead a life of service to others without unconsciously desiring our own success.

We live in a world of stark inequality and injustice. So did Jesus. Jesus had a deep concern for those who suffered and were marginalized. So should we. For the follower of Jesus, compassion is not an option; it's an obligation, as well as a sign our lives have been transformed into the healing presence of Christ.

> *Only when I'm able to see my own unholiness*
> *can I begin to see the sacredness of all creation.*

On his life's journey Francis took his own path. He made mistakes; and some of his actions were rather irrational. Some of his ideas were outrageous. One can easily imagine him as difficult to be with, at times being downright ornery. But no matter his mood, no matter what people thought of him, he kept his focus on God.

The deepest levels of self-denial that Francis reached present us with a huge gap in comparison to our feeble efforts at approaching perfect trust in God. What is it that keeps me from total surrender to the loving embrace of God? I know what God seeks, yet I hesitate. I know God loves me, and this love, I realize, does not spring from a reluctant heart; God stands always willing and waiting to love us even more deeply, yet we hesitate in accepting God's love out of fear of losing ourselves and being buried in God.

The only way to overcome this fear and grow in trust in and love of God is through a serious commitment to prayer. In poverty, Francis found a way into prayer. Nothing was more important to him than spending time in prayer. Prayer is about building a relationship with the source of love. For Francis, prayer was the way to learn how to live love. I've been walking in the footsteps of St. Francis for almost a quarter of a century, and I'm only now beginning to see, albeit dimly, the connection Francis made between poverty and prayer.

> *Contemplation leads to communion,*
> *communion with God and all creation.*

Contemplation leads to action, action that manifests and makes real God's mercy and compassion. Contemplation and poverty are natural partners. Contemplation helps us to see both inside us and to see around us. Our contemplative vision improves as our lives become more simplified. Our lives are cluttered with so much stuff, and we are so easily distracted by so many things, that our spiritual vision is severely diminished.

Silence is the soul of simplicity. Simplicity helps us see what is important, helps us see another's need, helps us see injustice and suffering, helps us see the need to be free from all attachments that limit our freedom and ability to love.

We live in a thick fog of materialism and escapism.

Poverty and simplicity help us see what is important, helps us see another's need, help us see injustice and suffering, help us see the need to be free from all attachments that limit our freedom and ability to love. We strive to amass wealth, but true wealth resides in creating fraternity.

The world is divided into two camps: the rich and the poor.

Between those two camps there is no communication, no shared life, no communion. The rich and the poor are strangers, and their mutual isolation gives birth to misunderstanding and mistrust. And the gap between the rich and the poor grows wider and deeper by the hour.

Jesus condemned the unnatural and unjust division between the rich and the poor, because the division causes pride, envy, jealousy, self-centeredness, and loneliness. The kingdom of God, Jesus tells us, is about unity, reconciliation, harmony, peace, and love.

The kingdom of God is about oneness.

Jesus calls us to a life of communion, communion with God and communion with each other. The life of communion helps us grow in knowledge and love of God and each other. Jesus is the bridge between the rich and the poor, the bridge between earth and heaven. The cross of Christ reconciles us to God and each other, and is a lived example of self-emptying love.

Contemplation and communion lead to action, call us to the margins of society, to the American urban jungles of deprivation, crime, and violence, to the dark corners around the world where people live in massive slums of overwhelming need clinging to life without clean water or electricity and barely enough food for survival. In these deprived places, not only do we give life but life is also given to us. It is here we see for the first time the oneness that has always been there, though obscured by our blindness.

Through contemplation we learn to see. Through communion we learn to share. Through action we learn to love.

Be still. Know God. Live love.

The Mystical Flame

We often talk about our sinfulness in terms of blindness, and our redemption in terms of seeing. We are blind to the needs of the poor; we do not want to see their plight. We turn away from the sight of those who endure the pain of living without the basic necessities of life.

No one wants to see what I filmed in Haiti. I don't want to see it. Because in seeing it, I can't forget it, and I must do something about it. But in the very doing of something for others, I discover myself and liberate my false self from the unseen prison of my own ego.

But many people today are also weary of how they've become accustomed to living. Many are disillusioned with institutional forms of religion. The crisis of belonging so many feel has given rise to a widespread spiritual hunger, a search for the mystical flame that long ago had been consumed by darkness and doubt and materialism.

For me, poverty road was the road back to God. I think everyone can benefit from spending time with the poor and with the saintly people who live their lives in service to the poor. They know about poverty and prayer; they can relight the flame of faith.

An ember of faith
fanned by
the holy breath of God
can turn into
a blazing fire of love.

The Blind Beggar

Be like the blind beggar at Jericho,
seated at the side of the road,
and stretch out open hands
to the silence of God.

St. Francis used to walk the streets of Assisi with a bowl in his hand, going door to door begging for food. An empty beggar's bowl is an apt metaphor for the receptivity and acceptance required in our relationship with God. An ancient Chinese script says, "Come before the divine with a bowl, an empty bowl, a beggar's bowl." Knowing only God could give him what he truly needed, St. Francis went to God with empty hands, divesting himself of all vestiges of self-will and self-interest in order to be fully receptive to God alone.

We are all blind beggars, and we all need to stretch out open hands to God, who will give us sight and teach us how to see things differently, how to see things as they are, in their fullness, wholeness, and connectedness.

Everyone's life and death affects God's creation.

Empty Hands

At the moment when Christ said, "Not my will, but yours be done," he experienced the true crucifixion and became a living sacrifice. We need to experience a crucifixion every day. We need to nail our wills to the cross and surrender our wills to the will of God. Are we living sacrifices?

Christ became poor and emptied himself of everything for us.

I go to God with my hands full . . . and ask for more. St. Francis of Assisi was willing to go to God with empty hands. For him, the only thing that mattered was utter trust in God, and the saint's adult life was a continual witness to the realization that total trust cannot exist until we have lost all self-trust and are rooted in poverty.

My efforts at approaching perfect trust are woefully feeble. St. Francis said the road to God is straight and narrow: the road is poverty. For us, that means we must be willing to go to God with empty hands, trusting God for everything.

A life of prayer and poverty helped St. Francis of Assisi unearth an essential spiritual truth: total trust in God cannot exist until we have lost all self-trust.

The most difficult of fasts does not involve abstinence from food. Far more difficult is to fast from your own selfishness. I once managed to stay on such a fast for two and a half hours, and it was hell.

To live in the reality of God is to live in trust, transparency, and compassion.
To live in the reality of God is to be embraced by God's tenderness.

Why Francis?

There are always flowers for those who wish to see them.
—Henri Matisse[44]

In time, we all see it, all know it . . . the world is often an ugly place, filled with violence and all forms of evil. We far too easily and far too often place personal or national gain above the good of the whole.

The beauty and innocence of childhood quickly fades, and we are left with isolation and loneliness. Life is hard, filled with dashed hopes and painful experiences. Suffering visits every life. Some lives know nothing else but suffering. It is all very confusing, and in the womb of darkness that surrounds so much of life, dreams of another world, a better world, are born. We dream of a world of justice and peace, a utopian world where people live in harmony as brothers and sisters.

But this dream, which is common among all people, is not new. In fact, it is a faint memory of something lost long ago. The Hebrew Bible tells us of an imagined paradise known as Eden, where Adam and Eve had everything they needed. Abundance was theirs. But it was not enough. Reaching for more was their original sin. And ours also. Through sin, paradise was lost, for them, for all of us.

But there was a man, so filled with a longing for God, who showed us that Eden was not lost forever, that Eden was simply a way of living. That man was, of course, Francis of Assisi.

In his innocence, Francis talked with birds. We have lost all sense of innocence, replaced by skepticism and doubt. In taming the wolf, Francis confronted the ferocity of evil that was within him and around him. The peace that was within Francis was so real, so genuine, people believed him when he preached of the importance of personal, social, and political peace. We accept the violence of war as a normal and needed part of life. Sometimes we feel we just need to kill, even though Jesus told us to put down the sword and to love our enemies.

Francis looked at the world we all look at, but he saw it differently. He saw the beauty of creation and the hand of the Creator. Where we might see a sunflower, if we are not too busy, Francis saw not only the flower but also the Love that created the flower, a love that grows best in the divinely fertile soil of harmony and community. And the flower became his sister.

In his new way of seeing and living, Francis overcame his fear of death. With God in his heart as a presence as real as the sun rising above Assisi, Francis rose above all fear, all anxiety. He lived in the moment, as each moment was filled with transformational grace. Francis demonstrated with his life that to be truly free he needed nothing except God. In poverty, he found richness. In his self-emptying of all that was not God, Francis became truly naked, as unashamedly naked as were Adam and Eve before they succumbed to desires beyond God.

Francis showed how the fullness of life is not just a dream or hopeless desire, but is something that can be experienced right here, right now, in this very moment. Francis showed us that those rare moments of our life when we are pure, serene, and peaceful are the most genuine, most truthful moments of life, and that these moments echo the essence of paradise we have lost but can still regain. Francis showed us that it is possible to see the beauty in everything and see the Creator in the creatures.

Francis trusted God fully. This is where we fail. We lack trust in God, do not believe God will give us all we need, that God will not withhold any good thing. Perhaps our pride gets in the way of our trusting. Perhaps our love of God has been supplanted by our love of self. Francis takes us back to Eden, back to a time of purity and innocence, a time when beauty and harmony grew in a garden of love.

Francis followed his heart and his passion for God. He was willing to surrender everything and to become nothing in order to embrace the fullness of God. In doing so, Francis discovered, in his weakness, something truly powerful. This poor man, this humble beggar, changed the course of Christian life and helped us to see the good in everything.

Why Francis? Why not us? Why not you? Why not me?

Far and Near

Speaking on behalf of the Lord, the prophet Isaiah said, "Hear, you who are far off, what I have done; you who are near, acknowledge my might" (33:13 NABRE).

There is a loneliness to the past and the future. I am not there; I am here in the present. I am far from who I was in the past and far from who I will be in the future. I am only near myself in this present moment.

God too is far and near. Far in the sense that God leaves us to ourselves in order for us to discover our own hearts and the heart of God. Yet God is as near as the next breath we take, as near as our very heartbeat. God is so near we do not see her. God seems so far because we do not know him. Because we do not see or know God who is so far and so near, we have the anguish of loneliness at the core of our being. We know emptiness not plentitude. Sadness is always around the corner; joy occasionally comes and quickly goes.

To discover God in your heart you must journey beyond all self-consciousness to an awareness of a reality greater than yourself. It is a long journey and a short journey. And on the journey, we must drop all notions of God and all notions of self. Only then can God reveal God to you and reveal you to yourself.

In loneliness and longing, we begin our journey to God. Stripped of everything, we have nothing, we take nothing. Yet our very loneliness is graced with the possibility to discover the transcendent. Even the silence of God is graced and speaks of the mystery of God and God's forgiving nearness, God's hidden intimacy.

In stillness and silence, we learn about a love that shares itself, an overflowing love that dissolves all alienation and fills the empty space within us. God is here in this moment, waiting with open and outstretched arms, waiting to embrace and caress you with endless love.

Kiss this moment for in it is perfect joy and all good.

Love Is the Key

Jesus asks us to love as God loves—without counting the cost or holding anything back. Love gives all away. Love frees us to act for the good of another rather than for ourselves. God's love is unbiased and all-embracing. It does not ask who we are or how successful we are at what we do.

Being an instrument of peace requires us to embrace the enemy in pardon.

To give freely what we have freely received—namely, God's love—is the purest form of evangelization. Following the example of Christ will lead some of us to go poor among the poor, without power, without purse, without provisions, with charity and respect for those they encounter. All of us must seek peace above all else and then do good at every opportunity. Our lives are our sermons, and our preaching should be benign and gentle, spoken with meekness and humility.

When I'm centered on God, I'm not distracted by my wayward self and am more easily absorbed in the presence of God. I think one of the basic messages gleaned from the life of St. John of the Cross is that inward stillness gives birth to outward peace. We see few signs of outward peace in the world. During Mass, after the consecration, we symbolically give each other a sign of peace by shaking hands or exchanging hugs. It is the most real moment in the liturgy. One hand reaching out to another. But we quickly pull back, retreating to our self-centered fortress that even God cannot penetrate.

A School of Love

> *The greatest accomplishment in life*
> *is to be who or what you are,*
> *and that is what God wanted you to be*
> *when he created you.*
> —Abbot Thomas Keating, ocso[45]

When we are young, we wonder what path our lives will take. In our late teens, we normally choose a path. Often in life, we make a complete change of direction and boldly head off into unknown territory. I think I'm on the road God wants me to be on. I guess the actual road we take isn't really all that important, as long as it leads us back to God. Returning to God is the destination of our life's journey. There are so many routes we can take. And there are lots of roads that take us the wrong way and we get lost.

The journey is replete with dead ends, detours, and roadblocks. Sometimes U-turns are essential.

Today it seems the path to God is the road less traveled. Our society is headed in the wrong direction. The ways of the Lord do not seem to be our ways. We want to consume more and more. We want to succeed in business, no matter the cost. We ignore the poor. We want to wage war. We hardly live as if we believe in God. Charles de Foucauld, the Christian contemplative and mystic who lived among the Tuareg people of Algeria, said, "As soon as I believed there was a God, I understood that I could not do anything other than live for him." If a poll were conducted that asked the question, "Who or what do you live for?" I would bet God would be near the bottom of the list of answers. The reason God would poll so low is that there is a rupture between what we believe and how we act.

It puzzles me how so many Christians (including me, a good deal of the time) live lives that bear no resemblance to the life of Christ. Am I a follower of Christ or a follower of the latest trend in society? The heartbeat of the Incarnation is generosity and love. In Christ, we see a God so generous he throws everything away out of love. While we busy ourselves striving for power and trying to control events and even people, the Gospel perpetually proclaims a far different approach to life: God has created us to live a life of dependence and receptivity, and our acceptance of that spiritual reality is required for true human growth and fulfillment.

To live the Gospel forces us to live with contradiction—for the Gospel requires a faith that believes that when one has nothing, one has everything. Moreover, it asks us to count poverty as riches and humiliation as an honor. Of course, this sounds like utter nonsense, even to those who profess to be followers of Christ. But even a casual reading of the Gospels reveals that Jesus denounced power, injustice, and poverty. Christ moved beyond justice to generosity. If the Gospel is not about love and justice, it has been reduced to mere sentimentality.

For followers of Christ, service to the poor and lowly is not optional—it is a requirement. Christ gave us an understanding of divine justice that is based on divine mercy. When we turn our back on the poor, we are turning our back on Jesus. We want a cozy Jesus; but Jesus is far from cozy. The core of Christianity is about the cross, suffering, renunciation, and sharing what we have with others. Yet our society proclaims a dramatically different message. It tells us to grab all we can, to live for ourselves. It urges us to be independent, to deny the interdependence of all living beings, and to ignore that we are dependent on God for every breath we take.

Independence is not a Gospel value. Interdependence is a Gospel value.

When Charles de Foucauld understood he could not do anything other than to live for God, he caught a glimpse of the ultimate truth: human beings by their nature are compelled to turn toward God and eventually devote themselves totally to God. The great Sufi mystic and poet Rumi wrote about how the "profession of God's unity" needs to reverberate through all our thoughts and actions. The prophet Mohammed said, "Knowledge without works is like a tree without fruit." When our hearts are enlightened by grace to the "knowledge" or awareness of God, we are driven to apply this interior knowledge to our everyday exterior life.

What the mystics and saints of all faiths came to realize is that to enter the heart of God is to enter a school of love. When we first experience God's love, our spirits are dazzled by delight and we are left in a state of bewilderment. In the wake of the experience all our previous thoughts and ideas are overturned, and we know that without love we are naught. And love must be shared, must be given away.

Love is a hunger for community.

There are so many paths we can take in life. No matter what path we choose, the path needs to be paved with love in order for it to lead us back to God. Where there is love . . . there is God. Everything we do needs to be done in love. That means we must continually strive to root out all anger and violence from our lives. Jesus said, "Peace be with you," because he knew that God is a God of peace, and that perfect peace is the fruit of perfect love. What God had in mind when he created each of us is that we would attain the perfection of love, becoming instruments of peace, mercy, kindness, and compassion. At the end of our individual journeys, God will ask us only one question: In the adventure of your life, did you learn to love?

Where Love Is

When we are enslaved by obsessive desires, we are not free to pray. When our interest in power, money, and material things is greater than our longing for God, we are still far from authentic prayer. The deeper we journey into prayer the less interested we are in thoughts rooted in worldly desires and sensory perceptions.

> *The altar of our spirit*
> *should be unadorned*
> *and free of*
> *false and unhealthy desires.*

Our prayer should be dressed in reverence and humility, unsoiled by a mind still cluttered, impassioned, and impure. Calm the restlessness of your mind by mindfulness of your breathing and by acts of compassion and mercy. We must imitate God, who stoops down in mercy to touch us. So we too must stoop down in mercy to touch others, even those who live far away.

The spiritual life is a twofold journey . . . an inward movement to the depths of our being and the source of love and an outward movement to the broken world, the margins of society, where love is expressed in acts of kindness.

> *Love is the most uplifting force in the universe.*

True Fellowship

Mercy is an essential ingredient of Christian spirituality. It is a sign of God's perfection and care. Mercy is the generous sharing with others of God's gift of mercy that we have experienced. Mercy allows forgiveness of failures, hurts, and sins. Mercy creates the possibility of true fellowship among all people; without mercy, genuine community is not possible. Mercy turns discrimination into reconciliation. Mercy gives us eyes to see all people as images of God and prompts us to share our lives and resources with each other. Mercy rejects no one and welcomes everyone to the Eucharistic table.

A Prayer: My Plans

*O Lord, my mind and heart
are centered on so many things
other than you.
Mostly good things,
but not you.
Help me this day
to desire you
first and foremost,
and not to be distracted
by all the things
that pull me
this way and that way,
fragmenting my being.
Teach me this day, O Lord,
how to forget
my fears and anxieties,
and to put all my trust and hope
in you alone.*

*O God, you know my plans.
Help me hear your plan for me.
Help me know when my plans
are rooted in my false self,
the "me" that does not see
its own weakness and pride.
Help me never forget that
the only bread I need is you.*

St. Francis Inn, Philadelphia, Pennsylvania

PART FIVE

Feeding Jesus

Going into Strange Countries

If our embracing stillness and silence
and occasionally entering into periods of solitude
does not lead us to a compassionate response
to cruel and unjust poverty,
then it has been a self-serving waste of time.

Thomas Merton recognized his spiritual journey as a metaphorical "going forth into strange countries." For Merton, even going nowhere was a pilgrimage. Day by day, our lives are a journey, a journey to nowhere, to God. I've been around the world, traveled to many "strange countries" in order to get nowhere, in order to arrive at an empty place within me where the fullness of life is hidden.

My encounter with St. Francis of Assisi changed my life. My journey with St. Francis has taken me to places I never imagined going. I've lived among the poor in India, Kenya, Brazil, Peru, El Salvador, Honduras, Mexico, Jamaica, Haiti, and the Philippines. As I traveled, I was stunned to learn that malnutrition causes the deaths of over six million children every year. More than a billion people lack safe drinking water. Half of humanity must survive on the equivalent of two dollars a day.

The horrors of the sprawling slums in those faraway places often brought me to tears. Naked kids being bathed in the streets with water laced with bacteria. Entire families squeezed into one room without electricity or a toilet. The nauseating stench of open sewers. I was haunted by the massive garbage dumps in the Philippines, where people live, scavenging like vultures through the rotting waste of others. I was shocked by the sight of hundreds of people with leprosy in a leper colony in the Amazon, people with mutilated faces, whose arms and legs had been eaten away by a vile disease I assumed had been eradicated long ago. I was saddened by the suffering in a home in Chaclacayo, Peru, where a saintly American doctor cares for fifty destitute kids with every disease imaginable. While filming a malnourished infant, I became sick to my stomach. The poverty-induced lethal violence I witnessed in Honduras frightened me. The despair and hopeless isolation I encountered in the massive refugee camps in Kenya and Uganda still haunts me.

Yet to my amazement, I liked being with the poor. The poor were teaching me about my own poverty, my own weakness. In all those distant places, I learned a lot about poverty and prayer, and the mystery of life and death.

But I didn't have to leave America to feel the pain of crippling poverty. In this country, 700,000 people are without shelter each night. In 2003, I filmed for six months in Skid Row in downtown Los Angeles, where 11,000 homeless people struggle for survival in the shadow of astounding affluence. Every day I witnessed an endless parade of misery, pain, rejection, and loneliness. People slept in cardboard boxes, under tarps, or in small tents. Every night in Skid Row more than 700 children are without shelter, forced to share space with the mentally ill and drug addicts.

In December of 2005, I spent two weeks in one of the worst slums in America, the Kensington section of Philadelphia, making a second film about the St. Francis Inn, a soup kitchen run by Franciscan friars. Known as "the Badlands," Kensington in those days was a dark, brooding, depressed area where poverty, pain, and drugs thrived. The mean streets of Kensington were littered with throwaway people, people marginalized, ignored, and forgotten, people whose lives were lived in fear, in overwhelming want, and without hope. It was a place of death and despondency. I spent part of a night in an abandoned building with a homeless man. The temperature was ten degrees. The windows were broken, and the wind howled through the empty, litter-strewn rooms. It snowed through the porous roof. The man was afraid to fall asleep, fearing a rat would crawl into his mouth seeking warmth. It was a nightmare.

Before shifting my focus from filming to serving the poor in Haiti, I traveled the country speaking and showing my films at universities, high schools, and churches, telling my audience they had a responsibility to help ease the pain of chronic poverty. I also shared the story of how I went from the soap opera tale of "Luke and Laura" on the run to running a nonprofit foundation that tried to put the power of film at the service of the poor.

Poverty is painful. But far beneath the surface, you find the priceless seed of hope. Not just a fairy-tale hope, but a gritty hope rooted in total dependency on God. As I walked with the poor, I encountered my own true poverty and the radical truth of the Gospel: only empty hands can hold God.

My encounter with the bloated belly of poverty helped me remove the veil of comfortability from the gospel and revealed the radical nature of Christianity. Jesus showed us how to love, how to love unconditionally and without limits. According to Christ, how we love the hungry, the lowly, and the lost is how we love him; and how we love Christ will be the only litmus test for our entrance into our heavenly home with God for all eternity. Until we enter our eternal home, we are all homeless, even if we live in a palace, because everything on earth is perishable, except love.

The Lines That Connect Us All

We are all brothers and sisters, children of the same Creator, and to set ourselves up as higher or better than others is a subtle form of blasphemy. We are all connected, one with all of creation and the Creator. If one among us is diminished, we are all diminished.

The Incarnation teaches us that God is humble. The richness of God is revealed in the poverty of Christ. God lives in our poverty and weakness. Jesus embraced and loved the poor and rejected. For Jesus, the poor are sacraments, because they offer a direct way to encounter God. The poor, broken, and rejected are portals through which we can enter fully into the life of Christ. Christ shows us that mercy is more than compassion or justice. Mercy requires us to become one with the poor and hurting, to live their misery as though it were our own. In Christ, we see a God so generous he gives himself away out of love. Christ moved beyond justice to generosity.

We must seek harmony in diversity as we rejoice in our humanness.

We all find God in different ways, but our whole lives are journeys toward God. On that journey to know God, Jesus makes it abundantly clear that

God is to be found in the hungry, the naked, the imprisoned, the homeless, the abandoned, and the downtrodden.

The Incarnation compels us to step to the back of the bus and choose to sit with the poor and learn to see life from their point of view in order to better share in their struggle for access to God's gift of freedom, oneness, and love that has been denied them by virtue of our selfishness.

We all know that poverty exists, that there are untold numbers of people living in unimaginably horrible conditions. The growing numbers of homeless people in America is on full display in every city. Most people would like to do something to ease the suffering. The sheer number of outstretched hands begging for our spare change is daunting. But we are busy. Modern life seems hopelessly complex, requiring everyone to become master jugglers, juggling job and family responsibilities. The demands on our time are at once maddening and frustrating. With so many things to do, and so many hands stretching out for help, I think we have developed a fatigue of compassion.

When we look beyond our borders, we are overwhelmed by the need. War, famine, brutal dictatorships, natural disasters, economic recessions, and corrupt governments have created a huge exodus of refugees living in squalor. We grow weary from stories on television and in newspapers documenting the plight of the poor in places such as Darfur, Kenya, Uganda, and Haiti, and the cumulative effect of all the tragic stories leaves us feeling helpless to do anything about it. So we turn away and keep busy.

But the Gospel tells us we cannot turn away, cannot divert our eyes and hearts from the suffering caused by chronic poverty. We need a new way to look and a new way to respond to the poor. We need to look through eyes of faith, no matter what faith we follow; and we need to respond with a heart of faith. It will not be easy. It will take time. Meditating on the plight of the poor, and on our role in their plight, and the spiritual response to the plight are vital.

I've learned the importance of relationships and how interdependent we are on each other. For St. Francis of Assisi prayers were not an escape from the world but an entrance into it. As St. Francis grew in relationship with God during prolonged periods of solitude and prayer his growing awareness of God's presence with himself gave him a new way to look at the world around him and helped him see God's presence within others. Because he had been touched and embraced by God's diffusive and self-giving love, Francis imitated God by becoming more loving to everyone he encountered. The growing awareness of God's presence within all creation and especially within all humanity reached its apex when the saint embraced and kissed a leper. For Francis, the Incarnation gave birth to compassion, which enabled him to see in the rotting flesh of a leper the self-giving love of God.

I've learned to see the poor and the marginalized, the alcoholic and the drug addict, the mentally ill and the homeless not as objects of pity and charity but as brothers and sisters with whom I'm intimately related. The longer I walk with the poor—and with Jesus—the more I see the need to put to death the idea of my own self-sufficiency. To think of myself as separate from God and all of creation, including the poor, is an illusion. We pay a high price for fidelity to our illusions.

As I traveled, I began to see more clearly how turning my back on the poor was turning my back on Jesus. My exposure to those saddled with extreme poverty uncovered my own clinging selfishness. I came to see how consuming more than I needed was stealing from those in need. Perhaps St. Francis understood that it would be hard for him to feel true compassion for the poor and the weak as long he sought comfort and required security for himself. St. Francis understood that compassion is far removed from pity and sympathy, and that compassion grows out of an awareness of our common humanity. For St. Francis service to the poor is not optional; it is a requirement for the follower of Christ.

The Gospels agree on one central point: Jesus calls us to love. Christ consistently dismantles the walls that divide us from each other. His love shimmers with words of affirmation, words of kindness. His love calls us into a life of service and sharing.

If the gospel is not about love and justice, it has been reduced to mere sentimentality. Jesus denounced power that leads to injustice and poverty; He asked us to share what we have with others. Christianity does not turn away from the cross and suffering; it enters it.

We have deceived ourselves into thinking we can follow Christ without becoming one with the poor, that we can know and love God without loving others, and not just friends and family and those who love us back! Jesus says that's easy, even pagans do that. Christ calls us to a different, deeper kind of love: a love for the unlovable, for those who cannot give back, even for our enemies. Christ said that at the end of our lives that is the litmus test, the judgment of our character we all will face.

Jesus identified with the poor and the rejected, showing us that God lies waiting where the world never thinks to look. St. Francis reminds me to look at my relationship to everything in my life. He makes me take a second look at what "ownership" means. He tells me that everything belongs to God, who in his infinite love allows me to use it. This prevents me from clutching to things as "mine," and instead fills me with gratitude for the generosity of God, who has lent me the things I need. That shift in consciousness lifts a tremendous burden from my heart. Rather than holding on to what I own, I enjoy what has been temporarily lent to me. Everything is gift; everything is God's. Francis teaches me that I'm merely a humble steward gently holding things in trust, enjoying God's bounty without becoming attached to anything.

Poverty of spirit does not refer to an economic condition. It reflects the human reality that we are poor before God and, consequently, we need to radically depend on God alone for true fulfillment. We must be on guard not to confuse the necessities of life with what is luxurious. The humble simplicity that embodies poverty of spirit stands in stark contrast with the uninhibited pursuit of comfort, power, pleasure, and riches that permeates a society that prizes possessions as a good in itself. Poverty of spirit is a means of maintaining a continual attitude of dying to self.

We need to die to self because it is the only way to be fully alive to God.

Christlike transformation is not concerned with acquiring more but with letting go of more, and becoming more present to those with less. The best way you can show your love of God is to be merciful to others. Every act of mercy and kindness brings us closer to the reality of God. Growing closer to God is our real job in life. We need to open our eyes and see the many blessings God has given us, and then we must share them freely with others.

Detroit (2002)

*No one can be sent by Jesus to heal the world who has not first
been called out of the world by Jesus to his side in solitude.*
—Erasmo Leiva-Merikakis[46]

Baby Steps

The Gospel presents us with profound social, economic, and political
challenges. Issues of global poverty and hunger, corporate corruption, and
national policies of war and nuclear arms are Gospel concerns. The Gospel
demands a response from us, which can be boiled down to three simple and
clear things that we, as the body of Christ, cannot tolerate in our private and
public lives: hunger, cheating, and violence. Moreover, we are compelled to
treat all with dignity and equality, constantly on alert to extend mercy and
compassion to all who are hurting.

The Gospel values of mercy, compassion, and love can be found in the core beliefs of all faiths. They are universal human values, and it is those virtues that can unite us as a human family and help us see and know that the chronically poor around the world are our brothers and sisters, and we must stand with them in fraternity and solidarity. We can begin to do this by taking at least baby steps toward defying political polarization, consumerism, and militarism, and putting our full trust in God's abundance, mercy, and love.

Looking to Heaven

So many people are obsessively concerned about salvation and the afterlife, but for the most part those concerns are merely distractions from this life, where so many are denied access to the basic things required to sustain life.

More important than
salvation and the afterlife
is that we love God
with the fullness of our attention
and love each other
as God loves us.

If you encounter a hungry person, and out of your love of God, give that person something to eat, you have begun to experience salvation in its purest form.

The road to authentic salvation
is to empty ourselves
of all desire
except for the desire
for God.

Heaven on Earth

Heaven is a hard word to pin down. What it is or where it is . . . is a mystery. Perhaps the simplest way to define it is: heaven is the reality of God. Heaven touches earth whenever we catch a glimpse of God, whenever we encounter

God in a truly real way. Heaven can be found in a tender touch, in a glass of water, a morsel of food given to a hungry person. Heaven is seen in an act of kindness, an act of compassion. Heaven is the reality of love, self-emptying, self-sacrificing love. We should not strive to get to heaven; we should strive to be heaven. The twentieth-century Carmelite nun Blessed Elizabeth of the Trinity said it best: "I have found my Heaven on earth, because Heaven is God and God is in my heart."[47]

Heaven is within all of us, and all of us can be in heaven if we enter our hearts, encounter and experience God, and then become God's ambassadors of love and peace.

Giving and Forgiving

The God whom Jesus reveals is not a God consumed with power, but a God interested in relationships of caring fidelity, a God who is in solidarity with the most vulnerable and most needy.

Jesus gives and forgives. When we walk with Jesus, God's generosity is guaranteed, making greed and the feverish pursuit of acquiring more and more of everything both inappropriate and unnecessary.

Jesus gives us new marching orders: love one another. And in the eyes of Jesus, a brother or a sister is everyone, even those who don't look like us, don't act like us, don't believe like us, and even make us uncomfortable or hate us.

> *Jesus calls us to an*
> *alternative way of life,*
> *a way that says no*
> *to control, power, and domination,*
> *a way that says yes*
> *to trusting in the abundance of God.*

Amazing George

This is George. He lives in Kingston, Jamaica. George spends his day praying for those in need. I took this photo in 2000, after spending a few hours with George. Before I left him, he said, "Gerry, do you want me to play my harmonica for you?" I said sure. With the stumps that were his fingers, he fished out his harmonica from his pants pocket. He then played the most soulful rendition of "Amazing Grace" that I have ever heard. For many years after that, when things in my life were not going right, and little things such as a flat tire managed to really agitate me, I would pause, think of George, and take a deep breath, thankful that my problems were so trivial.

Be Made Clean

I was recently drawn to the Gospel of Mark and the story of Jesus healing the leper. Since I filmed *Embracing the Leper* at a leprosarium in Manaus, Brazil, reading anything about lepers triggers deep emotions within me. St. Francis of Assisi had a great fear of lepers. He was so repulsed by them that he went to great lengths to avoid contact with them. Of course, God turned that very disdain into a means of transformation for Francis. When Francis surrendered to his fear and embraced a leper, it marked a turning point in the saint's life. I wrote about this crucial episode in *The Sun and Moon Over Assisi* but never fully appreciated the courage it took to embrace a leper. When I encountered lepers in the Amazon region of Brazil, I was shocked to learn that leprosy still exists. Leprosy can be found in more than a half-dozen nations. In the Amazon alone, more than forty-five thousand lepers struggle to survive. To spend time in a leprosarium is extremely unsettling. Initially, it is difficult to even look at a leper. The smell from someone with active leprosy defies description.

In Jesus's time and culture, lepers where considered "unclean." The term *leprosy* was not merely restricted to what we know as Hansen's disease. Back then, leprosy included any serious skin eruptions. Lepers were outcasts. And because they were "unclean," they were not permitted to enter the temple. Moreover, according to Jewish custom, if you touched someone "unclean" you became "unclean" and therefore you could not enter the temple. Yet Jesus elected to heal the leper by touching him. Jesus certainly could have healed the leper without touching him. The Gospels contain evidence of such healings without a physical touch from Jesus. In touching the leper, Jesus deliberately defiled himself according to Jewish custom. In touching the leper Jesus is symbolically telling us that God is willing to get down in the ditch where we are. We do not have to be clean to go to God. God comes to us in our uncleanliness. Whenever we pause long enough to really look at ourselves and we see something that needs to be cleaned up, we simply need to ask Jesus to touch us and heal us.

Early in Matthew's Gospel we read about a leper who approached Jesus, knelt before him, and pleaded, "If you wish, you can make me clean" (8:2 NABRE). Jesus was so moved by the leper, that he stretched out his hand in pity, touched him and said, "I will do it. Be made clean." In that instant, the leprosy vanished from the man's body. What in us is soiled, needs to be made clean? Do I believe that Jesus can heal me, can make me clean?

I certainly can understand how Jesus was moved to pity by the sight of a leper. Lepers' bodies have been eaten away by a loathsome disease; they have mutilated faces; their fingers, arms, and legs have been eaten away. In biblical times and down through the centuries, leprosy was considered the result of sinfulness. We know better. Nonetheless, is there some behavior of ours, whether we consider it "sinful," "unclean," or "unhealthy," that is eating away at our spiritual lives and needs to "be made clean"? Is there something in our lives that we need to surrender to Jesus?

I believe, as did the leper, that Jesus wishes nothing but the fullness of God for each of us. And for us to become full with God, we must become empty of all that is not God, must become clean of all that takes us away from God.

God chose to be born in us. In Jesus, God took on human form, took on human weakness. Jesus knows our weakness, knows how easy it is for us to be soiled. When we approach Jesus, he is moved by pity, compassion, and love to reach out and touch us and make us whole.

Jesus wants nothing else than to knock down the walls that separate us from God, wants nothing else than to root out the behaviors in our lives that erode our very humanity by disconnecting us from the divinity within us.

> *Come, Holy Spirit, enkindle within me the fire of your love*
> *that burns away everything within me that is unloving*
> *and help me see the ever-present spiritual reality of Christ*
> *who makes all things new.*

A Still Lake

The more aware I become of the perfection of Christ, the better I'm able to see my own imperfections. Being able to look beyond imperfections—your own and those of others—is the key to being happy.

> *The merciful see the best in everything.*

A pure heart is like a still lake that reflects the majesty of God.

Love Never Ends

Christianity is not about correct theology or conformity to dogma. Christianity is about love, and consequently it is about forgiveness and concern for others.

To love as Christ did—
that is, to love without regard
for the imperfections and faults of others,
even our enemies—
requires us to change.

Sadly, we are more interested in changing others than changing ourselves. In order for me to love those who have hurt me, I must fundamentally change myself, because my natural instinct is to fight back. Jesus had a different response; his response flowed from love.

Many years ago, I wrote this: "A friend hurt me. I'm finding it difficult to pray for him. But I must persevere, for in praying for him I will free myself from the bondage of anger that will only destroy me. Hatred is death to the soul. Our culture's preference for self-affirmation has transformed forgiveness into a sign of weakness."

We often find it very difficult to offer forgiveness. Not so God; for God, forgiveness is effortless. In fact, God takes joy in forgiveness because it generates new life.

To love others as Jesus loves them is an extremely difficult, if not impossible, task, yet it must be our primary goal as Christians.

The Test

The test of seeing the truth is your willingness and determination to conform your life to it. To know Christ is one thing; to live as Christ is something else entirely.

To choose to believe in God
and not live in accordance with that belief is torture.

Our main job in life is reconciliation with God, with ourselves, with each other, and with all of creation.

To be a follower of Christ
is to be open to
the grace of forgiveness.

Christ asks us to forgive those who have offended us; he goes so far as to say we must love our enemies. Reconciliation is the key to personal liberation.

A Prison

The best way to love God is to relieve the pain and suffering of others.

Pain and suffering truly shape our lives. No one can escape pain and suffering. They can either crush us or help us grow. Suffering either strengthens or kills. It is through suffering that we really get to know ourselves. But we need to do more than just endure the suffering that visits us. We need to reflect on it and allow it to enlighten and transform us.

Darkness, at times, surrounds all of us. It is impossible to calculate the amount of suffering that is endured each day. So often everything seems hopeless. Despair often shadows our days. We cling to a hope that things will change, that we'll catch a break.

How sad that we often decide to abstain from life, to hide ourselves because we have been hurt or rejected. Our inner shell of self-protection soon becomes a prison that robs us of the vitality of life.

To look deeply into the darkness of your own imperfect life is the surest way to be transformed by the hopeful light that springs forth from the mercy of God.

> *Our very woundedness*
> *is waiting to be transformed*
> *into compassion.*

Our emotional and physical pain helps us understand and respond to the suffering of another.

> *Compassion is as elegant*
> *as any cathedral.*

One with All

Christ was born in a world where there was no room for him. His first earthly home was with people who had no home, people who were regarded as weak and powerless. Christ belonged to people who did not belong.

And so, with people for whom there is no room in our world, Christ is present. Christ calls us to make our home among them, to be one with them, to love them as he does.

Not all of us literally need to make our home among the rejected, but all of us need "to be at home" with them—that is, to be comfortable among them, to spend time with them, to laugh with them, to cry with them, to embrace them, to be bound in fraternity with them, to have them present within us, always mindful of their needs.

To be one with God
is to be one with all.

Kids at Play

Seriousness stifles spirituality. Jesus said we must be like children: carefree, energetic, and playful. Children are alive and radiant; they live in the moment.

Spiritual growth requires a measure of relaxation, listening, and humor. We tend to visualize Christ with a sober countenance. We need to remember that Christ also smiled because his soul was imbued with joy. The holy is not confined to the solemn. Everything is holy.

God lives in laughter and in suffering.

Sharing and Serving

True human progress is not about the survival of the fittest. Human progress requires converging, uniting. The more energetically we are united with others, the more our different creative gifts work together to reach new heights of human development and consciousness.

We need each other to become whole. Human convergence comes through love. Love unites what has become disintegrated and isolated. And in our unity, we still keep our individuality, with each gift of life creating a beautiful particle that helps form the whole of life, the full body of Christ. God is unity.

God pulls us out of our isolation by showering us with the grace to see that our lives and gifts must be put to the service of others and all of creation. Through acts of sharing and serving, we'll move toward union.

In reaching out to others
we are reaching up to God.

We have not yet begun to tap the powerful and sacred energies of love, as Christ asks us to do, even to the point of loving our enemies.

Through love
we shall evolve
to what we were
created to be:
fully realized children
of God and heirs of heaven,
which can be materialized
right here on earth.

The spiritual dimension can't be separated from the social dimension. We need to heal both the spiritual and the material wounds of our society. Jesus makes it perfectly clear that compassion is to be our primary spiritual practice. To make visible the hidden love of God, to feel more intensely the inexpressible marvel of God, we need to spend time in prayer and time with the poor.

Radical Obedience

Mercy is the holiness of God made manifest. It is God's love in action. Mercy and God are inseparable, one and the same. Mercy is an act of creation, springing forth from unconditional love. God is the energy and passion that drives me to help the poor. But I do so very little in comparison to the people I have filmed, amazing people such as Dr. Tony in Peru and Fr. Tom in Haiti.

When I look at the lives of the truly holy people I've filmed, I see how radical obedience to Christ not simply is a matter of avoiding sin, though that is important, but also requires us to be identified with the poor. Jesus entered humanity in a state of weakness and powerlessness. Jesus gave himself to the weak, the despised, and the forsaken. In turn he became despised and rejected. Christ's life was marked by sorrow and pain. He didn't hang out with the poor for a few hours a week and then return to a comfortable home to relax with a glass of wine. He became one with the poor, fully sharing in their misery. He didn't become a leader of the poor; he became a servant of the poor. When the poor wanted to crown him their king, he fled. Jesus loved the lost and the lowly, and he loved being in their company in order to serve them more fully. He did so because it was the will of God.

I'm not implying that it is the will of God for everyone to devote themselves fully to the poor. I'm just trying to understand the very narrow path these servants of the poor are walking, and how that path seems to lead to a quicker and deeper encounter with God. I do, however, think their physical journey with the poor has symbolic lessons for the rest of us. We need to encounter our own true poverty and acknowledge our own weaknesses and powerlessness, and be more open to those moments when we can extend mercy in the daily events of our lives.

> *If my compassion is true, if it be a deep compassion of the heart and not a legal affair, or a mercy learned from a book and practiced on others like a pious exercise, then my compassion for others is God's mercy for me.*
> —Thomas Merton, *No Man Is an Island*[48]

Serving

We're being fed the lie that individualism is the pinnacle of human development. Christ certainly did not believe that. Competitive greed is not a natural part of human nature. Do not be conformed to the ways of the world, the fashions of the hour.

> *The ways of God transcend*
> *the ways of any society,*
> *culture, or age.*

To be a Christian means we must live a life of resistance—resistance to sin, compulsions, despair, injustice, and the lies of popular culture. To be a Christian, we must soak up the grace that liberates us from everything that holds us back from unity with God.

> *We are prisoners of consumerism.*

We want to be served. Jesus wanted to serve. When my priorities revolve around money and consumption, I have no time to be available to others— or God—and it will be impossible to live a life of surrender and service, which is to say the life of a Christian.

Tough Message

The widespread existence of hunger indicates a massive violation of human rights bordering on epidemic proportions. We are all outraged when human rights are violated by terrorism, repression, and murder. But where is the outrage when human rights are violated by the existence of dire conditions of extreme poverty and unjust economic structures that give rise to vast inequalities?

Am I a part of a system of oppression of the poor? Unless I stand with the poor, the answer is yes. To learn the causes of poverty, we must spend time with the poor. If we share in their struggles, we can share in their liberation.

Christ's message can be reduced to this: make every stranger, no matter how poor or dirty, no matter how weak or unlovable, your neighbor. Tough message.

The Common Good

> *We face a crisis about the common good because there are powerful forces at work among us to resist the common good, to violate community solidarity, and to deny a common destiny. Mature people, at their best, are people who are committed to the common good that reaches private interests, transcends sectarian commitments, and offers human solidarity.*
> —Walter Brueggemann, *Journey to the Common Good*[49]

The single-minded pursuit of profit has led the world economic system down a catastrophic blind alley. In the face of staggering unemployment rates, mass migration, widespread starvation, and global warming, it seems fair to question whether capitalism is conducive to fundamental and authentic human development. Capitalism, with its obsessive focus on the maximization of wealth, is not concerned with the common good or creating fraternity; its sole orientation is profit. Capitalism downplays human dignity, ethical concerns, and social justice.

A downside of our current market-driven economic system is that it tends to isolate people into individual consumers. Christianity, through its understanding of the Trinity, is relational. We are all connected, all sons and daughters of God. Jesus calls us to a personal relationship with God and our neighbor. Jesus reduced the entire law to a course of social action animated by a single word: charity. Jesus offers us a true and effective antidote to the ills of greed. Charity—given and received—is everything.

We were made for growth and creativity. The Creator designed us to be creators. What are we creating? Conflict and war? Justice and peace? These are our basic choices.

Materialism and consumerism are stumbling blocks to entering fully into the transcendent faith to which Christ calls us. Our society glorifies the amassing of individual wealth and an ever-growing greater accumulation of goods. In our society, anything that furthers our goal of individual material prosperity is considered good; and anything that hinders it is considered bad. Ethics and morality are not part of the equation. Economic individualism and the idea of free competition without reference to the common good goes against the spirit of the Gospels.

> *The more material abundance we have or seek, the more*
> *likely we are to starve from the scarcity of the Spirit.*
> —Parker J. Palmer, *The Company of Strangers*[50]

Political and Mystical

Our concern for the poor is both political and mystical, and bringing the two strands of human experience together is our great challenge in the face of the tsunami of soulless capitalism and class warfare that is washing over so much of society.

We can look the other way, but no one can say they are not aware of the depths of the poverty that is experienced by billions of people around the globe. In clear opposition to Catholic social teaching, we've made a god out of the market, which a dozen years ago collapsed. Sadly, the cost of recovery fell on the backs of the poorest, the very people who saw no gain during the giddy, greedy days of boom. The blind greed of bankers and Wall Street executives is pushing the poor, the unemployed, the elderly, and the disabled into a hole from which they'll never escape. There will be no bailouts for them.

The Jostle of the Market

We live in a world that undercuts community. Many of us live hectic, time-starved lives of anxiety and isolation. In our market-driven economy, we work longer hours and spend less time with our families. In our culture, where everything is negotiable and linked to the jostle of the market, reverence for the gift of life has been snuffed out by the satisfaction of immediate and individualistic consumer fantasies that are destructively addictive. The cycle of addictive desire and disappointment robs us of happiness.

> *The key to attaining happiness is to give it away.*
> *But we love hanging on to what we've got.*

In our obsession with happiness we easily forget that depression is part of the human condition and that all sorrow need not be numbed with antidepressants such as Prozac. No pill can get to the root of the multidimensional causes of depression.

> *Happiness grows only in the garden of unconditional love.*

A Dirty Word

For me capitalism is becoming a dirty word. I suppose the idea of capitalist-style competition has some merit—as long as corporate leaders and independent businesspeople at least make an attempt at remembering that the purest goal of all economic endeavors is the well-being of the entire human community, especially the weakest and poorest members. The capitalist system needs to be constantly on guard against the dangers of greed and structural injustice while at the same time fostering a sincere concern for distributive justice. It is sinful that so many people around the world do not have access to clean and safe water and enough food to at least prevent death by starvation.

According to Catholic social teaching the poor give insight to the Good News of the Gospel, and our concern for the poor should go far beyond mere moral concern. Nearly forty years ago, Pope Paul VI said that economic decisions should focus on the poor because in God's eyes they occupy a privileged place. In other words, our first concern should be the poor. Instead, profits are our first concern, and the poor are relegated to an afterthought if considered at all. Wealth rarely trickles down to the where the poor are: living on the mean streets of our big cities and hidden in massive slums around the world.

Given Away

The best way to lovingly serve our neighbor is to take our eyes off ourselves, to forget ourselves, to become unimportant to ourselves, and fix our eyes, hearts, and minds on Christ. We must let go of self-centeredness to love with true purity under all circumstances.

> *Justice should be moved by love*
> *to meet the needs of the poor.*

The emerging global economy has a strong tendency to foster soulless consumerism and mindless worship of technology. It often tramples the rights of workers and the poor. We need to be attentive to the human consequences and social impact of globalization.

> *We must become the poor Christ—*
> *offered up and given away.*

Christ relentlessly proclaims God's preferential love for those the world ignores and rejects.

> *The despised and the unimportant of the world*
> *are loved unconditionally by their Creator.*

By loving the poor and insignificant first and foremost, God demonstrates the extent and fullness of divine love for all of creation.

Made by Love

We do not know peace, because we do not know love. We do not know love, because we do not know God. God is love. We were made by love and for love. But we have turned our backs on love and have become unloving.

The world has been disfigured by our failure to love. The world will only be transformed when all people learn how to love each other. Pierre Teilhard de Chardin, the French Jesuit philosopher, paleontologist, and geologist, said, "Someday, after mastering the winds, the waves, the tides and gravity, we shall harness for God the energies of love, and then, for a second time in the history of the world, man will have discovered fire."

Our human love is limited, unable to reach beyond ourselves, our family, our friends. Our love is feeble, unable to withstand the storms of life. Our love is egocentric, unable to put others first.

Love requires humility, mercy, kindness, trust, patience, perseverance, and sacrifice. Sadly, these noble traits are underappreciated and in short supply in our troubled world.

Only divine love
allows us to embrace all,
even our enemies.
Peace can only flow
from self-emptying love.

Peace creates unity and works for the common good. Faith in God should unite us, lead us to a peace rooted in mercy and compassion. But our flawed faith divides us, pits one faith against another, says my religion is better than yours, my religion is the only true religion. So we pray and kill and ignore the poor, the weak, and the suffering. And cause God to weep.

God is neither Christian, nor Jewish, nor Muslim, nor Buddhist, nor Hindu. God is love. Different religions are different ways at trying to understand God. God is beyond all faiths, beyond all understanding.

Where there is hatred,
there is the absence of God.
Where there is love,
there is God.

My love for my Christian faith is enhanced by my embracing all religious faith. Every faith needs to root out hate and cultivate love.

Christ is not complete
without diversity.
Each person expresses Christ
in a unique way.

Every person is
a word of the Word.

Possessions

When we realize the emptiness of all material things, we are free to encounter God. All that is "self" must be abandoned if we are to follow Jesus. The road he travels is the road of self-emptying.

When profit is the aim and law of life, then humanity suffers a great loss. We all crave to be on the receiving end of a gift of love; but our very craving masks a deeper, more profound human need: to give love. The less you have, the less you have to distract you from God.

To become poor
is to know the richness of God.

The danger of building up riches is that an accumulation of wealth makes it easy to succumb to a self-complacency that makes God superfluous. Without clinging to anything, we must patiently stand before God with open hands. Jesus is not asking us to get rid of our possessions; he is asking us to lose our attachment to them. He knows an unfettered mind is essential to reaching the emptiness where God can meet us.

The impulse to accumulate all we can needs to be thwarted. We have no right to own more than we need. And we need far less than we want. Voluntary physical poverty is a means to a healthy spiritual poverty.

Exterior and interior poverty
are close friends.

A Few Dollars

A careful reading of the Gospels reveals that from God's point of view, true success in human life is measured by your ability to incarnate the Beatitudes. Christ mandates that we reach out a hand of help to those in need. When it comes to helping the poor, not knowing what to do is not an excuse not to do anything. Do what you can.

To turn your back
on the poor
is to turn your back
on Jesus.

Giving a few dollars to the poor is not the same as being one with the poor, which is what Christ requires. The moral measure of any society or community can be gauged by how it treats its weakest member.

Our streets are littered with homeless people because we seek comfort rather than compassion and love. The painful truth is that we serve our own individual, personal interests rather than the common good. We have much work to do.

Our attitude toward the poor
is linked to
our attitude toward God.
Our response to God's saving love for us
is reflected in
our love and service of the poor.

You often hear the statement that "God helps those who help themselves." That's nonsense. More accurate is this: "God helps those who put their trust in God." Besides, the first statement is essentially an excuse not to help those in need.

Called to Serve

The Gospels make it abundantly clear that God is on the side of the poor, the broken in body and spirit, and the outcasts of society, the lepers, the prostitutes, the orphans, and, today we must add, the addicted. Did you bring Good News to the poor today?

We have become so separated from the poor and the suffering that we have lost the chance to find true fulfillment by giving of ourselves and by serving the poor.

We are called to serve. The most truly authentic way to serve is to serve from our own weakness and not from our strength. For in our weakness we are more able to recognize the weakness in another. Sadly, we often look down on those we serve, because we are serving from a position of power. The Gospel is not calling us to this kind of service. We need to look directly into the eyes of those we serve . . . or better yet, in a spirit of humility, look up to them.

To walk with the poor is to walk with God.

The Pain of Others

The poor, the weak, and the hurting are God in skin.

We need to begin to think more seriously about the common good both at home and abroad and better understand that compassion is crucially essential to our survival. In the countless prisons of poverty around the world, God is hidden in the suffering, hidden in great and small acts of resurrection, hidden in a truly inexhaustible mystery.

But there is no mystery about this: the world is riddled with pain. No life can escape it. Even Jesus accepted it. Pain is universal. When we turn our attention away from our own pain, be it physical or emotional, we can see the pain of others, the pain of the world. Once we truly see and feel the pain of others, we are impelled to alleviate suffering wherever and whenever we encounter it. In the process, we will slowly come to realize we are not the center of the universe and that all living creatures possess an inviolable sanctity that binds us all together as sisters and brothers.

Over and over again, Christ tells us that love is the sole criterion for eternal unity with God. The love Christ is talking about is far from a mere humanitarian concern for abstract justice and the anonymous "poor." Christ calls us to a concrete and personal love for all people, including our enemies, and for all of creation. He calls us to be his helping, healing hands. Christ someday will say to us, "When I was hungry, you gave me something to eat." When we soothe the trials of others, we encounter Christ. We are called to be angels of compassion, to be God's messengers delivering food and hope to those living with hunger and despair.

God humbly and continuously bends down in love to embrace us in our weakness and vulnerability. God's love is different from our love. God's love means being willing to love someone more than your own life, for the sake of the other. Every moment of every day, God the all-powerful willingly becomes powerless and risks becoming a beggar of love patiently waiting for us to respond by loving not only God but all of God's creation, especially the poor and rejected. Compassion is the fullest expression of the luminous force of intentional love and kindness.

The chronically poor in Haiti have no leverage for an alternative, for a life without constant insufficiency. They are in free fall toward premature death. We need to be holding out our hands to them. In doing so, our limited and very conditional love becomes a conduit for God's unlimited and unconditional love to touch and heal the people of Port-au-Prince.

Helping the poor, whether in Haiti or in your own city, is a sacramental gesture in which we touch a sacred reality here and now. We touch God through God's creatures.

When we become aware of the suffering caused by unmindful consumption, we begin to take baby steps toward cultivating more mindful eating, drinking, and consuming in an attempt to preserve peace, well-being, and joy in not only our own consciousness but also in the collective body of humanity and the consciousness of society. Moreover, we slowly begin to transform the violence, fear, and anger we find within ourselves and society through acts of healing and peace.

Mercy, compassion, and love are human values, and it's those virtues that can unite us as a human family, and help us see and know that the poor of Haiti and countless other developing nations are our brothers and sisters, and we must stand with them in fraternity and solidarity. And we can begin to do this by taking at least baby steps toward defying political polarization, consumerism, and militarism and putting our full trust in God's abundance, mercy, and love.

The longer I walk with the poor—and with Jesus—the more I see the need to put to death the idea of my own self-sufficiency.

The Hiddenness of God

In Haiti, my false ideas and values are shattered into thousands of little pieces, and I see clearly the pain and suffering of Christ, the pain and suffering of the human condition. In Haiti, human misery is raw and real. In Haiti, I see things in their utter nakedness. The cross is around every corner. The cross has no place to hide. We either close our eyes to the cross or we confront and embrace the cross. In Haiti there are no diversions, no false idols to avert my gaze from the misery. There is no place to turn. All you can see is the hiddenness of God. Here the presence of God takes on the form of absence.

In this void, one slowly prepares to humbly approach the consciousness of God. In the absence of God, the presence of God awaits. Detachment is the path to wholeness. In the slums of Haiti, I feel closer to God than I do at Sunday Mass in my home parish. In Haiti, I'm detached from the world yet not fully attached to God. It is a place of dreadful inner anguish for me. I can't believe or not believe in anything.

Yet in Haiti I feel God is hidden in the insignificant and the unassuming. The poor feel their own fragility and understand their dependency. Somehow, in Haiti I feel the way to God is through the misery and nothingness of my false self. It is here that I see more clearly my true self and my complete dependence on God. It is here that I feel more tangibly God's love.

Love is a mystical force that pushes open the door to forgiveness and mercy.

Jesus invited the poor and the outcasts to sit at his banquet table. Who are our dinner guests?

Giving food to the poor is easy. Eating with the poor is much harder. And more rewarding. Jesus ate with the poor, and he asks us to do the same. Communion with the poor is an enriching source of healing.

In the Sermon on the Mount, Christ said the hungry will be satisfied. It can happen—but only if we stand in solidarity with the poor and accompany them on their journey. As we walk together, common concern will overcome the destructive tendencies of individualism and greed.

The Cries of God

We pray for our daily bread. Yet for millions of people around the world, their daily bread consists of violence, famine, and destruction. Did God hear our prayer and not theirs? No. God hears the cries of the poor. We do not hear the cries of God asking us to be divine hands tending to the needs of the poor.

God took on human form as a vulnerable baby, the child of homeless refugees, needing human help in the ongoing work of creation.

We are God's messengers
delivering food and hope
to those living with hunger and death.

The Cries of the Poor

Around the world, so much of life is so unjustly ordered that it stands in the way of God's hope for humanity. The reign of God, which is a reign of peace, justice, and mercy, is being blocked by the disorder we have created by our indifference to social justice, the plight of the poor, and our lack of mercy. We have suppressed the liberating energies of the Gospel and ignored the witness of Mary who, as stated in *Lumen Gentium*, is a "promoter of the justice that liberates the oppressed and the charity that succors the needy, but above all is an active witness to the love that builds Christ in hearts."

God wants us to be poor. But not poor in the sense that we don't have enough money to buy food or secure housing. The poverty God wishes for us is not monetary poverty. The poverty God wishes for us is that we live a radical dependence on God alone, willing to respond, like Mary, in purity and fullness to the divine will. To be poor in God's eyes is to have the attitude of a servant of the Most High: "Let this happen to me as you say" (Luke 1:38 NCV).

The social message of the Gospel isn't some theoretical ideal. It's a call to action. Justice requires us to change systems of institutionalized injustice that imprison people in chains of poverty and hunger. Institutionalized injustice can be found everywhere, in every nation. Cité Soleil in Port-au-Prince is no different from Skid Row in Los Angeles. Both are abominations in the eyes of God, and God demands we dismantle those prisons and set the captives free. Sadly, we avert our eyes and pretend Cité Soleil and Skid Row are not there. But they are there, and people are suffering.

We need more than an emotional response to the plight of the poor; we need more than feelings of sorrow and regret. We need to be moved by grace to action. When we hear the cries of the oppressed, the cries of the poor, we hear the voice of God. Where there is weakness, there is God.

We need to ask God
to shatter our complacency,
to strip us of our need
for comfort.

In the Risen Humanity of Christ

In the risen humanity of Christ, I find peace and love. But it is not enough for me to simply experience that peace and love within myself or only for myself. It is something that must be shared with all of humanity, all of creation. In every encounter, in every relationship, I should attempt to convey the risen humanity of Christ through my words and deeds. This experience of the risen humanity of Christ makes all things always new, always presenting fresh opportunities to transform ourselves and our world by following the self-emptying example of Jesus, who constantly renews everything he touches because he is always pointing us back to God, back to the true source of life.

> *Fix your mind and thoughts on Christ.*
> *In doing so, you will know the peace of Christ.*
> *Go to Christ in prayer and thanksgiving.*
> *Listen to his words in the Gospels and stay true to them.*
> *With Christ, you will never be alone and you will always be loved.*

At its root, there is only one reason for the existence of poverty: selfishness, which is a manifestation of a lack of authentic love. Sadly, we tend to think of the homeless as social nuisances. Jesus had a different point of view and suggested that the poor are pathways to God. By serving the poor we are not only practicing Christian charity but also reforming ourselves. We don't have to solve all the problems for the poor; just being with them goes a long way toward lightening their burden. The witness of love lived in voluntary poverty has the peaceful power to change hearts. The infancy story of Christ tells us we can have hope and joy, can overcome our immense loneliness and can find unity, integration, solidarity, and reconciliation of all, with all.

Destitution grinds people down. According to Christ, the poor are a profound, redeeming revelation of God's presence and grace. But our culture tends to separate us from the poor who live out of sight in hidden pockets of despair and want. We are blinded to the needs of the poor by our own desire for property, comfort, and acquiring more material goods for ourselves.

Peter Maurin, cofounder with Dorothy Day of the Catholic Worker, said, "On the Cross of Calvary Christ gave His life to redeem the world. The life of Christ was a life of sacrifice. We cannot imitate the sacrifice of Christ on

Calvary by trying to get all we can. We can only imitate the sacrifice of Christ on Calvary by trying to give all we can. What we give to the poor for Christ's sake is what we carry with us when we die."[51]

Exhausting Yet Rewarding

Working with the homeless is exhausting and frustrating work. To be on the frontlines of charity, justice, and peace requires heroic goodwill, a deep and prophetic faith. Yet at the same time it is profoundly rewarding and gives birth to a deeper awareness of self and love of God.

I never imagined that spending six months on the streets of Skid Row while making my film *Rescue Me* would teach me more about spirituality than homelessness. While walking those mean streets, where more than eleven thousand people, including hundreds of children, live in cardboard boxes, tents, and in overcrowded missions, I frequently encountered deep-seated anger and hostility. A woman threw a bottle at me; it landed at my feet and shattered into hundreds of pieces of flying glass. A guy threatened to hit me with a metal pipe. A shadowy figure emerged from the darkness wielding a baseball bat in a very threatening manner. These and other scary moments made me angry. At first, it was easy and natural to harshly judge a hostile homeless person. Slowly I learned not to do so. Instead of judging, I learned to look at their hostility differently. They are simply having a hard time trying to find happiness and avoid suffering, and it just so happened that when they were going about doing so, I got in the way.

When I learned to see myself in the homeless person, my anger at their attacking me began to melt away. I learned that my love of God required me to take a stance of gentleness, reverence, and respect in my attitude toward all other beings. I especially needed to cultivate respectful and gentle mindfulness of the needs of the poor.

The more time you spend with the chronically poor,
the easier that becomes.

A Humble Disguise

We long to find God in some moment of spiritual ecstasy, looking for the divine in some spectacular or extraordinary event. Yet God comes to us, if we are to believe—fully believe—what Scripture says, in a humble disguise, in unexpected places. God comes to us poor, hungry, thirsty, diseased, imprisoned, alone, and lonely. God comes to us in a homeless old woman forced to use a public street for a toilet. God comes to us in people, places, and ways that make it difficult for us to see him or receive him.

We don't find God where we expect or want to find him.

The real sin hidden within the plague of global poverty where millions upon millions are suffering from hunger and curable disease is our inexplicable indifference, our complicity and complacency. The Gospel tells us we must not look away from the suffering, must not ignore the poor. The Gospel tells us to embrace the suffering and the weak, to be God's healing hands.

According to Jesus, you cannot honor God and dishonor the poor at the same time, nor can you wage war and worship God at the same time.

Watch how a person treats the poor and the hungry, the sick and the stranger, and you will know that person's view of life.

You can measure the value of spiritual experiences by the extent to which they returned the individual to the physical world with an enhanced sense of responsibilities to others.

A Human Landslide of Misery

The following four reflections were all written in 2006 during the making of The Fragrant Spirit of Life, *which was set in Uganda. Making the film required three grueling trips to East Africa.*

We live in a tempestuous, havoc-ridden world. Our lives as Christians need to be a healing balm that soothes the countless wounds and suffering that torment the lives of so many people. The violence of war and the violence of hunger and preventable diseases need to be surrendered to the peace of Christ.

Within each of us, a war rages. This is where the first negotiated peace plan must be implemented. Once compassion, mercy, peace, and love have been incorporated within us, we will be able to reach out to the wounded of the world around us.

Christianity without passion for peace and justice is not Christianity.

The wounded abound in Uganda. In Uganda, you see a human landslide of misery, countless fragile lives tumbling into despair. The word *compassion* comes from two Latin words that together mean "to suffer with." To suffer with someone, you need to go where it hurts, to places of pain and brokenness, to places of anguish and misery. To suffer with someone, you need to enter their weakness; you need to be vulnerable with the vulnerable, powerless with the powerless.

We want to think of ourselves as compassionate, yet we want no part of suffering, want nothing to do with misery, want to avoid feeling weak and ineffective. We don't look to enter pain. We avoid pain at all costs. We have a ready supply of painkillers.

Our society is based on competition, not compassion. Yet Jesus tells us to be as compassionate as God. God is so compassionate that the divine entered into our humanity and shares in our weakness and suffering.

God, the All-Compassionate, is with us . . . even in our misery and pain. And so we too must enter into and be with those who are alone in the world, alone in their misery and pain, even if all we can offer is only our presence.

The Baby Jesus

> *Christ, who shared in the ultimate power of the divine,*
> *was born into the condition of powerlessness of an infant.*

On the first Christmas Day God not only became a human being, but God also became an infant human being. As a baby, Jesus needed to be fed, clothed, sheltered, and protected. God as a baby was not only weak but also totally dependent on human help. As an adult, Christ said that whenever you feed the least of God's children you are feeding him. Because God is present within each of us, God still needs to be fed, which is why it is so important to learn to see Christ in the poor, because when you feed the poor you are truly feeding Christ. God is still helpless, patiently waiting for us.

Christian compassion is rooted in the discovery of Christ in the suffering people of the world. Moreover, solidarity with the poor and the oppressed is the very essence of Christian mysticism. Still, when I see the vastness of the problem of global poverty, I feel absolutely helpless. But that feeling gives insight into the Good News, for "With God's power working in us, God can do much, much more than anything we can ask or imagine" (Ephesians 3:20 NCV). The power of God is the power of love, which invites, but never coerces. This love, whether we are conscious of it or not, is the longing of all our desire and restlessness. But that is such a hard truth to learn. I still harbor ungodly desires, and my heart is still often restless.

At Christmas, we need to ponder the infant Jesus lying powerless in the manger and wonder at the divine humanity we are all graced with. If we see ourselves as being as full of God's beauty as the infant Jesus was, we could no longer continue to hurt each other, and all acts of violence would cease to exist. God's outrageous love, manifested in the planned vulnerability of Jesus, would lead Christ to the cross that awaited him on Calvary, and Christmas should lead us to embrace the vulnerability of love that is forever beckoning us.

Mary's Song

While in Haiti during Advent of 2010, I began to hear more clearly the subversive and prophetic words of the Canticle of Mary. In the Magnificat Mary boldly proclaims God has "brought down the powerful from their thrones, and lifted up the lowly" (Luke 1:52 NRSV). Mary sings about the hungry, those who have been denied access to stable food supply, because she believes God promise that the weak and vulnerable will be lifted up. We may sing those words, but we don't really take them seriously. But the reality is that the birth of God will turn everything upside down.

Mary prophesies a new world in which no one is hungry or exploited, when all the lowly are lifted to a place of dignity. (The word that has been translated as "lowly" was often used in Septuagint to refer to the sexual humiliation of women.) Choosing a virgin to be the Mother of God was no accident; in fact, it spoke loudly to God's preference for the lowly and the outcast. Christ, of course, befriended the weak and fragile. The deeper message here is that God makes our barrenness fruitful. Mary sings of a time when all who are poor will be filled with the rich bounty of God. That song becomes our song as we feed the hungry and lift up the lowly.

Living Saints and Pious Frauds

I wrote the following in Advent of 2009, just days before leaving on my first trip to Haiti. I was struggling to live the Gospel more fully. I still am. What I wrote then still sounds like a tough message. I suppose Christianity is an all-or-nothing venture. A lukewarm follower of Christ does not become a light to the world, does not become the change that changes everything. I was a pious fraud for far too long, saying all the right things, but not changing the things within me that desperately needed to be changed. During Lent 2017, I began making serious changes.

I once rejected Christianity because the message of Christ had been so misrepresented and distorted that it was impossible to believe. Instead of encountering living saints who embodied the spirit of Christ, I saw pious frauds. Christianity seemed to be more interested in supporting and reassuring its followers that living for themselves was perfectly fine in the eyes of God. The Good News that Jesus proclaimed had been so adulterated that its strength, power, and joy had been almost completely eradicated.

As I filmed in slums around the world, I slowly saw and felt the power the Gospel had to transform lives. I began to see, ever so dimly, that the ethos of seeking security and comfort for oneself and one's family in the midst of widespread poverty and suffering around the world had caused a spiritual crisis. Like so many Christians, I was guilty of ignoring the spiritual values Christ taught. I still ignore them. Truly following Christ is very, very hard.

The Gospel requires us to turn our backs on the dominant culture of our time and follow a whole new way of life that frees us from the constraints of the pressure of conformity to the consumer culture and the constant preoccupation with the appearance of success and security. The Lord became flesh among the poor, and so what better place to be in order to prepare for the coming of the Lord at Christmas than among the poor?

Walking Toward the Light

In my book *Thoughts of a Blind Beggar*, I wrote,

> I am a sinner not immune from temptation. I stumble often, often succumb to the deception of my ego. My heart is fickle, my faith weak. Holiness seems beyond my reach. Yet, each day, I pick myself up and keep walking toward the Light, toward the day when I have finally emptied myself of all that is not God. Unity with God does not happen in a flash, is not won by a lottery ticket, instantly bestowing the riches of heaven upon you. Unity with God takes time, as day by day, month by month, year by year we slowly and deliberately let go of more stuff cluttering our tiny hearts in order to make room for the infinite source of love and life.[52]

In late April 2019, I had to journey to California to empty out a storage unit I could no longer afford to keep. It contained over a thousand DVDs of my films and over a thousand copies of my earlier books, as well as boxes of memorabilia from my ministry. I tossed out thousands of letters from people writing to me about a film or a book or a presentation I gave. It was not easy, but after the task was complete it felt good to let go of all that stuff. It was a lesson in emptying.

Because we are so easily self-deceived, we have no problem dismissing the fact that we are sinners and that we sin daily. In order to grow closer to God, we need to awaken a healthy sensitivity to our own sinfulness. When we are honest with ourselves and God, healing and transformation can occur.

As Christians, we are penitents, but not guilt-ridden. We are sinners, but we are forgiven. Feeling negative about yourself is not pleasing to God. Humility is truth. We know we are sinners; we know we are forgiven.

The Splendor of Poor Things

We are all poor, all in need of something beyond ourselves. Poverty is our true reality, which we try to disguise with riches. The Nicaraguan priest and poet Ernesto Cardenal said, "There is a splendor in poor things, the splendor of what is real."[53] In the places where I've filmed, especially in Africa, I saw the splendor of simple, poor things, things made of clay, straw, and plain wood, homespun things that are coarse, rough, and rudimentary, yet they reveal the majestic, naked splendor of matter.

Cardenal reminds us that it is easy for us to confuse what we have with what we are. We are not more because we have more. Nor are we less if we have less. St. Francis called poverty a great treasure. He possessed nothing but a pair of sandals and a sack fastened about his waist with a rope. By owning nothing he came to possess everything.

Our entire economy is based on greed. We worship money and property. We have fallen far from God. Jesus said we should resist the temptation of self-preservation and privilege. He made it perfectly clear that those who seek self-preservation are lost. Jesus gave up everything and became nothing; he held nothing back for himself.

Cathedrals of the Poor

When I was in Uganda in 2008, I saw the spiritual importance of being with the poor. The far-too-numerous and massive slums that dot the landscape of so many developing nations are cathedrals of the poor, places so real and raw that they pulsate with the presence of God. In these slums, you are on holy ground because Jesus is there in the form of people suffering from hunger and curable diseases.

Christ wants us to live a life of detachment and expectation. But we cling to the countless things we think are important. We chase after what we don't have; we lust after what is beyond our reach. We have turned greed and hoarding into virtues. Consumed by our need for comfort and security, we have become blinded to the needs of the poor. We do not share, and our selfishness is the cause of much of the poverty we see.

Economic policies in affluent nations often have a devastating impact on destitute people living in destitute countries, making basic human dignity something that is far beyond their reach. The people in the slums in Africa where I filmed have no voice, no power, no rights, and no way to make their plight known.

We are driven by economic success. We worship at the altar of consumerism. Christ showed us a different way—a way of simplicity, dependence on God, and extending goodwill to others. Our commodity economy is not in harmony with the teachings of Jesus.

Holy Simplicity

These are complex times. We lead complex lives. We live in a hectic, fast-paced society that is filled with moral dilemmas, financial worries, ecological disasters, criminal violence, racial bigotry, corporate greed, decaying inner cities, global political unrest and economic instability, and deadly wars fueled by religious differences that pit neighbor against neighbor. We are stressed and anxious, as we breathlessly chase after more and more possessions. Our passion to possess blinds us to the reality that much of the world is enduring poverty and starvation on a scale unmatched in human history. Every day thousands of people die of starvation. This seems unthinkable. But the sad truth is that millions of malnourished and aimless people are living on the edge of extinction.

What can I do? I think St. Francis would recommend that I take a close look at the virtue of simplicity. By way of simplicity, Francis was able to enter into the deep silence of his heart.

Simplicity is hard. Attaining it will not eliminate the complexity of modern life and all its intricate personal and global problems. I think simplicity allowed Francis to live in harmony with the ordered complexity of his day. As his heart grew in simplicity, he was better able to understand the Lord and the world around him.

Pope John XXIII said, "The older I grow, the more clearly I perceive the dignity and winning beauty of simplicity in thought, conduct, and speech: a desire to simplify all that is complicated and to treat everything with the greatest naturalness and clarity."[54]

François Fénelon, in his book *Christian Perfection*, wrote, "It is a wise self-love which wants to get out of the intoxication of outside things."[55] Before I can free myself from the lure of material things, I have to become more sensitive to the things of the spirit, which will diminish my chances of being dazzled by the superficial, such as the latest sports car from BMW. More important will be the latest revelation from God on how I can love my neighbor while at the same time deflecting my own self-centered greed. Through simplicity we learn that self-denial paradoxically leads to true self-fulfillment. Simplicity allows us to hold the interests of others above our self-interest. Real simplicity is true freedom. The constant drumbeat of materialism is no longer deafening. We desire less, and are happy with less.

Simplicity is the best method of stripping away excess baggage that weighs us down and all nonessential adornments that surround us. As these distractions disappear, the reality of God becomes clearer. Simplicity is a much more profound concept than voluntary poverty, which is much smaller in scope, because simplicity not only reduces your material possessions but also diminishes your desire for them.

Simplicity immunizes you from the plague of consumerism.

Aleksandr Solzhenitsyn said, "On our crowded planet there are no longer any internal affairs."[56] Our future depends on more and more people learning to live more simply. Mahatma Gandhi once said that the world has enough resources to meet everyone's need, but not enough to match everyone's greed. Americans make up 6 percent of the world's population, yet we gobble up more than 30 percent of the globe's resources. If the rest of the planet follows our greedy example it will spell disaster for humanity. Large segments of the world's population are already living without hope, tottering on the brink of cruel deaths by starvation. Simplicity is not an option; it is a vital necessity. Reckless, out-of-control consumption must be curtailed before it destroys us. Unlimited growth, which fosters a throwaway culture, is a dangerous illusion. Voluntary denial is liberating. As Christians we must become advocates of the poor and the forgotten. We must become poor ourselves, living simply so others can simply live.

A Question

The radical message for which Christ died is dramatically opposed to our culture of selfish individualism and unchecked consumerism. Should not our Christian faith compel us, by means of our transformed hearts, to live differently from the rest of our culture, whose values are rooted in the material realm and are far from the teachings of Christ?

We have reduced Christ to a sublime abstraction,
making it possible to ignore the very truth of Christ.

We Walk Away

The Gospel is countercultural in countless ways. Take the story in Mark's Gospel of the rich man, who has observed all the laws of his Jewish faith, who asks Jesus what more he must do to gain entrance into eternal life. Jesus tells him to sell all he has, give away the proceeds to the poor, and follow him. The countenance of the rich man's face turns sullen. He turns and walks away. Jesus turns to his disciples and tells them that it would be easier for a camel to pass through the eye of a needle than for a rich person to enter the kingdom of God.

On the face of it, the story says a rich person will find it impossible to get into heaven. But actually, the story has less to do with money than with surrender. I'm certainly not rich, at least by the American standards; but compared to the two-thirds of the world's population locked in the cruel prison of poverty, I'm indeed a rich man. I might not have much money in the bank, and my salary barely covers my modest living expenses, but my extensive time among the chronically poor has certainly shown me how rich I am. Even though I feel as if I have given my life in service of the poor, is Christ asking me to literally sell my house (if I owned a house) and give everything I own away? I don't think so.

In the Jewish culture at the time of Jesus, being rich was a sign of God's blessing; conversely, being poor indicated God was not pleased with you. The rich felt secure in their knowledge of their future eternal bliss. Jesus turned that idea upside down, saying that our external possessions are not a sign of our internal harmony with God. God's capital, according to Jesus, is love, not money. We will be judged not by what we have but by what we give away in love.

The rich man in the story walked away said because "he had many possessions." He was unable to let go of the things he valued, the things that made him feel safe and secure. Jesus is saying that security is detrimental in the spiritual life because it thwarts full surrender to God. As I walk with the poor, I have come to see how so much of what I once thought was important or valuable has turned out to be rather worthless. In our culture, even those of us who are hardly considered rich have so many resources at our disposal that we feel no need for God. Our culture tells us to be strong, to be independent. The ever-countercultural Jesus says God is found in weakness, that we are all connected, all one in the loving and merciful eyes of God. Perhaps Jesus was asking the rich man to become poor in order for him to experience the deepest need and longing of his heart: unity with the Creator, the source of all life. Whether we admit it or not, we need God. None of us is truly rich because we lack the fullness of God. I think Jesus was telling the rich man that self-reliance is detrimental to the spiritual life and that spiritual growth requires surrender and total dependence on God.

Christ is asking us to give away all that is blocking us from the deepest longing of our hearts—unity with God. That could be money, or it could be any of a litany of things that we hold onto for dear life, things like excessive worry, the need to control, the urge for unrestrained carnal pleasure, addiction to drugs or alcohol (or any addictive behavior), the need to consume more and more, the unrelenting desire to succeed at all costs, the need to be constantly entertained, the need to be always on the move, always striving for something we don't have . . . the list is endless. So much of modern life distracts us from God. Every day we face an onslaught of images and messages hurled at us from the media, Hollywood, and the world of business. Life has become a whirling dervish of furious activity. We live life in fast-forward. There is no time for stillness and silence, no time for reflection. No time for God. We are too rich, too busy, too preoccupied with satisfying our own desires. Jesus is saying: stop, stop everything that leads us away from God.

Life has become so frenetic and fragmented
that stillness and wholeness have become the impossible dream.

The more we are focused on the material world, the less we will be focused on the spiritual realm. Jesus was telling the rich man to give away all he was clinging to and to cling to God alone. Jesus is asking us to becoming radically dependent on him alone. I'm slowly learning that I can accomplish nothing on my own, but with Christ, nothing is impossible. I easily forget that truth. Following Christ is truly hard because it is truly countercultural. I once met a humble Franciscan friar who had dedicated his entire life to serving the poor. He told me the only thing he owned were his sins. Sin, at its root, is nothing more than a failure to love. This ultimately is what Christ is asking us to give away: anything that hinders love. A Buddhist monk once said, "If you have compassion, you cannot be rich. . . . You can be rich only when you can bear the sight of suffering." He understood what Christ was saying to the rich man in Mark's Gospel. God is calling us to deeper and deeper levels of love, mercy, and compassion, and we need to give away anything that thwarts our response to that call. And so, our faces turn sad and we walk away because we have so much. But without God, we have nothing.

The spiritual life has more to do with subtraction than addition.

A Broken Heart

Before deciding to try to help poor kids in Haiti, I had my heart broken countless times as I filmed severe poverty around the world. The Hasidic Jewish tradition suggests that only someone with a broken heart is a whole person. Some interpret that to mean that when a person has a broken heart, the presence of God rushes in to heal and love the broken heart. While I believe that to be true, I think there is more to it. When my heart is broken by the sight and reality of the desperately poor around the world, I am taken out of myself and am made whole by virtue of my realization that I am connected not only to these people but to all of creation. I am whole when I realize I am part of the whole creation of God. In the wholeness of my humanity I can see more clearly the huge gap between human misery and human compassion.

In reference to the civil rights movement and the war in Vietnam, Rabbi Abraham Joshua Heschel never tired of saying, "In a free society, some are guilty, but all are responsible."[57]

The people in the slums where I filmed had only one agenda: survival. Seeing so many people nearly half dead from hunger filled me with sadness. I was distressed and ashamed. Yet for most of my life I too was half dead from my own hunger, hunger for power, status, and money. I was half dead to the suffering world around me.

There are no easy answers to the endless questions that arose from what I saw and filmed in desperately poor places throughout Africa, South America, Central America, the Philippines, and the Caribbean. There are no quick fixes, no good theological excuses either.

Answers and solutions will only come from a broken heart. We need our hearts broken in order for us to truly step outside of our own ego, to strip ourselves of our own need for comfort and security and enter fully into the pain and suffering of our African sisters and brothers and to walk in solidarity with them, demanding that they be set free from poverty, hunger, and disease and be allowed to live in peace, simplicity, and dignity.

As they walk with all their fears and hopes, the chronically poor of the world (and in our own backyard) breathlessly await our response to their unjust plight.

Love is service. It is the emptying of self. It is losing in order to find.

The Epicenter

In March of 2010 I took my third trip to Haiti, less than three months after the deadly earthquake had taken place.

In the abandonment, despair, and conflict of Holy Saturday I drove to Léogâne, which was the epicenter of the quake. Along the way we saw evidence of much hardship and destruction. We stopped at a tent serving as an Episcopal Church as the altar servers prepared and practiced for the Easter Sunday liturgy. The main church was destroyed. Léogâne is about a ninety-minute drive west of Port-au-Prince. What we found when we arrived was shocking.

The level of devastation was frightening. Very little of the town remained standing. Yet amid the massive amounts of rubble, people were busy clearing the debris. I filmed at the destroyed home of the parish priest where at least seventy-five people had gathered together under the blazingly hot sun to undertake the painstakingly hard, backbreaking job of breaking up the large pieces of concrete and then hauling them away in buckets and wheelbarrows. The young and old, men and women, and kids all pitched in. A number of teenage boys wore Boy Scout uniforms. Everyone was working together, doing what had to be done, in order to start over.

Many of the mountains of rubble were tombs. On Holy Saturday we remember Christ's time in the tomb. In the paschal mystery, suffering and hope are intertwined. The suffering of Good Friday was a portal to the hope of Easter Sunday. The area surrounding Léogâne is coastal farmland, and its pastoral setting, though still blighted with tents, was a welcome relief to the sprawling urban chaos of Port-au-Prince.

In creation, we contemplate a manifestation of God's face, of God's presence—and our souls are set a fire with charity for all of creation, leading us to embrace the whole world, a world deformed by sin yet transfigured by grace. An incredibly beautiful world lies silently all around us all of the time, and it remains unseen, a lost paradise, until some quiet miracle opens our eyes and we see everything afresh. By grace, seeing deeply into a flower we catch a glimpse of paradise, a vestige of God. As we divest all vestiges of self-will and self-interest and become more God-centered, we will begin seeing all of creation and all people as Jesus did: as our brothers and sisters.

In humility, we need to see ourselves as children of God, and hence connected to and equal with all of creation, a delicately interwoven tapestry of wonder and awe, lovingly stitched together by the Master Weaver. If we do not recapture our original connectedness, do not return to the garden of paradise, we are doomed.

We are slowly killing the poor and the weak.
We are slowly destroying planet Earth.
We need to recapture a sense of awe and wonder,
to look at the vastness and beauty of creation
and know that God entrusted
the beauty and bounty of creation to us,
to sustain us, to sustain all of us.

A Future Full of Hope

God is beyond the world yet God can be found in and through the world, especially the world of the marginalized and the weak.

The prophet Jeremiah proclaimed, "I know well the plans I have in mind for you, says the Lord, plans for your welfare, not for woe! Plans to give you a future full of hope. When you call me, when you go to pray to me, I will listen to you. When you look for me, you will find me. Yes, when you seek me with all your heart, you will find me, says the LORD, and I will change your lot" (Jeremiah 29:11–14 NAB).

On the surface you don't see much hope in the slums and refugee camps of Uganda, Kenya, and Haiti where I have filmed. Beyond those three impoverished nations, almost half of humanity faces poverty, hunger, and disease on a daily basis. Many of them also face terrorism and war that results in their displacement. Others are caught up in the nightmare of human trafficking, sold into slavery.

Where is God in this picture? Where is the hope God promises?

Reflecting on Psalm 23 Leonardo Boff writes, "There is indeed a dark valley, a valley of death; there are enemies and persecutions. It is within this darkness that God comes to us as a shepherd and host, and assures us: I am with you."[58]

Spiritual darkness is not the same as spiritual disbelief.

Those who trust in God despite their sorrows and tragedies know this hope, know God will bring them through the darkness. When we know this hope we want to share it and bring the light of hope to those living in the darkness of chronic poverty. God calls us to be love for one another. When we reach out in love to someone, we give them the gift of hope, the gift of life.

God in Exile

In January 2012, I made my fifth trip to Africa. It came just three weeks after celebrating the incarnation of God. Still fresh in my mind was the reality that Jesus was the son of homeless refugees. He was born not to riches, but to poverty. During his life on earth, Jesus knew hunger and thirst; he knew squalor, insecurity, and danger; he knew isolation and loneliness; he knew betrayal and exile. Jesus knew the debilitating destitution of dire poverty. He knew extreme suffering, enduring death by crucifixion. His incarnation is in us, in the suffering world in which we live.

On my way to Africa, I crossed many borders. But one border was wide and invisible; it was the border between superabundance and extreme destitution. Going to Africa to explore the plight of the refugees fleeing starvation and violence in places such as Somalia was a very natural progression on my personal journey of documenting chronic poverty.

In the face and presence of the poor we can learn to see the face and presence of Christ. God is at home among the poor. Jesus was born in the midst of their poverty and rejection. Like the poor and oppressed, Jesus was despised and rejected. Like the poor and oppressed, Jesus was hungry and discouraged. Jesus did not come as a royal ruler, as king of the universe. He was born into poverty and lived among the poor. He was an outcast, living among outcasts, living among people with no privilege or rights. His message was so radical, so unsettling, he was quickly put to death for threatening to turn the established power structure upside down.

The Jesus that most of us see is a Jesus created in our own image and likeness, a Jesus who reflects our need for power, our need for a messianic Savior. This imperial Jesus bears no resemblance to the historical Jesus. Jesus was a countercultural revolutionary who questioned and challenged the core beliefs of his time and culture. He sided with the marginalized and oppressed, and he was put to death because the empire was threatened by his dangerous ideas.

Within centuries of his death the patriarchal church elevated Jesus to the lofty pedestal of ruler of the universe, and as a result, our authentic incarnational connection to him has been buried under centuries of mistruth.

Life is always unfolding and evolving, always generously sprinkled with ambiguity and untidiness. The same can be said for the life of faith. Yet we seek one tidy, uniformed answer to all our questions and doubts. We've forgotten we're all on a journey to the common good. It is a mutual journey toward a growth that is beyond private, sectarian, and national interests—a journey toward human solidarity.

Around the world, poverty is choking people to death. Poverty gives birth to hunger and despair. Poverty means one bad thing after another. Worse, poverty often also means death. Death by poverty blasphemes the reign of life proclaimed by Christ.

Jesus established the kingdom of God based on the Jubilee principles of the Old Testament. These principles called for a political, economic, and spiritual revolution in response to human need. Jesus intended nothing less than an actual revolution, with debts forgiven, slaves set free, and land returned to the poor. Of course, this revolution threatened the vested interests of the powerful and therefore put Jesus on the road to Calvary.

Human need—be it physical, emotional, spiritual, or social—was Jesus's reason for being . . . and should be ours. Christ wants us to respond to the suffering that torments the poor. Jesus wants a new social order where human lives are dignified with justice, uplifted in compassion, and nurtured by peace.

The ever-increasing world of violence that threatens us all can only be defeated by love, by the reaching out of a hand in a moment of darkness. Compassion is the most effective response to hatred and violence. Because of the birth, life, death, and resurrection of Jesus Christ, we know that every birth, every life, and every death matters to God . . . and must matter to us.

See How They Love Each Other

The cross is that ultimate self-emptying which is our only way into the kingdom, into that transformed world of oneness which is already at hand, just under the iron grasp of the ego.
—James W. Douglass, *Lightning East to West*[59]

Through living the Gospel, we can change the social order by changing the lives we touch. Catholic Worker cofounder Peter Maurin wrote, "In the first centuries of Christianity the hungry were fed at a personal sacrifice, the naked were clothed at a personal sacrifice, the homeless were sheltered at a personal sacrifice. And because the poor were fed, clothed and sheltered at a personal sacrifice, the pagans used to say about the Christians, 'See how they love each other.'"[60]

We tend to look to governmental policies to create social change. Perhaps we should be looking to the corporal works of mercy, whose roots can be traced to the twenty-fifth chapter of Matthew's Gospel. You don't change the world by trying to change the world; you change the world by changing yourself. Change comes from within, moving from internal to external. Slowly, I'm learning that change is constant. Moreover, the task of transformation is infinitely difficult, requiring endless time and dedication. Every day I must surrender more. When surrender becomes a way of life, every day graces you with many opportunities to die to yourself so others may live.

In making my poverty films, I was graced with the chance to be around many people who gave without measure and without hope of reward, and this forced me to look at love in an entirely different way. In their presence,

I learned that each of us has a far greater and more generous heart with which to love God than we realize. This takes time, but we can learn to see that everyone, especially the poor, has value because each and every person is made in the image and likeness of God. When you spend time in places of chronic impoverishment, you are eventually shaken out of your sense of self-assurance, your destructive habits, and—most important—your egocentric torpor.

> *Jesus gives [his disciples] a simple, clear example of what right discipleship is all about: service. Washing one another's feet, feeding the hungry, clothing the naked—here is the core of the Eucharist, our great miracle of love. . . . God's table is large, as large as creation. All are invited, all are to have access to the necessity of food and the miracle of love. Both are essential to the fullness of life. Without food, the body languishes and dies; without love, our souls wither and are filled with despair. The leftovers of our lives? What are they and who will get them? So many people can live off our leavings if we would only share. This is hardly sufficient. Disciples of Christ give abundantly in imitation of the Master who gave his very self.*
> —Robert F. Morneau, *Ashes to Easter*[61]

A History of Sacrifices

> *Someday after mastering the wind, the waves, and gravity, we shall harness for God the energy of Love, and then for the second time in history we will have discovered fire.*
> —Pierre Teilhard de Chardin

Monsignor Luigi Giussani, who was the founder of the ecclesial movement Community and Liberation, wrote, "To recognize the presence of another is always the beginning of a history of sacrifices—always. When a mother gives birth to a baby, it's the beginning of a history of sacrifices; when a boy marries a girl, it's the beginning of a history of sacrifices. But this is like the dawn of an ever more intensely laden day when man recognizes God made man as present, present in his life."[62] I would add: when a man becomes a priest or a woman becomes a nun, it's the beginning of a history of sacrifice.

We don't like the word *sacrifice*. Yet nothing happens without some measure of sacrifice. When we become aware of the ultimate Presence, it changes our lives and demands a litany of sacrifices as we struggle to give up attachments, habits, and fears that diminish the Presence in our lives.

We are all bundles of need. To engage with another is to come face-to-face with his or her need, which requires a decision: Do I help or do I walk away? When I adopted three Haitian kids (Bency, Judeline, and Peter Francis), it required a major sacrifice of my time, energy, and resources. But their presence in my life has blessed me more than money ever could.

In his book *Mystical Passion*, William McNamara, a Trappist monk, wrote, "Capacity for love is perhaps the only indispensable natural foundation for holiness. I must possess the power and impetus, the wings of the soul, to forget myself for another's sake, to prize another more than myself, to face fear and pain for another, and to risk my life. Friendship with God depends on this."[63]

Friendship with Christ requires us to be filled with compassion for those for whom suffering from lack of basic necessities, such as clean water, has become a way of life. To grow in compassion requires sacrifice and real love—love for God and one another. It is love that will move us to action on behalf of the poor, and it is love that will give us the courage to make the necessary sacrifices and not to be overcome by fear.

Love often takes us by surprise, a surprise that is expressed by the notion of falling in love. When we fall, we lose control. When we fall in love, whether with God or another, we become vulnerable and lose our sense of separateness. In love, we fall into wonder and awareness, joy and anguish. We all want love, but we also fear the cost of love, the price of being awake to a deeper reality. Love takes work. Love is not a commodity whose cost can be measured. Many ignore the bliss of love in order to avoid the pain of love, preferring the false safety of their own finely crafted inner world of isolation. But the heart longs for what the heart longs for: love . . . no matter the cost, no matter the hurt. We were made by Love and for love. Slowly, the distinction between the Beloved and the lover dissolves and Presence becomes communion. In Love, the poor are my brothers and sisters, along with all of creation. In Love we know the fullness of life that transcends even our physical death.

So instead of loving what you think is peace, love other men and love God above all. And instead of hating the people you think are warmakers, hate the appetites and the disorder in your own soul, which are the causes of war. If you love peace, then hate injustice, hate tyranny, hate greed—but hate these things in yourself, not in another.
—Thomas Merton, *New Seeds of Contemplation*[64]

Hidden in the Rubble

My second trip to Haiti came just days after the earthquake. I flew in with a medical team on a private jet. We landed in the middle of an absolute nightmare of twisted, broken bodies. I saw crushed arms and legs being amputated. I saw death and destruction on an unimaginable level. I saw streets littered with corpses. I saw the skeletal remains of a person burned to death.

On my last day in Haiti I managed to work my way back to Cité Soleil. Much of what I had seen there the previous December was destroyed. I was unable to do any substantial filming because I was scared. The place felt very dangerous as the escalating frustration level of the people seemed to have reached a boiling point. I heard that people were fighting over the limited amount of food being distributed by relief agencies.

As I worked my way home during three flights, I could not get the images of all I had captured on film and tape out of my head. While I was in Haiti, there was hardly any time to process what I saw and felt. My thoughts drifted back to the painful memory of the collapsed grammar school. The haunting sight of a young boy's decaying foot sticking out from the rubble was almost more than I could bear.

Where was God? God was hidden in the rubble, the magnificence and mystery of God's humanity at its worst. God was in the rubble, suffering too. I thought how God is often buried under the rubble of our lives, buried under so many trivial and unimportant things that prevent us from loving God. Loving God is of paramount importance in the life of a Christian.

I'm not sure how long it will take to make any sense out of what I saw in Haiti. Maybe it will never make any sense. But I do know that the presence of so many wonderful men and women who rushed into this hell of suffering was truly inspirational, for they became living symbols of the compassion

God calls each of us to embody, even in the smallest details of our personal lives.

I do think God was hidden in the rubble of Haiti. But God was also visibly present in the arms that pulled others out of the rubble, in the hands of those who treated an injury. God is in the messiness of human life, reaching out in love to lift us from the rubble of our lives, rubble created by our faults, failures, and mistakes. God is with us in our suffering.

I made a mess out of most of my life; I made lots of bad decisions and succumbed far too often to my weaknesses. But God was there, even if I was unaware. Even when a person becomes more deeply aware of God's presence and makes a sincere effort to become more fully united with God, progress is usually very slow, so slow some give up along the way.

Progress along the spiritual road requires vigilant patience. Patience is in short supply in our society. Try surfing the internet on a computer with a dial-up connection (if that were even possible anymore) and see just how impatient you become. Haiti's recovery will be very slow and will take a very long time. Decades, I would guess. As in the life of faith, there will be no quick fixes in Haiti. All we know is God is there and God wants us there.

As I boarded the small plane to Miami, somehow I knew I would return.

An Unfathomable Mystery

Fewer than three months later, I did in fact return to Haiti, landing in Port-au-Prince the day before Palm Sunday. Holy Week in Haiti seemed like the exact right place for me to prepare for the death and resurrection of Christ. During the week, I visited the site of the destroyed major seminary where many professors and seminarians lost their lives. I paused to pray at a mass grave where many of the deceased were buried.

The quiet of the deserted and destroyed seminary afforded me a few minutes of silence to pray and ponder all that I had seen. To be back in the middle of intense suffering, in the middle of death, was deeply distressing. Despite some of the good things happening since the day the earthquake struck, Haiti seemed to be pushing me toward a sense of absolute hopelessness. What am I doing? Are any of my films, my books, my speaking engagements making any difference?

It's my hope that my work has added a little something to the reality of God's all-inclusive love and mercy. Still, how can I even begin to fix the poverty I see around me when I do not truly see the poverty within me? The more I see of life, the fewer answers I have. It is all such an unfathomable mystery . . . life and death, love and hatred, joy and sadness, health and sickness, prosperity and poverty, laughter and tears. Yet God, through Christ, is in all of it, except hatred, of course. It is all part of the magnificent complexity of the mystery of creation.

A Tabernacle of God

My wealth lies in God's love for me; my poverty lies in my lack of love for God.

For St. Francis of Assisi, the essential ingredient of Gospel poverty is "living without grasping." For most of us today, our lives are marked by a hunger to grab all we can. To become vulnerable and powerless is to become totally dependent on God.

The danger of our thirst for individualism is that it weakens our awareness of the needs of others.

The seduction of property blinds us to the needs of the poor. The poor can teach us to see the barrenness of affluence and the emptiness of consumerism.

As long as I enjoy comfort and require security, I will have a hard time feeling true compassion for the poor and the weak. Acknowledging my own weakness increases my ability to be more merciful toward others. Relinquishing the possessions of the ego we all amass inside ourselves is the most demanding form of poverty.

Our greatest violation of poverty is to hold the good God gives—goodness has to flow. Acts of charity are the wings of Love. We can only love truly when our hearts are free of the self-centered desires of pride, ambition, and lust. Acts of love give flesh to faith and hope.

The despised and the unimportant of the world are loved unconditionally by their Creator. Both the New and the Old Testament reveal God's preferential love for those the world ignores and rejects. The universality of God's love excludes no one. All life is a cry to God. We must all work to help create a society that is founded on welcome and respect, embracing the most vulnerable among us. In our encounters with the poor, we must move from pity to love, from charity to justice.

The life of Christ makes it clear that God choose humility over majesty, that infinity dwells in the finite. God hides in a piece of broken bread and in the broken life of a slum-dweller. God wants us to see each other as tabernacles, as secret hiding places for the divine. Pray for the grace to be able to see a homeless person as a tabernacle of God.

God did not create poverty. People did. Because people created poverty, people can also end it. The incarnation and life and death of Christ teaches us not to place any limits on forgiveness and sharing.

Angels of Compassion

Anyone alive can be an angel.

It is within the space of our limitations that God shows us more of God's love. Until we see, understand, and admit our limitations, the noise of our desires and wishes keeps us focused on ourselves and our needs. Our lives become centered on our achievements, reputations, and winning respect and approval from others. It is in our limitations, our weaknesses, our flaws and failures that God unexpectedly emerges with an unabashed, loving hug.

Within the walls of the Santa Chiara Children's Center in Haiti, my vulnerability became more visible to me and I saw my own need for healing and further transformation. God the Creator came in his love to embrace each of us in our most vulnerable moments. Our limitations, finitude, suffering, shortcomings, weakness, disability, and frailty can be gifts if our hearts are open to the transformative love of God. These unwelcomed conditions do not rob of us of our humanity; instead, they give us a grace-filled opportunity to confer dignity on someone else through self-emptying acts of mercy and compassion. No matter our own inadequacies and defects, we are all called to be angels of compassion.

Grace is God's way of talking to us. We can best experience grace and therefore hear God more clearly when we stop living for ourselves and instead give ourselves in loving service to others.

A Prayer: The Canvas of My Soul

O God, I have not yet
truly begun to paint
the canvas of my soul.
Help me find the vivid brush strokes of
love, tenderness, compassion,
wonder, poetry, and purity
needed to create a portrait
inspired by you
to be given as a gift
to all who see it.

Help me replace
the dark, hidden tones
of my life
with the numinous hues
that reveal harmony and balance.
May the borders
of my canvas
not be so small
as to exclude
the richness and diversity
of all humanity
and the endless paths
to the divine.

Fresco, Basilica di San Francesco, Assisi

PART SIX

PRAYERS

A Journey to Weakness

O God, help me follow
wherever you lead me.

I believe my spiritual life
is essentially a journey
in which I move from what I am
to what I will become.
I am just beginning
to learn that life is
a journey to weakness.
The saints truly learned to live
when they began to explore
their own weaknesses.
By your unmerited grace,
every experience of weakness
is an opportunity of growth
and renewed life.
The emptiness I often feel stems
from not realizing
I am made for communion
with you.
If I am not growing toward
unity with you,
my God,
I am then growing apart
from you.
Help me learn
to be still,

to be humble
in order to move into
a greater union with you.
Only in stillness and humility
can I enter into
a dialogue with you,
sweet Jesus.
I need to bring to you
what I am
so that in time
I might become
more like what you are.

In following you, Lord Jesus,
I have seen with my own eyes
in so many places around the world
how life is filled to overflowing
with pain and struggle.
Your way leads to the cross,
and it doesn't offer
an easy way around it.
To become your disciple
means accepting
a spirituality of the cross
and renouncing
a spirituality of glory.

You humbled yourself
in order to love me.
You gave of yourself
in order to love me.
Help me give myself
in order to love you
and all of creation.

I Hand It All to You

O my God, help me
to stop picking away
at the sore of my guilt
over my past misdeeds,
the many times
I failed to love.
Help me instead
fix my gaze on
your endless love.

Help me see
how my sins are
merely manifestations
of my own inner emptiness
and an indication
of how far I am from you,
the true source of love.

I give you, my God,
everything that is within me.
I also surrender
all of my past.
I hand it all to you
and accept your
total forgiveness,
your overflowing mercy,
and your boundless love.

I also give you
all the wounds life
has inflicted on me.
Give me, please, the grace
to look at them honestly,
to feel them fully,
and then entrust them
to your divine care.

Help me also forgive
all who have harmed me,
and allow me to forget
the painful memories
that only allow the harm to live.

This day, I see my past,
my faults, my wounds, my shame . . .
and I let them go.
I give them to you.
I seek your Spirit
in order to have
the faith and strength
to live fully
in the present day,
consciously aware
of each precious,
life-giving moment.

The Narrow Path

O God, you know
I want to fulfill
your holy desire
for my life,
want to take the path
you wish I would take.
O God, you know also
that I not only stray
from the narrow path
you have chosen for me
but that sometimes
I choose to take
a totally different path.
And you, O Lord, are so
gentle and kind

you give me the freedom
to go the way I wish to go.
But more than that,
you still walk with me,
still love me
and long to guide me.
Your gift of grace
makes my new path
a new way to you.

You never abandon me
no matter which way I go.
And when I go the wrong way,
a way that would
lead me away from you,
you do not withdraw your grace
and still gently offer me
opportunities to turn around,
to change my misguided way.
You are a God of endless chances.

Thank you, dear Lord,
for turning my life around.
Please help me
stay on the narrow path
back to your heart.
Please help me
embrace
more and more of you.

Bitter Cross

O sweet Lord
I want so very much
to avoid the bitter cross
you ask me to carry,
the cross of putting aside

everything that is outside
the realm of your love.
Actually, nothing is outside
the realm of your love,
because you so long for us,
so thirst for us,
that you follow us
into the darkest corners
of our lives
looking to embrace us
with your mercy and compassion.
Yet I so often
want to embrace things
that you find
unhealthy and unfitting
for a seeker of God.

O Lord help me see, feel, and know
that outside of you
there is nothing of any worth,
and that with you
all is priceless.
Help me nail to the cross
the secret things in my heart
that I must sacrifice
in order to follow you
more closely
and love you
more dearly.

Endless Love

You alone, my God, are faithful
to your promises.
I know you are with me,
walking beside me,
and I have no reason

to fear or doubt . . .
but I am weak
and I need your strong arm.

I appeal to your gentleness,
O God of mercy.
I seek your divine help,
O God of compassion.
I cling to your faithfulness,
O God of endless love.

My Refuge

God, you have been my refuge
from year to year;
you are my refuge
from day to day,
even from hour to hour.
Blessed are you, Lord.
Show me, I beg, what you want
me to do,
who you want me to become.
I am yours.
Yet, I still need to learn your will,
learn what you desire for me,
for you are my God.
You are the source and sustainer
of all life.
Yet I still stray from you.
You are the only light
to lead me out of my own darkness.
Lord have mercy on me a sinner.

Show Me the Way

Lord God, I give you permission to be
the Lord of my life

and the Lord of my ministry.
You, Lord, are the creator
and sustainer of the universe,
yet you have no power
over my life unless
I allow you to help me.
You are all powerful
and yet you are a
God of poverty
out of respect for my free will.
You give me, a weak pauper,
the power to say yes or no
to the abundance of grace
you wish to shower on me
every moment of my life.

Every day, in countless small ways,
I mount the throne of my life and
make myself the Lord of my life.
I say you are Lord,
but I do not relinquish my throne.
I do things my way.
Your way is often an untaken path.

You want to be the Lord of my life.
Not because you like being Lord,
or need or want to be Lord.
You want to be the Lord of my life
because you know that is
what is best for me.
And because you love me
you only want what is best for me.

O my God, I am tired of being
lord of my life.
My way is a dead end.
Your way leads to eternal life.

O my God, I give you permission
to be the Lord of my life.
Show me the way.
Amen.

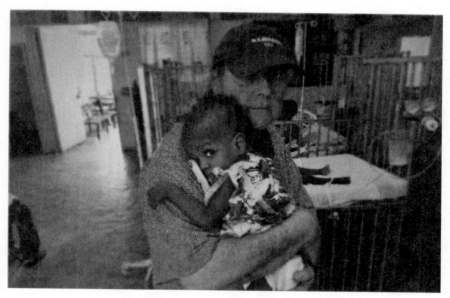

Gerry and Tamysha at Grace Hospital in December 2016
Photo: Stanley "Billy" Alexandré

EPILOGUE

My Soul Is Thirsting for God

My soul has been wounded,
gravely so.
I am unable to heal myself.
You, O God, alone know
the source of my hidden ailments.
You know all my doubts, my confusions,
and the endless contradictions that spring
from my meager life.
You know my weaknesses,
my faults, and my many failures.
You, O God, alone know
how parched and dry
my inner life is,
how I desperately thirst
for the only water
that can quench my intense longing.

I am comforted by the fact
that I know that you know
that I do want to know you
more fully,
to love you
more completely.
I truly do want
to be one with you
and to please you always.
But through my fault,
my most grievous fault,
I do not always act
as I wish to act.
I am not always aware
of your presence

because I am too focused
on myself,
on my own wounds,
my own ideas,
my own selfish desires.
I am bounced around
too easily
by the thoughts of others
that appear to sparkle with truth
yet often are merely distractions
or, worse, dreadful diversions.
The path to your door
and the fullness of life
is straight and narrow,
yet I keep veering off onto
culs-de-sac of empty promises
and phantom illusions.

My God, my God,
your way is so confusing
and hard to follow.
Yet it is so clear
and so easy to follow.
You simply and only want
me to love,
always, everywhere, everyone.
You want me to do as you do,
to make myself invisible and silent,
to make myself weak and poor,
to give myself away, completely
and without reservation,
so that only you can shine.

In my time of early morning prayer,
in the stillness and silence
that blankets the coming of dawn,

I get it and want to do it.
But then I get up,
and I am no sooner out of the house,
than my resolve begins to dissolve.
I argue and become petty.
My temper flares,
my joy flees.
Resentments rise,
faith falls.
Doubts and confusions
encamp around me.
By nightfall,
I have been reduced to ashes,
a smoldering heap of anguish
tormented by my own mediocrity.

But you love me,
always, everywhere,
even when my behavior
turns its back on you.

O my God, I beg you
to heal my wounds,
to help me go through this day
more in harmony with you.
Help my faith and actions
have smaller and smaller gaps
between them.
Give me, please, my God,
the grace to pause
often during the whirlwind
of the day,
and tell you that I love you,
that I need you,
that I want to do your will.
Shower the parched, dry, waterless

terrain of my inner life
with your abundant grace
that will keep you
in my heart and mind
all day long,
especially during those times
when I am at my weakest.

I know it is impossible for you
to withhold your love from me.
It is the one thing you can't do,
for loving is the essence of your being.
Yet all too often, sadly,
it is possible for me
to reject your perfect
and all-embracing love.
I don't mean to reject your love,
for who would reject
the most perfect love of all?
But I do sometimes forget it,
I get distracted
or beset by doubts
or desires for things
not rooted in you.
Please, dear Lord,
increase your unmerited grace
during those moments
of weakness and confusion.

You know and I know
that I will fail again.
O how that thought pains me.
Please continue to reach out
your hand and help me
get back up.

Without you
I am
nothing.

With you
I lack
nothing.

You are the fullness of life,
the fullness of love.
In you are endless mercy,
endless compassion,
endless forgiveness.
You alone are holy,
you alone are Lord.

Lord, have mercy on me,
a lowly sinner.

NOTES

1. Thomas Merton, "Preface to the Argentine Edition of *Obras Completas I*" in *Honorable Reader: Reflections on My Work,* ed. Robert E. Daggy (New York: Crossroads, 1991), 42–43.

2. Henri Nouwen, *Compassion: A Reflection on the Christian Life* (New York: Doubleday Image, 1992), 114.

3. Thomas Merton, "Letter to Ernesto Cardenal August 15, 1959," *The Courage for Truth: Letters to Writers,* ed. Christine M. Bochen (New York: Farrar, Straus and Giroux, 1993), 113

4. Marcus J. Borg, *Reading the Bible Again for the First Time* (New York: HarperCollins, 2001), n.p.

5. Karl Barth, *The Epistle to the Romans*, trans. E. C. Hoskyns (London: Oxford University Press, 1968), 33–34.

6. Karl Rahner quote found in Ronald Rolheiser, *The Holy Longing* (New York: Doubleday, 1999), n.p.

7. Thomas Merton, *New Seeds of Contemplation* (New York: New Directions, 1972), 21.

8. Eckhart Tolle, *Stillness Speaks* (Navato, CA: New World Library, 2003), 3.

9. Thomas Merton, *No Man Is an Island* (New York: Harcourt, Brace, 1955), 260.

10. Evelyn Underhill, *The Ways of the Spirit*, ed. Grace Aldophsen Brame (New York, Crossroads, 2000), 50.

11. John Dear, sj, *Living Peace: A Spirituality of Contemplation and Action* (New York: Doubleday, 2001), 25.

12. Thomas Keating, *Invitation to Love: The Way of Christian Contemplation* (New York: Bloomsbury Atlantic, 1994), n.p.

13. Parker J. Palmer, *The Active Life: Wisdom for Work, Creativity, and Caring* (New York: HarperCollins, 1970), 17.

14. Madeleine Delbrêl, *We, the Ordinary People of the Street* (Grand Rapids, MI: Eerdmans, 2000), 100.

15. Thomas Merton, *Conjectures of a Guilty Bystander* (New York: Doubleday Image, 1989), 19.

16. Max Picard, *The World of Silence* (Chicago: H. Regnery, 1952), n.p.

17. Thomas Merton, *New Seeds of Contemplation,* 82–83.

18. Thomas Merton, *Thoughts in Solitude* (New York: Farrar, Straus and Giroux, 1956), 79.

19. Thomas Merton, *Dialogues with Silence,* ed. Jonathan Montaldo (HarperSanFrancisco, 2001), 5.

20. Carlo Carretto, *Letters from the Desert* (Maryknoll, NY: Orbis, 1972), 73, 130.

21. Thomas Merton, *Seeds of Contemplation* (New York: New Directions, 1949), 59.

22. Thomas Merton, *Thoughts in Solitude*, 82.

23. Eckhart Tolle, *The Power of Now* (Novato, CA: New World Library, 2004), n.p.

24. Thomas Merton, *Thoughts in Solitude* (New York: Farrar, Straus and Cudahy, 1958), 85–86.

25. Thomas Merton, *No Man Is an Island*, 258.

26. Thomas Merton, *The Living Bread* (New York: Farrar, Straus and Giroux, 1956), 147.

27. Walter Brueggemann, *The Prophetic Imagination* (Minneapolis: Fortress Press, 2001), 40.

28. Thomas Merton, *The Inner Experience: Notes on Contemplation* (HarperSanFrancisco, 2003), 36.

29. Robert Llewelyn, *Why Pray?* (Brewster, MA: Paraclete Press, 2019), 27.

30. Richard Rohr, *Radical Grace* (Cincinnati, OH: St. Anthony Messenger Press, 1995), n.p.

31. Daniel O'Leary, "Windows of Wonder," *The Tablet*, May 17, 2008.

32. Sr. Ruth Fox, OSB, Blessing delivered at Dickinson State University graduation in 1985 (*PRAY TELL: Worship, Wit & Wisdom* website, July 15, 2015).

33. Tim Shriver, "A Call to Prayer: Father Thomas Keating's Parting Wisdom," *America* magazine, January 7, 2019.

34. Thomas Merton, *The Asian Journal of Thomas Merton* (New York: New Directions Press, 1973), 341–42.

35. Ruth Burrows, OCD, *Guidelines for Mystical Prayer* (London: Bloomsbury Press, 2007), n.p.

36. Oliver Clement, *Three Prayers* (Yonkers, NY: St. Vladimir's Seminary Press, 2000), 30.

37. Susan Clark Studer, *The Teacher's Book of Days: Inspirational Passages for Every Day of the Year* (CA: Prima Publishing, 1999), 27.

38. *Daily Readings with Mother Teresa,* ed. Teresa de Bertodano (New York: HarperCollins, 1994), from *Daily Dig* website, *Plough Quarterly Magazine,* April 26, 2020.

39. Henri Nouwen, *Compassion: A Reflection on the Christian Life*, 24–25.

40. Michael Casey, *Strangers to the City* (Brewster, MA: Paraclete Press, 2013), 176.

41. Paul Tillich, *The Shaking of the Foundations* (Eugene, OR: Wipf & Stock, 2012), n.p.

42. Jonathan Montaldo, *Always Stretching Forward Toward Christ: Thomas Merton's Restless Journey.* Unpublished manuscript, 2016.

43. Jonathan Montaldo, "Loving Winter When the Plant Says Nothing" (Unpublished Manuscript, 2003).

44. Henri Matisse, *Jazz* (London: Thames and Hudson, 2013), n.p.

45. Quoted in Wayne Teasdale, *The Mystic Heart: Discovering a Universal Spirituality in the World's Religions* (Novato, CA: New World Library, 1999), 127.

46. Erasmo Leiva-Merikakis, *The Way of the Disciple* (San Francisco: Ignatius Press, 2003), n.p.

47. Blessed Elizabeth of the Trinity, quoted in Wayne Teasdale, *The Mystic Heart*, 3.

48. Thomas Merton, *No Man Is an Island*, 212.

49. Walter Brueggeman, *Journey to the Common Good* (Louisville, KY: Westminster John Knox Press, 2010), 1.

50. Parker J. Palmer, *The Company of Strangers* (New York: Crossroad, 1983), 100.

51. Peter Maurin, *Easy Essays*, quoted in Mark Zwick and Louise Zwick, *The Catholic Worker Movement: Intellectual and Spiritual Origins* (Mahwah, NJ: Paulist Press, 2005), n.p.

52. Gerard Thomas Straub, *Thoughts of a Blind Beggar* (Maryknoll, NY: Orbis Books, 2007), 29.

53. Ernesto Cardenal, *Abide in Love* (Maryknoll, NY: Orbis Books, 1995), 92.

54. *Journal of a Soul: The Autobiography of Pope John XXIII*, trans. Dorothy White (New York: Image Books, 1999), 278–79.

55. François Fénelon, *Christian Perfection: Devotional Reflections on the Christian Life* (New Jersey: Dimension Books, 1976), n.p.

56. Aleksandr Solzhenitsyn, *Détente, Democracy, and Dictatorship* (Abingdon, OX, UK: Routledge, 2009), 54.

57. Rabbi Abraham Joshua Heschel, *Moral Grandeur and Spiritual Audacity*, ed. Susannah Heschel (New York: Farrar, Straus and Giroux, 1996), 224–26.

58. Leonardo Boff, *The Lord is My Shepherd: Divine Consolation in times of Abandonment* (Maryknoll, NY: Orbis Books, 2006), 29.

59. James W. Douglass, *Lightning East to West* (Eugene, OR: Wipf & Stock, 2006), 53.

60. Peter Maurin, *Easy Essays* (Eugene, OR: Wipf & Stock, Catholic Workers Reprint Series, 2010), 110.

61. Robert F. Morneau, *Ashes to Easter* (New York: Crossroad, 1997), 107–08.

62. Luigi Giussani, *Is it Possible to Live this Way?: An Unusual Approach to Christian Existence*, Vol. 3, "Charity" (Montreal: McGill-Queen's University Press, 2009), 101.

63. William McNamara, *Mystical Passion: The Art of Christian Loving* (Rockport, MA: Element Books, 1991), n.p.

64. Thomas Merton, *New Seeds of Contemplation*, 122.

AUTHOR CONTACT INFORMATION

Gerry Straub with Baby Ruth, April 19, 2019
Photo: Stanley "Billy" Alexandré

If you wish information on how to purchase any of Gerry's films, all of which are available as DVDs or video downloads, please contact:

Pax et Bonum Communications, Inc.
P.O. Box 970
Ft. Pierce, FL 34954

www.PaxEtBonumComm.org

If you wish to support Gerry's work with abandoned kids in Haiti, please contact:

The Santa Chiara Children's Center
P.O. Box 970
Ft. Pierce, FL 34954

www.SantaChiaraCC.org